Intermediate Italian

Edited by

Laura Riggio and Giuseppe Manca

Content in this program has been modified and enhanced from Starting Out in Italian and Complete Course Italian: The Basics, both published in 2008.

Living Language and colophon are registered trademarks of Random House, Inc.

Published in the United States by Living Language, an imprint of Random House, Inc.

www.livinglanguage.com

Editor: Laura Riggio
Production Editor: Ciara Robinson
Production Manager: Tom Marshall
Interior Design: Sophie Chin
Illustrations: Sophie Chin

First Edition

Library of Congress Cataloging-in-Publication Data

Intermediate Italian / edited by Laura Riggio and Giuseppe Manca. — 1st ed.
   p. cm.
  ISBN 978-0-307-97157-9
 1. Italian language—Textbooks for foreign speakers—English. 2. Italian language—Grammar.
3. Italian language—Spoken Italian. I. Riggio, Laura. II. Manca, Giuseppe.
  PC1129.E5I58 2011
  458.2'421—dc23
                              2011021874

This book is available at special discounts for bulk purchases for sales promotions or premiums. Special editions, including personalized covers, excerpts of existing books, and corporate imprints, can be created in large quantities for special needs. For more information, write to Special Markets/ Premium Sales, 1745 Broadway, MD 3-1, New York, New York 10019 or e-mail specialmarkets@ randomhouse.com.

PRINTED IN THE UNITED STATES OF AMERICA

20 19 18 17 16 15 14 13 12

Acknowledgments

Thanks to the Living Language team: Amanda D'Acierno, Christopher Warnasch, Suzanne McQuade, Laura Riggio, Erin Quirk, Amanda Munoz, Fabrizio LaRocca, Siobhan O'Hare, Sophie Chin, Sue Daulton, Alison Skrabek, Carolyn Roth, Ciara Robinson, and Tom Marshall.

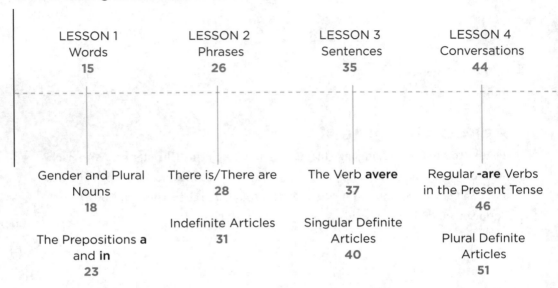
COURSE

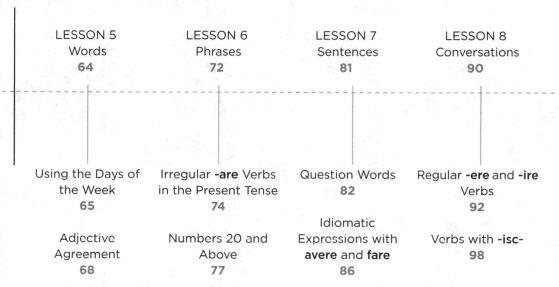
OUTLINE

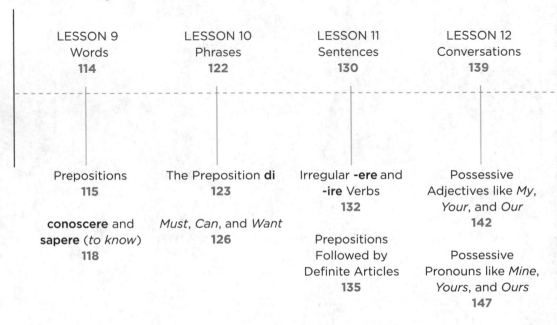
C O U R S E

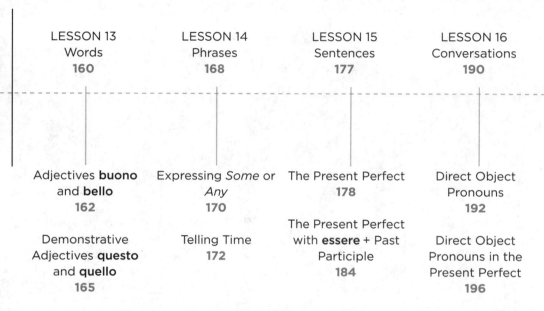
OUTLINE

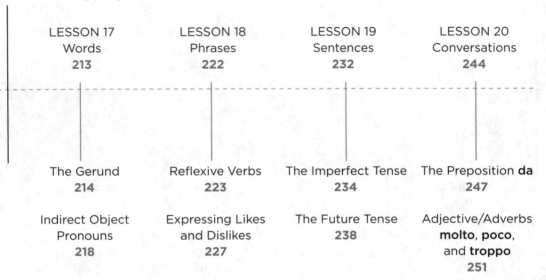

How to Use this Course

Benvenuto! Welcome to *Living Language Intermediate Italian*!

Before we begin, let's take a quick look at what you'll see in this course.

CONTENT

Intermediate Italian is a continuation of *Essential Italian*. It will review, expand on, and add to the foundation that you received in *Essential Italian*. In other words, this course contains:

- an in-depth review of important vocabulary and grammar from *Essential Italian*;

- an expanded and more advanced look at some key vocabulary and grammar from *Essential Italian*;

- an introduction to idiomatic language and more challenging Italian grammar.

UNITS

There are five units in this course. Each unit has four lessons arranged in a "building block" structure: the first lesson will present essential *words*, the second will introduce longer *phrases*, the third will teach *sentences,* and the fourth will show how everything works together in everyday *conversations*.

At the beginning of each unit is an introduction highlighting what you'll learn in that unit. At the end of each unit you'll find the Unit Essentials, which reviews the key information from that unit, and a self-graded Unit Quiz, which tests what you've learned.

LESSONS

There are four lessons per unit for a total of 20 lessons in the course. Each lesson has the following components:

- **Introduction** outlining what you will cover in the lesson.

- **Word Builder 1** (first lesson of the unit) presenting key words and phrases.

- **Phrase Builder 1** (second lesson of the unit) introducing longer phrases and expressions.

- **Sentence Builder 1** (third lesson of the unit) teaching sentences.

- **Conversation 1** (fourth lesson of the unit) for a natural dialogue that brings together important vocabulary and grammar from the unit.

- **Word/Phrase/Sentence/Conversation Practice 1** practicing what you learned in Word Builder 1, Phrase Builder 1, Sentence Builder 1, or Conversation 1.

- **Grammar Builder 1** guiding you through important Italian grammar that you need to know.

- **Work Out 1** for a comprehensive practice of what you saw in Grammar Builder 1.

- **Word Builder 2/Phrase Builder 2/Sentence Builder 2/Conversation 2** for more key words, phrases, sentences, or a second dialogue.

- **Word/Phrase/Sentence/Conversation Practice 2** practicing what you learned in Word Builder 2, Phrase Builder 2, Sentence Builder 2, or Conversation 2.

- **Grammar Builder 2** for more information on Italian grammar.

- **Work Out 2** for a comprehensive practice of what you saw in Grammar Builder 2.

- **Drive It Home** ingraining an important point of Italian grammar for the long term.

- **Tip** or **Culture Note** for a helpful language tip or useful cultural information related to the lesson or unit.

- **How Did You Do?** outlining what you learned in the lesson.

- **Word Recall** reviewing important vocabulary and grammar from any of the previous lessons in *Intermediate* or *Essential Italian*.

- **Take It Further** sections appear throughout the lessons, providing extra information about new vocabulary, expanding on certain grammar points, or introducing additional words and phrases.

UNIT ESSENTIALS

You will see **Unit Essentials** at the end of every unit. Vocabulary Essentials present the English translations of key vocabulary that you've learned, so they give you a chance to test yourself on the most important words and phrases that you've learned. Grammar Essentials summarizes the key grammar that you've learned and acts as a "cheat sheet" that will remind you of the key structures you've learned.

UNIT QUIZ

After each Unit Essentials, you'll see a **Unit Quiz**. The quizzes are self-graded so it's easy for you to test your progress and see if you should go back and review.

PROGRESS BAR

You will see a **Progress Bar** on each page that has course material. It indicates your current position within the unit and lets you know how much progress you're making. Each line in the bar represents a Grammar Builder section.

AUDIO

Look for the symbol ▶ to help guide you through the audio as you're reading the book. It will tell you which track to listen to for each section that has audio. When you see the symbol, select the indicated track and start listening. If you don't see the symbol, then there isn't any audio for that section. You'll also see ⏸, which will tell you where that track ends.

You can listen to the audio on its own, when you're on the go, to brush up on your pronunciation or review what you've learned in the book.

PRONUNCIATION GUIDE, GRAMMAR SUMMARY, GLOSSARY

At the back of this book you will find a **Pronunciation Guide, Grammar Summary,** and **Glossary**. The Pronunciation Guide provides information on Italian pronunciation and spelling. The Grammar Summary contains an overview of key Italian grammar, some of which is covered in *Essential* and *Intermediate Italian,* and some of which you won't formally learn until *Advanced Italian.* The Glossary (Italian–English and English–Italian) includes vocabulary that's covered throughout this course, as well as vocabulary introduced in *Essential* and *Advanced Italian.*

FREE ONLINE TOOLS

Go to **www.livinglanguage.com/languagelab** to access your free online tools. The tools are organized around the units in this course, with audiovisual flashcards, and interactive games and quizzes for each unit. These tools will help you to review and practice the vocabulary and grammar that you've seen in the units, as well as provide some bonus words and phrases related to the unit's topic.

Unit 1:
Talking about Yourself and Your Home

In this unit, you'll learn how to talk about yourself, your house, and your hometown. You'll review some key Italian grammar, and expand your vocabulary and conversation skills. By the end of the unit, you'll be able to:

☐ use key vocabulary related to cities and towns

☐ talk about more than one of something

☐ use key vocabulary to talk about your house or apartment

☐ express *in*, with cities and countries

☐ say *there is* and *there are* in Italian

☐ use indefinite articles **un, uno, una**, and **un'**

☐ use the very important verb **avere** (*to have*)

☐ use the singular definite articles **il, lo, la**, and **l'**

☐ talk about actions with regular **-are** verbs

☐ use the plural definite articles **i, gli**, and **le**

Lesson 1: Words

In this lesson, you'll learn how to:

☐ use key vocabulary related to cities and towns

☐ talk about more than one of something

☐ use key vocabulary to talk about your house or apartment

☐ express *in*, with cities and countries

Word Builder 1

▶ 1A Word Builder 1 (CD4, Track 1)

(la) città	*city*
(il) paese	*town, country*
(il) museo	*museum*
(l')edificio	*building*
(il) centro	*center, downtown*
(la) mostra	*exhibit*
(la) biblioteca	*library*
(la) libreria	*bookstore, bookshelves (in a house or office)*
(il) ristorante	*restaurant*
(il) parco	*park*
(l')albero	*tree*
(l')aria	*air*
(la) vista	*view*
(la) chiesa	*church*

Ⅱ

Take It Further

▶ 1B Take It Further (CD4, Track 2)

You first came across the full conjugation of the verb **essere** (*to be*) back in Lesson 4 of *Essential Italian*. But let's take a moment to review it now.

io sono	*I am*	noi siamo	*we are*
tu sei	*you are (infml.)*	**voi siete**	*you are (infml., pl.)*
lui è, lei è	*he is, she is*	**loro sono**	*they are*
Lei è	*you are (fml.)*	**Loro sono**	*you are (fml., pl.)*

Don't forget that **tu** is the informal or familiar form of *you*, used when addressing one person, and **Lei** is the formal or polite form. In the plural, **voi** is familiar, and **Loro** is formal. In writing, it's important to capitalize the **L** in **Lei** and **Loro**, to distinguish them from **lei** (*she*) and **loro** (*they*). And of course it's common to drop the pronouns in Italian if they're understood from context.

Io sono americano./Sono americano.
I'm an American.

Sei uno studente.
You're a student.

La professoressa è di Roma o di Verona?
Is the professor from Rome or from Verona?

Siamo a casa in vacanza.
We're at home on vacation.

Siete fortunati!
You're lucky!

Stanno bene.

They're well.

⏸

💡 Tip!

Remember that there are quite a few different ways to memorize new vocabulary, so it's a good idea to try a few out to see what works for you. Simply reading a word in a list isn't going to make you remember it, though. Write down your new vocabulary in a notebook, then try written or spoken repetition to make it sink in. (You can use the recordings for that, too.) You could also make flash cards, with the Italian on one side and the English on the other. Start going from Italian into English and once you've mastered that, go from English into Italian, which will be harder. Of course, don't forget about the online flashcards at **www.livinglanguage. com/languagelab**, designed specifically for this program. You could also label things in your home or office. Experiment and explore, but whatever you do, try to make vocabulary learning as active as possible!

✏ Word Practice 1

Translate the new vocabulary that you've just learned. Use the definite articles **il**, **la**, or **l'**.

1. restaurant	
2. museum	
3. city	
4. park	
5. country	
6. building	
7. church	

8. library	
9. tree	
10. bookstore	
11. view	
12. center, downtown	

ANSWER KEY

1. il ristorante; 2. il museo; 3. la città; 4. il parco; 5. il paese; 6. l'edificio; 7. la chiesa; 8. la biblioteca; 9. l'albero; 10. la libreria; 11. la vista; 12. il centro

Grammar Builder 1

▶ 1C Grammar Builder 1 (CD4, Track 3)

GENDER AND PLURAL OF NOUNS

Remember that all nouns in Italian have gender. Nouns ending in **-o** are typically masculine, nouns ending in **-a** are typically feminine (although some, especially of Greek origin, are masculine), and nouns ending in **-e** can be either masculine or feminine. Some of those nouns are predictable, though. Nouns that end in **-ione**, such as **stazione** (*station*) and **televisione** (*television*) are typically feminine. Nouns that end in **-ore**, such as **signore** (*gentleman*) and **dottore** (*doctor*), are always masculine. For other nouns ending in **-e**, though, the best thing to do is simply memorize the gender. In the vocabulary lists, the gender of nouns will be shown with an article, as in Word Builder 1, or with (*m.*) or (*f.*).

In *Essential Italian*, you learned about indefinite articles, corresponding to *a* or *an*, and definite articles, corresponding to *the*. We'll come back to that and do a quick review later in this unit. For now, let's take another look at how to form plurals in Italian, reviewing what you've already learned, and adding some new information.

A feminine noun that ends in **-a** will change the final **-a** into an **-e**.

chiesa *(church)*	**chiese** *(churches)*

A noun that ends in **-o** will change the final **-o** into an **-i**. Similarly, masculine nouns ending in **-a** will also change the final **-a** into an **-i**.

albero *(tree)*	**alberi** *(trees)*
programma *(program)*	**programmi** *(programs)*

A noun that ends in **-e**, whether it's feminine or masculine, will change the final **-e** into an **-i**.

ristorante *(restaurant)*	**ristoranti** *(restaurants)*

Note that a noun ending with an accented vowel, such as **città**, will not change in the plural.

città *(city)*	**città** *(cities)*

Also, a noun ending in **-io** will not end in a double **i**, but instead ends in one **i**, unless the **i** carries the stress.

edificio *(building)*	**edifici** *(buildings)*
zio *(uncle)*	**zii** *(uncles)*

⑪

✎ Work Out 1

A. Give the gender of the following nouns.

1. **studente** _____

2. **vacanza** _____

3. **professore** _____

4. **casa** _____

5. **ragazzo** _____

6. **lavoro** _____

B. Now give the plural of the following nouns.

1. **paese** _____

2. **mostra** _____

3. **città** _____

4. **museo** _____

5. **negozio** _____

6. **vista** _____

7. **ristorante** _____

8. **caffè** _____

ANSWER KEY
A. 1. m.; 2. f.; 3. m.; 4. f.; 5. m.; 6. m
B. 1. **paesi**; 2. **mostre**; 3. **città**; 4. **musei**; 5. **negozi**; 6. **viste**; 7. **ristoranti**; 8. **caffè**

Word Builder 2

▶ 1D Word Builder 2 (CD4, Track 4)

(l')appartamento	apartment
(la) via	street
(la) stanza	room
(la) camera	room, chamber, cabinet
(il) soggiorno	living room
(la) cucina	kitchen
(il) bagno	bathroom
(il) letto	bed
(la) camera da letto	bedroom
(l')armadio	armoire, closet
(il) tavolo	table
(il) divano	sofa, couch
(la) televisione	television
(il) televisore	television

⏸

✎ Word Practice 2

Fill in the floor plan below with the names of as many rooms as you can come up with, based on the vocabulary you've just learned.

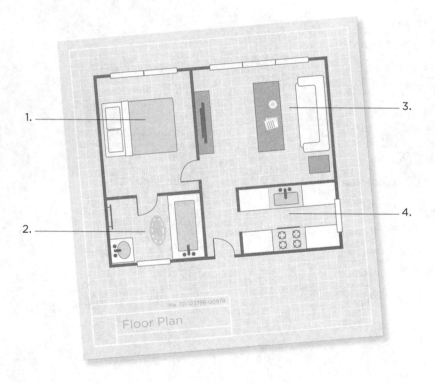

1. _____

2. _____

3. _____

4. _____

ANSWER KEY

1. la camera da letto; 2. il bagno; 3. il soggiorno; 4. la cucina

Grammar Builder 2

▶ 1E Grammar Builder 2 (CD4, Track 5)

THE PREPOSITIONS A AND IN

The prepositions **a** and **in** both mean *in*, *at*, and *to* but are not interchangeable. The preposition **in** is always used before a country, while **a** is used before a city.

Noi siamo a Roma, in Italia.
We are in Rome, in Italy.

In addition, different places will use either **a** or **in**, for no obvious reason. For instance, Italians use **in** in front of **ufficio**, but **a** in front of **casa**, and they always say **in vacanza** when on vacation.

⏸

✏ Work Out 2

Insert either the preposition **in** or **a** appropriately.

1. **Noi siamo _____ Roma.**

2. **Io sono _____ vacanza.**

3. **Il professore non è _____ ufficio.**

4. **I signori Giannini sono _____ casa.**

5. **Verona è _____ Italia.**

ANSWER KEY
1. a; 2. in; 3. in; 4. a; 5. in

✎ Drive It Home

By now, you're familiar with Drive It Home exercises, which may seem easy, but are meant to make grammatical structures more automatic by helping you establish grammatical patterns through practice and repetition. So don't skip over these exercises! They'll help you in the long run.

A. First, give the plural of each of these nouns. They all follow the same pattern, but write out each answer and say it aloud.

1. **centro, albero, giorno, bagno, letto, divano, appartamento** _____

   _____

2. **mostra, vista, chiesa, stanza, cucina, via, camera** _____

   _____

3. **paese, ristorante, studente, dottore, televisione, televisore** _____

   _____

B. Now, use the correct preposition, **a** or **in**, with the following places. Form sentences starting with **"Siamo …"** (*We are …*)

1. **Firenze, Napoli, Venezia, Milano, Parigi, Perugia** _____

   _____

   _____

   _____

2. **Italia, Francia, Spagna, Brasile, Giappone, Australia** _____

   _____

   _____

   _____

ANSWER KEY
A. 1. centri, alberi, giorni, bagni, letti, divani, appartamenti; 2. mostre, viste, chiese, stanze, cucine, vie, camere; 3. paesi, ristoranti, studenti, dottori, televisioni, televisori
B. 1. Siamo a Firenze., Siamo a Napoli., Siamo a Venezia., Siamo a Milano., Siamo a Parigi., Siamo a Perugia.; 2. Siamo in Italia., Siamo in Francia., Siamo in Spagna., Siamo in Brasile., Siamo in Giappone., Siamo in Australia.

🔆 Tip!

As you might have already realized, prepositions in Italian, as in any language, are very idiomatic, and therefore it's not always easy to decide which preposition to use. The best way to learn them is to learn prepositions in phrases. Note the prepositions and which nouns they go with each time they come up in expressions you read or hear. Eventually they will come to you more easily.

How Did You Do?

Let's see how you did in this lesson. By now, you should be able to:

☐ use key vocabulary related to cities and towns (Still unsure? Jump back to page 15.)

☐ talk about more than one of something (Still unsure? Jump back to page 18.)

☐ use key vocabulary to talk about your house or apartment (Still unsure? Jump back to page 21.)

☐ express *in*, with cities and countries (Still unsure? Jump back to page 23.)

✏️ Word Recall

The following are key nouns that you've learned in this first lesson. Translate each one, and indicate whether you'd find it in **una città** (*a city*) or in **una casa** (*a house*).

1. museo _____

2. chiesa _____

3. bagno _____

4. divano _____

5. edificio _____

6. soggiorno _____

7. letto _____

8. biblioteca _____

9. stanza _____

10. parco _____

11. tavolo _____

12. via _____

ANSWER KEY

1. *museum* (**città**); 2. *church* (**città**); 3. *bathroom* (**casa**); 4. *sofa* (**casa**); 5. *building* (**città**); 6. *living room* (**casa**); 7. *bed* (**casa**); 8. *library* (**città**); 9. *room* (**casa**); 10. *park* (**città**); 11. *table* (**casa**); 12. *street* (**città**)

Lesson 2: Phrases

By the end of this lesson, you should be able to:

☐ say *there is* and *there are* in Italian

☐ use indefinite articles **un, uno, una,** and **un'**

Phrase Builder 1

▶ 2A Phrase Builder 1 (CD4, Track 6)

Che bello!	*How beautiful!*
bene	*well*

c'è	*there is*
ci sono	*there are*
in questo periodo	*in this period, currently*
abbastanza	*enough*
perfetto	*perfect*
non c'è	*there isn't*
lì vicino	*near there*
vicino a	*near, close to*
in centro	*to/in the city, in the center of town, downtown*

Take It Further

Here is some more key vocabulary that will come in handy as you go through Unit 1. Much of it will probably be familiar to you, but a little review is a good thing!

l'uomo	*man*
la donna	*woman*
il ragazzo	*boy*
la ragazza	*girl*
il professore	*professor (m.)*
la professoressa	*professor (f.)*
americano	*American*
inglese	*English*
italiano	*Italian*
il lavoro	*work*
la vacanza	*vacation, holiday*
stanco	*tired*
l'ufficio	*office*

perché	why, because
ma	but
qui	here

✎ Phrase Practice 1

Translate the following phrases from Italian into English.

1. c'è _____

2. Che bello! _____

3. lì vicino _____

4. in questo periodo _____

5. ci sono _____

6. in centro _____

7. vicino a _____

8. non c'è _____

ANSWER KEY
1. *there is*; 2. *How beautiful!*; 3. *near there*; 4. *currently, in this period*; 5. *there are*; 6. *to/in the city, in the center of town, downtown*; 7. *near, close to*; 8. *there isn't*

Grammar Builder 1

▶ 2B Grammar Builder 1 (CD4, Track 7)

THERE IS/THERE ARE

The phrases **c'è** and **ci sono** correspond to the English *there is* and *there are*, and are used to describe what is present or exists in a particular place. **C'è** is used with a singular noun, while **ci sono** is used with plural nouns.

C'è una mostra su Leonardo.
There is an exhibit about Leonardo.

Non ci sono molti alberi in centro.
There aren't many trees in the center of town/ in the city.

✎ Work Out 1

Complete the following sentences with either **c'è** or **ci sono**. The translations are given below each item if you need help, but first try to figure out the correct answer by simply looking for singular or plural nouns after each blank.

1. **Al museo degli Uffizi _____ molti quadri.**

    (*At the Uffizi Gallery _____ a lot of paintings.*)

2. **_____ molti studenti in questa classe.**

    (_____ *a lot of students in this class.*)

3. **_____una cucina grande in questa casa.**

    (_____ *a big kitchen in this house.*)

4. **Nel mio appartamento _____ due camere da letto.**

    (*In my apartment _____ two bedrooms.*)

5. **Non _____ un parco in città.**

    (_____ *not a park in the city.*)

6. **_____una televisione nella camera da letto.**

    (_____ *a television in the bedroom.*)

ANSWER KEY
1. **ci sono**; 2. **Ci sono**; 3. **C'è**; 4. **ci sono**; 5. **c'è**; 6. **C'è**

Phrase Builder 2

▶ 2C Phrase Builder 2 (CD4, Track 8)

Dov'è ?	Where is … ?
Dove sono?	Where are … ?
abbiamo	we have
non ho	I don't have
abito	I live
Com'è … ?	How is … ?, What is … like?
Come sono … ?	How are … ?, What are … like?
studiamo	we study
in un appartamento	in an apartment
in via Mazzini 13	in/at Mazzini street, number 13

⏸

✎ Phrase Practice 2

Translate the following phrases into English.

1. Come sono … ? _____

2. Dov'è? _____

3. Com'è … ? _____

4. Dove sono? _____

ANSWER KEY
1. *How are … ?, What are … like?* 2. *Where is … ?* 3. *How is … ?, What is … like?* 4. *Where are … ?*

Grammar Builder 2

▶ 2D Grammar Builder 2 (CD4, Track 9)

INDEFINITE ARTICLES

You first came across indefinite articles way back in Lesson 2 of *Essential Italian*. Let's take a moment to review them, and add a little more information. As you know, **un** is used before most masculine nouns, and **una** is used before most feminine nouns. But there are two other forms that you should know as well. **Uno** is used before masculine nouns that begin with s + consonant (**studente**, *student*); z- (**zaino**, *backpack*); ps- (**psicologo**, *psychologist*); or gn- (**gnomo**, *gnome*). The feminine **una** is shortened to **un'** before nouns that begin with a vowel. Here's a summary.

MASCULINE		
un	**un libro** (*a book*)	in front of a consonant or vowel
uno	**uno studente** (*a male student*)	in front of s + consonant, z-, ps-, or gn-

FEMININE		
una	**una casa** (*a house*)	in front of a consonant
un'	**un'amica** (*a female friend*)	in front of a vowel

✎ Work Out 2

Write the correct indefinite article in front of the following nouns.

1. _____ museo

2. _____ letto

3. _____ avvocato

4. _____ poeta (*poet, m.*)

5. _____ musicista (*musician, m.*)

6. _____ lavoro

7. _____ vacanza

8. _____ studente

9. _____ aria

10. _____ zaino

ANSWER KEY
1. un; 2. un; 3. un; 4. un; 5. un; 6. un; 7. una; 8. uno; 9. un'; 10. uno

✎ Drive It Home

Let's practice indefinite articles once more, so that this aspect of grammar becomes automatic. Write in the correct form of the indefinite article. Read each word out loud.

A.

1. _____ museo

2. _____ appartamento

3. _____ atleta (*athlete, m.*)

4. _____ **elettricista** (*electrician, m.*)

5. _____ **treno**

B.

1. _____ **mostra**

2. _____ **via**

3. _____ **madre**

4. _____ **zia**

5. _____ **sorella**

C.

1. _____ **zio**

2. _____ **studente**

3. _____ **sbaglio** (*mistake, m.*)

4. _____ **sport** (*sport, m.*)

5. _____ **studio** (*study, m.*)

D.

1. _____ **amica**

2. _____ **assemblea** (*assembly, f.*)

3. _____ **atleta** (*athlete, f.*)

4. _____ **attività** (*activity, f.*)

5. _____ **associazione** (*association, f.*)

ANSWER KEY
A. 1. un museo; 2. un appartamento; 3. un atleta; 4. un elettricista; 5. un treno
B. 1. una mostra; 2. una via; 3. una madre; 4. una zia; 5. una sorella
C. 1. uno zio; 2. uno studente; 3. uno sbaglio; 4. uno sport; 5. uno studio
D. 1. un'amica; 2. un'assemblea; 3. un'atleta; 4. un'attività; 5. un'associazione

How Did You Do?

By now, you should be able to:

☐ say *there is* and *there are* in Italian (Still unsure? Jump back to page 28.)

☐ use indefinite articles **un**, **uno**, **una**, and **un'** (Still unsure? Jump back to page 31.)

✎ Word Recall

Let's practice some of the vocabulary and phrases you have learned so far.
Translate the following sentences into English.

1. **Nell'appartamento ci sono due camere da letto.** _____

_____

2. **In città ci sono i musei.** _____

_____

3. **Al museo c'è una mostra.** _____

_____

4. **Abito in centro.** _____

5. **In soggiorno ci sono il divano e la televisione.** _____

_____

6. **Dov'è la stazione?** _____

7. **Siamo di Roma.** _____

8. **Dove sono gli studenti?** _____

_____

ANSWER KEY

1. *In the apartment there are two bedrooms. 2. In the city there are museums. 3. In the museum there is an exhibition. 4. I live in the center of town. 5. In the living room there is the couch and the TV. 6. Where is the station? 7. We are from Rome.*
8. *Where are the students?*

Lesson 3: Sentences

By the end of this lesson, you should be able to:

☐ use the very important verb avere (*to have*)

☐ use the singular definite articles il, lo, la, and l'

Sentence Builder 1

▶ 3A Sentence Builder 1 (CD4, Track 10)

Oggi visitiamo il museo degli Uffizi.	*Today, we'll visit the Uffizi museum.*
C'è una mostra su Leonardo.	*There's an exhibit on Leonardo.*
Abbiamo abbastanza tempo?	*Do we have enough time?*
Sì, abbiamo quattro ore.	*Yes, we have four hours.*
Non c'è tempo per la biblioteca.	*There's no time for the library.*
Mangiamo con Gianni.	*We're eating with Gianni.*
C'è un parco vicino al museo?	*Is there a park by the museum?*
Non ci sono molti alberi.	*There aren't many trees.*
A Fiesole l'aria è pulita.	*In Fiesole the air is clean.*

⏸

✎ Sentence Practice 1

Fill in the missing words in each of the following sentences. The translations are given to help you, but try to identify the missing words without looking at the translations first.

1. Non _____ tempo per _____ biblioteca.

   (*There's no time for the library.*)

2. _____ un parco vicino _____ museo?

   (*Is there a park near the museum?*)

3. Mangiamo _____ Giovanni.

   (*We're eating with Giovanni.*)

4. _____ una mostra su Leonardo.

   (*There is an exhibition on Leonardo.*)

5. Non _____ alberi.

   (*There aren't many trees.*)

   ANSWER KEY
   1. c'è, la; 2. C'è, al; 3. con; 4. C'è; 5. ci sono, molti

Grammar Builder 1

▶ 3B Grammar Builder 2 (CD4, Track 11)

THE VERB AVERE

Let's review the very common verb avere (*to have*), which you first came across in Lesson 3 of *Essential Italian*. Remember that just like essere, avere is an irregular verb.

io ho	I have
tu hai	you have
lui ha	he has
lei ha	she has
Lei ha	you have (fml.)
noi abbiamo	we have
voi avete	you (pl.) have
loro hanno	they have
Loro hanno	you have (fml. pl.)

Abbiamo abbastanza tempo?
Do we have enough time?

Sì, abbiamo quattro ore.
Yes, we have four hours.

Lui ha un appartamento grande.
He has a large apartment.

Lui ha un appartamento grande?
Does he have a large apartment?

Ha un appartamento grande?
Does (he/she) have a large apartment?

(II)

✎ Work Out 1

Unscramble the following sentences.

1. **piccola/loro/una/casa/hanno/?** _____

_____

2. **appuntamento/voi/al/un/avete/museo/.** _____

_____

3. **ha/un/interessante/libro/lei/?** _____

_____

4. **professoressa/di/tu/una/italiano/hai/simpatica/.** _____

_____

5. **abbiamo/tempo/abbastanza/noi/?** _____

_____

6. **signora/ha/oggi/scusi/molto/lavoro/Lei/?** _____

_____

ANSWER KEY

1. Loro hanno una casa piccola?/Hanno una casa piccola loro? 2. Voi avete un appuntamento al
museo. 3. Lei ha un libro interessante?/Ha un libro interessante Lei? 4. Tu hai una professoressa
di italiano simpatica. 5. Noi abbiamo abbastanza tempo?/Abbiamo abbastanza tempo noi? 6. Scusi
signora, Lei ha molto lavoro oggi?/Scusi signora, ha molto lavoro Lei oggi?

Sentence Builder 2

▶ 3C Sentence Builder 2 (CD4, Track 12)

Dov'è la tua casa?	*Where is your house?*
Abito in un appartamento.	*I live in an apartment.*
Quante stanze ci sono?	*How many rooms are there?*
Ci sono soggiorno e la cucina.	*There's the living room and the kitchen.*
C'è anche lo studio.	*There's also a study.*
Com'è la tua camera da letto?	*How's your bedroom?*
È bella e spaziosa.	*It's beautiful and spacious.*
Ci sono lo stereo e la televisione.	*There's a stereo and a television.*

⏸

✎ Sentence Practice 2

Fill in the missing words in each of the following sentences. Again, the translations are given to help you, but try to identify the missing words first.

1. C'è _____ lo studio.

   (There is also a study.)

2. _____ la _____ casa?

   (Where is your house?)

3. C'è _____ stereo e _____ televisione.

   (There's a stereo and a TV.)

4. _____ stanze _____ sono?

   (How many rooms are there?)

5. _____ la tua camera _____ letto?

(How is your bedroom?)

ANSWER KEY
1. anche; 2. Dov'è, tua; 3. lo, la; 4. Quante, ci; 5. Com'è, da

Grammar Builder 2

▷ 3D Grammar Builder 2 (CD4, Track 13)

SINGULAR DEFINITE ARTICLES

Now let's review singular definite articles in Italian. Remember that **il** is used before most masculine singular nouns, but **lo** is used in the same cases where **uno** is used. That is, before masculine singular nouns beginning with **s** + consonant (*stereo*, *stereo*); **z**- (**zaino**, *backpack*); **ps**- (**psicologo**, *psychologist*); or **gn**- (**gnomo**, *gnome*). **La** is the feminine singular article. But for both masculine and feminine nouns that begin with a vowel, the form **l'** is used.

MASCULINE		
il	**il soggiorno** (*the living room*)	in front of a consonant
lo	**lo stereo** (*the stereo*)	in front of **s** + consonant, **z-**, **ps-**, or **gn-**
l'	**l'appartamento** (*the apartment*)	in front of a vowel

FEMININE		
la	**la cucina** (*the kitchen*)	in front of a consonant
l'	**l'aria** (*the air*)	in front of a vowel

✎ Work Out 2

Complete with the appropriate singular definite article:

1. _____ casa

2. _____ ufficio

3. _____ camera da letto

4. _____ studio

5. _____ televisione

6. _____ museo

7. _____ armadio

8. _____ divano

ANSWER KEY
1. la; 2. l'; 3. la; 4. lo; 5. la; 6. il; 7. l'; 8. il

✎ Drive It Home

Now let's get some more practice with the definite articles. Write in the correct form of the definite article. Read each word out loud.

A.

1. _____ museo

2. _____ parco

3. _____ televisore (note, this is another word for *TV*)

4. _____ soggiorno (*living room, m.*)

5. _____ balcone (*balcony, m.*)

B.

1. _____ aria

2. _____ appartamento

3. _____ atleta (*athlete, m.*)

4. _____ elettricista (*electrician, m.*)

5. _____ italiano

C.

1. _____ mostra

2. _____ via

3. _____ madre

4. _____ zia

5. _____ sorella

D.

1. _____ zio

2. _____ studente

3. _____ sbaglio (*mistake, m.*)

4. _____ zaino

5. _____ psicologo

ANSWER KEY

A. 1. il museo; 2. il parco; 3. il televisore; 4. il soggiorno; 5. il balcone

B. 1. l'aria; 2. l'appartamento; 3. l'atleta; 4. l'elettricista; 5. l'italiano

C. 1. la mostra; 2. la via; 3. la madre; 4. la zia; 5. la sorella

D. 1. lo zio; 2. lo studente; 3. lo sbaglio; 4. lo zaino; 5. lo psicologo

⊕ Culture Note

The **Museo degli Uffizi** holds, among other works of art, an extraordinary collection of Medieval and Renaissance masterpieces, including works by Giotto, Simone Martini, Botticelli, Leonardo, Michelangelo, Raffaello, and many other world renowned painters.

How Did You Do?

By now, you should be able to:

☐ use the very important verb **avere** (*to have*) (Still unsure? Jump back to page 37.)

☐ use the singular definite articles **il**, **lo**, **la**, and **l'** (Still unsure? Jump back to page 40.)

✎ Word Recall

Translate the following words into Italian.

1. *enough* _____

2. *today* _____

3. *the library* _____

4. *the museum* _____

5. *time* _____

6. *the study* _____

7. *the office* _____

8. *the apartment* _____

9. *the kitchen* _____

10. *the bedroom* _____

ANSWER KEY
1. abbastanza; 2. oggi; 3. la biblioteca; 4. il museo; 5. il tempo; 6. lo studio; 7. l'ufficio;
8. l'appartamento; 9. la cucina; 10. la camera da letto

Lesson 4: Conversations

By the end of this lesson, you should be able to:

☐ talk about actions with regular -are verbs

☐ use the plural definite articles i, gli, and le

Conversation 1

▶ 4A Conversation 1 (CD4, Track 14 - Italian; Track 15 - Italian and English)

Stephanie:	Che bello essere a Firenze! È una città fantastica e sono fortunata che tu sei la mia guida!
Guido:	Bene, oggi visitiamo il museo degli Uffizi. È in un edificio rinascimentale in centro. Ci sono quadri di Botticelli, Leonardo da Vinci, Michelangelo, Raffaello e Tiziano, tutti gli artisti importanti del Rinascimento. Inoltre in questo periodo c'è anche una mostra su Leonardo.
Stephanie:	Perfetto! Abbiamo abbastanza tempo?
Guido:	Sì, abbiamo quattro ore.
Stephanie:	E la biblioteca?
Guido:	Non c'è tempo per la biblioteca. Pranziamo con Gianni. Il ristorante è in una strada lì vicino.
Stephanie:	C'è un parco vicino al museo?
Guido:	No, non ci sono molti alberi in centro. Ma domani visitiamo Fiesole, un paese vicino a Firenze. A Fiesole l'aria è pulita e la vista, le chiese, gli alberi e i prati sono bellissimi.

Stephanie:	How beautiful to be in Florence! It's a fantastic city, and I'm fortunate you're my guide!
Guido:	Well, today we'll visit the Uffizi Gallery. It's in a Renaissance building in the center of town. There are paintings by Botticelli, Leonardo da Vinci, Michelangelo, Raphael and Titian, all the important Renaissance artists. And right now, there's also an exhibit on Leonardo.
Stephanie:	Great! Do we have enough time?
Guido:	Yes, we have four hours.
Stephanie:	And the library?
Guido:	There's no time for the library. We're eating with Gianni. The restaurant is on a street nearby.
Stephanie:	Is there a park near the museum?
Guido:	No, there aren't many trees in the center of town. But tomorrow, we'll visit Fiesole, a town near Florence. In Fiesole the air is clean, and the view, the churches, the trees, and the meadows are very beautiful.

Take It Further

Again, note the use of the propositions **a** and **in** in certain expressions: Italians use the preposition **in** to indicate where things are in a city: **in centro** (*in the center of town*); **in un edificio** (*in a building*); **in una strada** (*in a street*); and with actual addresses: **in via Mazzini** (*in Mazzini street*). However, they often use the preposition **a** to indicate where things are located with respect to other objects: **vicino a** (*near*); **davanti a** (*in front of*); **di fronte a** (*facing*), etc.

✎ Conversation Practice 1

Fill in the blanks in the following sentences with the missing words. If you're unsure of the answer, listen to the conversation on your audio one more time.

1. Che bello essere _____ Firenze!

2. È _____ un edificio rinascimentale _____ centro.

3. Ci _____ quadri di Botticelli, Leonardo da Vinci, Michelangelo, Raffaello e Tiziano ...

4. Perfetto! _____ abbastanza tempo?

5. _____ Fiesole l'aria è pulita ...

ANSWER KEY
1. a; 2. in, in; 3. sono; 4. Abbiamo; 5. A

Grammar Builder 1

▶ 4B Grammar Builder 1 (CD4, Track 16)

REGULAR -ARE VERBS IN THE PRESENT TENSE

You were introduced to **-are**, **-ere**, and **-ire** verbs in *Essential Italian*. But since verbs can be difficult to master, we'll review the basics and introduce you to a few more common and useful verbs. Let's start with **-are** verbs. Remember that you add the following endings to the verb stem after taking off the infinitival **-are**.

io	-o	noi	-iamo
tu	-i	voi	-ate
lui/lei/Lei	-a	loro/Loro	-ano

Let's see an example with **abitare** (*to live*).

io abito	*I live*
tu abiti	*you live*
lui abita	*he lives*
lei abita	*she lives*
Lei abita	*you live (fml.)*

noi abitiamo	we live
voi abitate	you (pl.) live
loro abitano	they live
Loro abitano	you (fml. pl.) live

Here are some common Italian **-are** verbs.

abitare	to live	chiamare	to call, to telephone
arrivare	to arrive	comprare	to buy
ascoltare	to listen to	giocare (a)	to play (a game, a sport)
aspettare	to wait for	parlare	to speak
ballare	to dance	suonare	to play (an instrument), to ring (a bell)
cantare	to sing	(ri)tornare	to return, to go back

Verbs ending in **-care** and **-gare**, such as **giocare** and **pagare**, add an **h** between the stem of the verb and the **tu** ending, **-i**, as well as the **noi** ending, **-iamo**. This preserves the hard /k/ and /g/ sound of the verb stem. Remember that **c** is pronounced *ch* before **i** (or **e**), and **g** is pronounced *j* before **i** (or **e**).

Noi giochiamo a tennis.
We play tennis.

Tu non paghi mai il conto.
You never pay the bill.

✎ Work Out 1

Complete the following sentences with the correct form of the verbs given in parentheses.

1. Maria _____ (abitare) in centro.

2. Giovanni e Roberto _____ (mangiare) in un ristorante italiano.

3. Io _____ (visitare) il museo degli Uffizi.

4. Noi _____ (lavorare) in un ufficio in centro.

5. Tu e Giulia _____ (giocare) a tennis.

6. Rossella, tu _____ (parlare) italiano?

7. Tu ed io _____ (aspettare) l'autobus.

8. Enrico _____ (ritornare) in Italia ogni anno.

ANSWER KEY
1. abita; 2. mangiano; 3. visito; 4. lavoriamo; 5. giocate; 6. parli; 7. aspettiamo; 8. ritorna

✎ Drive It Home

Let's practice those -are verbs now. For each subject or subject pronoun below, give the correct form of each of the verbs. Don't forget about -gare and -care verbs!

1. (io) cantare, tornare, ascoltare, giocare, parlare, pagare _____

_____

2. (noi) cantare, tornare, ascoltare, giocare, parlare, pagare _____

_____

3. (Carlo) cantare, tornare, ascoltare, giocare, parlare, pagare _____

_____

4. (tu) cantare, tornare, ascoltare, giocare, parlare, pagare _____

_____

5. (Gianni e Maria) cantare, tornare, ascoltare, giocare, parlare, pagare _____

_____

ANSWER KEY
1. canto, torno, ascolto, gioco, parlo, pago; 2. cantiamo, torniamo, ascoltiamo, giochiamo, parliamo, paghiamo; 3. canta, torna, ascolta, gioca, parla, paga; 4. canti, torni, ascolti, giochi, parli, paghi; 5. cantano, tornano, ascoltano, giocano, parlano, pagano

Conversation 2

4C Conversation 2 (CD4, Track 17 - Italian; Track 18 - Italian and English)

Lorenzo: Mirella, dov'è la tua casa?

Mirella: Abito in un appartamento in via Mazzini 13. L'appartamento è molto grande.

Lorenzo: Quante stanze ci sono?

Mirella: C'è il soggiorno e la cucina, ci sono due bagni, tre camere da letto e c'è anche lo studio che condivido con mio fratello.

Lorenzo: Com'è la tua camera da letto?

Mirella: È bella e spaziosa. Ci sono due letti, un armadio, un tavolo e quattro librerie. C'è anche un piccolo divano, lo stereo e la televisione.

Lorenzo: È veramente molto grande!

Mirella: Sì, sono fortunata!

Lorenzo: *Mirella, where's your house?*

Mirella: *I live in an apartment, at 13 Mazzini Street. The apartment is very big.*

Lorenzo: *How many rooms are there?*

Mirella:	*There's the living room and the kitchen, there are two bathrooms and three bedrooms, and there's also a study that I share with my brother.*
Lorenzo:	*What is your bedroom like? (lit., "how is your bedroom?")*
Mirella:	*It's beautiful and spacious. There are two beds, a closet, a table, and four bookcases. There's also a small couch, a stereo, and a television.*
Lorenzo:	*It's really very big!*
Mirella:	*Yes, I'm lucky!*

Conversation Practice 2

Unscramble and then translate the following sentences, all of which you've just heard in Conversation 2.

1. appartamento/molto/l'/grande/è. _____

    _____

2. è/tua/casa/dov'/Mirella/la/? _____

    _____

3. stanze/ci/quante/sono/? _____

    _____

4. la/com'/da/tua/letto/camera/è /? _____

    _____

5. grande/veramente/è/molto/! _____

    _____

ANSWER KEY

1. **L'appartamento è molto grande.** (*The apartment is very big.*) 2. **Mirella, dov'è la tua casa?** (*Mirella, where is your house?*); 3. **Quante stanze ci sono?** (*How many rooms are there?*); 4. **Com'è la tua camera da letto?** (*How is your bedroom?*); 5. **È veramente molto grande!** (*It's really very big!*)

Grammar Builder 2

▶ 4D Grammar Builder 2 (CD4, Track 19)

PLURAL DEFINITE ARTICLES

In the previous lesson, you reviewed the singular forms of the definite article, il, lo, la, and l'. Let's spend a little time reviewing the plural forms now. Remember that for the masculine, the plural of il is i; and the plural of lo and l' is gli. The feminine la and l' both become le in the plural.

i	i soggiorni (*the living rooms*)	in front of consonants
gli	gli studi (*the studies*) gli appartamenti (*the apartments*)	in front of s + consonant, z-, ps-, gn-, and vowels.
le	le cucine (*the kitchens*) le amiche (*the friends*)	in front of consonants and vowels

(II)

✎ Work Out 2

Complete with the appropriate plural definite article:

1. _____ case

2. _____ uffici

3. _____ camere da letto

4. _____ studi

5. _____ televisioni

6. _____ musei

7. _____ armadi

8. _____ divani

ANSWER KEY
1. le; 2. gli; 3. le; 4. gli; 5. le; 6. i; 7. gli; 8. i

✎ Drive It Home

Let's get some more practice with the definite plural article. Write in the correct form of the definite article. Read each word out loud.

A.

1. _____ musei

2. _____ parchi

3. _____ televisori

4. _____ soggiorni

5. _____ balconi

B.

1. _____ studi

2. _____ appartamenti

3. _____ atleti

4. _____psicologi

5. _____ italiani

C.

1. _____ mostre

2. _____ vie

3. _____ amiche

4. _____ stanze

5. _____ chiese

ANSWER KEY

A. 1. i musei; 2. i parchi; 3. i televisori; 4. i soggiorni; 5. i balconi

B. 1. gli studi; 2. gli appartamenti; 3. gli atleti; 4. gli psicologi; 5. gli italiani

C. 1. le mostre; 2. le vie; 3. le amiche; 4. le stanze; 5. le chiese

🌐 Culture Note

Italians count the floors in their buildings differently than Americans. What Americans call the first floor is always called **pian terreno** or **piano terra** (lit., *ground floor*) in Italy, and what Americans call the second floor is **primo piano** (*first floor*). The thirteenth floor isn't skipped the way it is in some American buildings, because according to Italian tradition the number 13 (**tredici**), brings good luck rather than bad luck. The penthouse is called **l'attico** and the basement is called **il seminterrato**. If you go to visit somebody in Italy, make sure you ring the bell on the right floor!

How Did You Do?

By now, you should be able to:

☐ talk about actions with regular **-are** verbs (Still unsure? Jump back to page 46.)

☐ use the plural definite articles **i**, **gli**, and **le** (Still unsure? Jump back to page 51.)

✎ Word Recall

Translate the following words into English.

1. fortunata _____

2. **guida** _____

3. **edificio** _____

4. **Rinascimento** _____

5. **biblioteca** _____

6. **strada** _____

7. **paese** _____

8. **prati** _____

9. **casa** _____

10. **appartamento** _____

11. **soggiorno** _____

12. **cucina** _____

13. **camere** _____

14. **studio** _____

15. **librerie** _____

ANSWER KEY

1. *lucky*; 2. *guide*; 3. *building*; 4. *Renaissance*; 5. *library*; 6. *street*; 7. *town, country*; 8. *meadows* (note: **prato** also means *lawn*); 9. *house, home*; 10. *apartment*; 11. *living room*; 12. *kitchen*; 13. *rooms*; 14. *study*; 15. *bookcases* (note: **libreria** also means *bookstore*.)

Don't forget to practice and reinforce what you've learned by visiting **www.livinglanguage.com/ languagelab** for flashcards, games, and quizzes!

Unit 1 Essentials

Vocabulary Essentials

Test your knowledge of the key material in this unit by filling in the blanks in the following charts. Once you've completed these pages, you'll have tested your retention, and you'll have your own reference for the most essential vocabulary.

AROUND TOWN

	country
	city
	building
	museum
	library
	bookstore
	church
	restaurant
	park

[pg. 15]

AT HOME

	apartment
	room
	living room
	kitchen
	bathroom

[pg. 21]

	bedroom
	bed
	table
	sofa, couch
	television

[pg. 21]

VERBS

	to live
	to arrive
	to listen to
	to wait for
	to dance
	to sing
	to call, to telephone
	to buy
	to play (a game, a sport)
	to speak
	to play (an instrument), to ring (a bell)
	to return, to go back

[pg. 47]

If you're having a hard time remembering this vocabulary, don't forget to check out the supplemental flashcards for this unit online. Go to **www.livinglanguage.com/languagelab**.

Grammar Essentials

Here is a reference of the key grammar that was covered in Unit 1. Make sure you understand the summary and can use all of the grammar in it.

ESSERE *(TO BE)*			
io sono	*I am*	noi siamo	*we are*
tu sei	*you are*	voi siete	*you are*
lui è, lei è	*he is, she is*	loro sono	*they are*
Lei è	*you are (fml.)*	Loro sono	*you are (fml. pl.)*

AVERE *(TO HAVE)*			
io ho	*I have*	noi abbiamo	*we have*
tu hai	*you have*	voi avete	*you have (pl. infml.)*
lui ha, lei ha	*he has, she has*	loro hanno	*they have*
Lei ha	*you have (fml.)*	Loro hanno	*you have (fml. pl.)*

CONJUGATION OF REGULAR -ARE VERBS

io	-o	noi	-iamo
tu	-i	voi	-ate
lui/lei/Lei	-a	loro/Loro	-ano

EXAMPLE: ABITARE *(TO LIVE)*

io	abito	noi	abitiamo
tu	abiti	voi	abitate
lui/lei/Lei	abita	loro/Loro	abitano

VERBS ENDING IN -CARE, -GARE LIKE GIOCARE AND PAGARE

io	gioco, pago	noi	giochiamo, paghiamo
tu	giochi, paghi	voi	giocate, pagate
lui/lei/Lei	gioca, paga	loro/Loro	giocano, pagano

PLURALS

	SINGULAR	PLURAL
Nouns ending in -o → i	albero	alberi
Nouns ending in -a → e	chiesa	chiese
Masculine nouns ending in -a → i	programma	programmi
Nouns ending in -e → i	ristorante	ristoranti
Nouns ending in -io (unstressed i) → i	edificio	edifici
Nouns ending in -io (stressed i) → ii	zio	zii
Nouns ending in stressed vowel → no change	città	città

INDEFINITE ARTICLES

MASCULINE		
in front of a consonant or vowel	un	un libro
in front of s + consonant, z-, ps-, gn-	uno	uno studente

FEMININE		
in front of a consonant	una	una casa
in front of a vowel	un'	un'amica

DEFINITE ARTICLES: MASCULINE

	SINGULAR	PLURAL
in front of a consonant	il soggiorno	i soggiorni
in front of s + consonant, z-, ps-, gn-	lo studio	gli studi
in front of a vowel	l'appartamento	gli appartamenti

DEFINITE ARTICLES: FEMININE

	SINGULAR	PLURAL
in front of a consonant	la cucina	le cucine
in front of a vowel	l'amica	le amiche

Unit 1 Quiz

Let's put the most essential Italian words and grammar points you've learned so far to practice in a few exercises. It's important to be sure that you've mastered this material before you move on. Score yourself at the end of the review and see if you need to go back for more practice, or if you're ready to move on to Unit 2.

A. Give the plural of the following nouns.

1. chiesa _____

2. città _____

3. negozio _____

4. ristorante _____

B. Insert either the preposition in or a appropriately.

1. Carla è _____ Milano.

2. Giovanni è _____ cucina.

C. Complete the following sentences with either c'è or ci sono.

1. A Firenze _____ molti musei.

2. _____ una chiesa rinascimentale.

D. Write the correct indefinite article in front of the following nouns.

1. _____ biblioteca

2. _____ professore

3. _____ studio

4. _____ amica

E. Complete with the appropriate forms of the definite article.

1. _____ case

2. _____ musei

3. _____ studenti

4. _____ strada

F. Complete the following sentences with the correct form of the verbs given in parentheses.

1. Loro _____ (abitare) a Firenze.

2. Carlo _____ (visitare) la mostra su Leonardo.

3. Io _____ (lavorare) in centro.

4. Paul, tu _____ (giocare) a tennis?

How Did You Do?

Give yourself a point for every correct answer, then use the following key to tell whether you're ready to move on:

0-7 points: It's probably a good idea to go back through the lesson again. You may be moving too quickly, or there may be too much "down time" between your contact with Italian. Remember that it's better to spend 30 minutes with Italian three or four times a week than it is to spend two or three hours just once a week. Find a pace that's comfortable for you, and spread your contact hours out as much as you can.

8-12 points: You would benefit from a review before moving on. Go back and spend a little more time on the specific points that gave you trouble. Reread the Grammar Builder sections that were difficult, and do the work outs one more time. Don't forget about the online supplemental practice material, either. Go to **www.livinglanguage.com/languagelab** for games and quizzes that will reinforce the material from this unit.

13-17 points: Good job! There are just a few points that you might consider reviewing before moving on. If you haven't worked with the games and quizzes on **www.livinglanguage.com/languagelab**, please give them a try.

18-20 points: Great! You're ready to move on to the next unit.

		points

Unit 2:
Everyday Life

In this unit, you'll learn how to talk about your everyday life, including both your work (**il lavoro**) and your free time (**il tempo libero**). Hopefully you're **fortunato** or **fortunata** (*lucky*) and have plenty of **tempo libero**! We'll be very **occupati** (*busy*) learning lots of Italian, and by the end of the unit, you'll know:

- ☐ the days of the week
- ☐ how to talk about your weekly routine
- ☐ common and important descriptive words
- ☐ how to use **gli aggettivi** (*adjectives*) in conversation
- ☐ essential irregular verbs
- ☐ how to use higher numbers
- ☐ how to ask questions with key question words
- ☐ idiomatic expressions with **avere** (*to have*) and **fare** (*to do, to make*)
- ☐ how to use **-ere** verbs
- ☐ how to use **-ire** verbs

Lesson 5: Words

By the end of this lesson, you'll know:

☐ the days of the week

☐ how to talk about your weekly routine

☐ common and important descriptive words

☐ how to use **gli aggettivi** (*adjectives*) in conversation

Word Builder 1

▶ 5A Word Builder 1 (CD4, Track 20)

la settimana	*the week*
il giorno	*the day*
lunedì	*Monday*
martedì	*Tuesday*
mercoledì	*Wednesday*
giovedì	*Thursday*
venerdì	*Friday*
sabato	*Saturday*
domenica	*Sunday*
il lavoro	*work*
la moda	*fashion*

⏸

✎ Word Practice 1

Translate the following into Italian.

1. *Saturday* _____

2. *the day* _____

3. *the days* _____

4. *a week* _____

5. *the weeks* _____

6. *Monday* _____

7. *fashion* _____

8. *Wednesday* _____

ANSWER KEY
1. **sabato**; 2. **il giorno**; 3. **i giorni**; 4. **una settimana**; 5. **le settimane**; 6. **lunedì**; 7. **la moda**; 8. **mercoledì**

Grammar Builder 1

▶ 5B Grammar Builder 1 (CD4, Track 21)

USING THE DAYS OF THE WEEK

In this lesson, you'll review **i giorni della settimana** (*the days of the week*) and learn how to use them to talk about your routine. Notice that in Italian the names of weekdays are not capitalized. Also, remember that all the names of weekdays are masculine, with the exception of **domenica**, which is feminine. Another important rule to remember is that, in Italian, when talking about what's happening *on* a specific day, prepositions are omitted.

Non lavoro lunedì.
I'm not working on Monday. (This coming Monday)

When talking about something that always happens on a specific day of the week, use the definite article in front of the day of the week.

Non lavoro il lunedì.
I don't work on Mondays. (Every Monday)

Work Out 1

Translate the following sentences into Italian. Note that you can express upcoming events in the near future by using the present, just as in English.

1. *I'm not working on Monday because I'm on vacation.* _____

   _____

2. *On Wednesdays we eat at the restaurant.* _____

   _____

3. *On Tuesday they're calling Maria.* _____

   _____

4. *He's visiting Florence (**Firenze**) on Thursday.* _____

   _____

5. *On Sundays there's an exhibit.* _____

   _____

ANSWER KEY
1. **Lunedì non lavoro perché sono in vacanza.** 2. **Il mercoledì mangiamo al ristorante.** 3. **Martedì chiamano Maria.** 4. **Giovedì visita Firenze.** 5. **La domenica c'è una mostra.**

Word Builder 2

▶ 5C Word Builder 2 (CD4, Track 22)

terribile	*terrible*
bello/bella	*beautiful*
nervoso/nervosa	*nervous*
malato/malata	*sick*
piccolo/piccola	*small*
grande	*big*
carino/carina	*cute/pretty*
brutto/brutta	*ugly*
rumoroso/rumorosa	*noisy*
pieno/piena	*full*
silenzioso/silenziosa	*silent*
solo/sola	*lonely*
depresso/depressa	*depressed*
felice	*happy*
vero/vera	*true*
falso/falsa	*false*
molto	*a lot, many; very*
tanto	*a lot, many; very*

⏸

✎ Word Practice 2

Translate the following adjectives and write their opposites in Italian.

1. *beautiful* _____

2. *false* _____

3. *depressed* _____

4. *noisy* _____

5. *small* _____

ANSWER KEY
1. **bello/a, brutto/a**; 2. **falso/a, vero/a**; 3. **depresso/a, felice**; 4. **rumoroso/a, silenzioso/a**;
5. **piccolo/a, grande**

Grammar Builder 2
▶ 5D Grammar Builder 2 (CD4, Track 23)

ADJECTIVE AGREEMENT

In Lesson 5 of *Essential Italian* you were introduced to adjective agreement. Let's review the basics again and then expand on what you know. Recall that there are two basic groups of adjectives: adjectives whose singular masculine form ends in -o (such as **piccolo**) with four possible endings (-o, -a, -i, -e), and adjectives whose singular masculine form ends in -e (such as **felice**) with two possible endings (-e, -i).

	SINGULAR	PLURAL
Masculine	piccolo	piccoli
Feminine	piccola	piccole
Masculine/Feminine	felice	felici

un bambino piccolo
a small child (male)

una bambina piccola
a small child (female)

i bambini piccoli
the small children (male, or both male and female)

le bambine piccole
the small children (female)

un bambino felice
a happy child (male)

una bambina felice
a happy child (female)

i bambini felici
the happy children (male, or both male and female)

le bambine felici
the happy children (female)

Notice that when we talk about a mixed gender group, both the noun and the adjective will take the masculine plural ending **-i**. **Molto** and **tanto** in Italian can be used both as adverbs and adjectives. When used as adverbs, they both mean *very* and they are invariable:

molto fortunata
very lucky (f. sg.)

molto fortunati
very lucky (m. pl.)

When used as adjectives, they both mean *a lot (of)*, *much*, or *many* and, like the other adjectives, they agree in gender and number with the nouns they modify:

molta pasta
a lot of pasta, much pasta

molti bambini
a lot of children, many children

Ⓘ

✎ Work Out 2

Complete the following sentences with the right form of the adjective given in parentheses.

1. **È una professoressa** _____. (simpatico)

2. **I dottori sono molto** _____. (occupato)

3. **Noi abbiamo una casa** _____. (rumoroso)

4. **È una bambina molto** _____. (grande)

5. **Silvia e Ilaria sono** _____ **per il colloquio di lavoro.** (nervoso)

6. **Mario è molto** _____. (malato)

ANSWER KEY
1. simpatica; 2. occupati; 3. rumorosa; 4. grande; 5. nervose; 6. malato

✎ Drive It Home

Give the correct form of each of the following adjectives for each subject.

1. **Gianni è ... (malato, bello, nervoso, grande, carino, solo, silenzioso, felice)**

_____

2. **Laura è …** (malato, bello, nervoso, grande, carino, solo, silenzioso, felice)

_____

3. **I ragazzi sono …** (malato, bello, nervoso, grande, carino, solo, silenzioso, felice)

_____

4. **Le ragazze sono …** (malato, bello, nervoso, grande, carino, solo, silenzioso, felice)

_____

ANSWER KEY

1. malato, bello, nervoso, grande, carino, solo, silenzioso, felice. 2. malata, bella, nervosa, grande, carina, sola, silenziosa, felice. 3. malati, belli, nervosi, grandi, carini, soli, silenziosi, felici. 4. malate, belle, nervose, grandi, carine, sole, silenziose, felici.

💡 Tip!

If you look at an Italian calendar, you will notice that the week in Italy begins on lunedì (*Monday*), not on domenica (*Sunday*). After all, domenica is one of the days of the week-*end*, not of the week-*beginning*!

How Did You Do?

Let's see how you did in this lesson. By now, you should know:

☐ the days of the week (Still unsure? Jump back to page 64.)

☐ how to talk about your weekly routine (Still unsure? Jump back to page 65.)

☐ common and important descriptive words (Still unsure? Jump back to page 67.)

☐ how to use gli aggettivi (*adjectives*) in conversation (Still unsure? Jump back to page 68.)

✎ Word Recall

A. Translate the following words from Italian into English.

1. grande _____

2. silenzioso/a _____

3. carino/a _____

4. solo/a _____

5. vero _____

B. Translate the following words from English into Italian.

1. *terrible* _____

2. *small* _____

3. *nervous* _____

ANSWER KEY
A. 1. *big*; 2. *silent*; 3. *cute*; 4. *lonely*; 5. *true*
B.1. **terrible**; 2. **piccolo/a**; 3. **nervoso/a**

Lesson 6: Phrases

By the end of this lesson, you should know:

☐ essential irregular verbs

☐ how to use higher numbers

Phrase Builder 1

▶ 6A Phrase Builder 1 (CD4, Track 24)

fai	you do, you make
faccio	I do, I make
andiamo	we go
magari	I wish, perhaps
mi dispiace	I'm sorry
ho bisogno di	I need
ho fame	I'm hungry
ho fretta	I'm in a hurry
un colloquio di lavoro	a job interview
lavoro part-time	part-time job
non credo	I don't think so
purtroppo	unfortunately

✏ Phrase Practice 1

Match the English in the right column with the Italian in the left.

1. **non credo**   a. *I do, I make*

2. **mi dispiace**   b. *we go*

3. **fai**   c. *I wish, perhaps*

4. **faccio**   d. *I'm sorry*

5. **ho fretta**   e. *I need*

6. **purtroppo**   f. *I'm hungry*

7. **ho fame**   g. *I'm in a hurry*

8. **magari**   h. *you do, you make*

9. **andiamo**

10. **ho bisogno di**

i. *I don't think so*

j. *unfortunately*

ANSWER KEY

1. i; 2. d; 3. h; 4. a; 5. g; 6. j; 7. f; 8. c; 9. b; 10. e

Grammar Builder 1

▶ 6B Grammar Builder 1 (CD4, Track 25)

IRREGULAR -ARE VERBS IN THE PRESENT TENSE

There are only four irregular -**are** verbs: **andare** (*to go*), **dare** (*to give*), **fare** (*to do, to make*), **stare** (*to stay*). But if you take a look at the endings, you'll see that they're not terribly different from regular verbs.

ANDARE *(TO GO)*			
io vado	*I go*	noi andiamo	*we go*
tu vai	*you go*	voi andate	*you (pl.) go*
lui/lei/Lei va	*he/she goes, you (fml.) go*	loro/Loro vanno	*they go, you (fml. pl.) go*

DARE *(TO GIVE)*			
io do	*I give*	noi diamo	*we give*
tu dai	*you give*	voi date	*you (pl.) give*
lui/lei/Lei dà	*he/she gives, you (fml.) give*	loro/Loro danno	*they give, you (fml. pl.) give*

FARE *(TO DO, TO MAKE)*			
io faccio	*I do/make*	noi facciamo	*we do/make*
tu fai	*you do/make*	voi fate	*you (pl.) do/make*

FARE *(TO DO, TO MAKE)*			
lui/lei/Lei fa	*he/she does/ makes, you (fml.) do/make*	loro/Loro fanno	*they do/make, you (fml. pl.) do/make*

STARE *(TO STAY)*			
io sto	*I stay*	noi stiamo	*we stay*
tu stai	*you stay*	voi state	*you (pl.) stay*
lui/lei/Lei sta	*he/she stays, you (fml.) stay*	loro/Loro stanno	*they stay, you (fml. pl.) stay*

Quando vai al supermercato?
When do you go to the supermarket?

Susanna dà una festa il sabato.
Susanna gives a party on Saturdays.

Che lavoro fai?
What (job) do you do?

Note that stare, in addition to its literal meaning *to stay*, is used idiomatically to mean *to be feeling*, as you've seen in previous dialogues.

Giovanna come stai?
Giovanna, how are you?

✎ Work Out 1

Complete the following sentences with the correct form of either andare, dare, fare, or stare.

1. Loro _____ al cinema il sabato.

2. Il professore _____ un libro ai suoi studenti.

3. Maria, come _____ ?

4. _____ bene, grazie, e tu?

5. Voi _____ un lavoro molto interessante.

6. Noi _____ in ufficio alle 8:30.

7. Questa sera tu _____ al ristorante o _____ a casa?

ANSWER KEY
1. vanno; 2. dà; 3. stai; 4. Sto; 5. fate; 6. andiamo; 7. vai, stai

Phrase Builder 2

▶ 6C Phrase Builder 2 (CD4, Track 26)

alle sette	*at seven*
mille cose	*tons of things, a thousand things*
cinquantaquattro	*fifty-four*
una giornata piena	*a full day, a busy day*
un momento	*a moment, wait a second*
di mattina	*in the morning*
di pomeriggio	*in the afternoon*
di sera	*in the evening*
di notte	*at night*
ho ragione	*I'm right*

ho torto	*I'm wrong*
fare spese	*to shop*

✎ Phrase Practice 2

Match the English in the right column with the Italian in the left.

1. di mattina	a. I'm right
2. ho ragione	b. a full day
3. mille cose	c. in the evening
4. ho torto	d. in the morning
5. fare spese	e. I'm wrong
6. una giornata piena	f. at night
7. di sera	g. at seven
8. di notte	h. in the afternoon
9. alle sette	i. to shop
10. di pomeriggio	j. a thousand things

ANSWER KEY

1. d; 2. a; 3. j; 4 e; 5. i; 6. b; 7. c; 8. f; 9. g; 10. h

Grammar Builder 2

▶ 6D Grammar Builder 2 (CD4, Track 27)

NUMBERS 20 AND ABOVE

In Lesson 9 of *Essential Italian* you learned the numbers up through **venti** (*twenty*). Let's continue counting with some higher numbers.

venti	*twenty*
trenta	*thirty*

quaranta	*forty*
cinquanta	*fifty*
sessanta	*sixty*
settanta	*seventy*
ottanta	*eighty*
novanta	*ninety*
cento	*one hundred*
mille	*one thousand*
milione/i	*million/s*
miliardo/i	*billion/s*

To form all other numbers, you just need to add uno, due, tre, etc., up through nove, as in cinquantaquattro (*fifty-four*). Note that you need to drop the final vowel of numbers venti through novanta when you add the numbers uno and otto, as in ventuno, ventotto. When adding the number tre to those numbers, -tré takes a written accent, as in quarantatré (*forty-three*).

The numbers *one hundred* and *one thousand* are cento and mille, respectively. Note that mille has an irregular plural: mila, as in duemila (*two thousand.*) As you write higher and higher numbers, notice that you get longer and longer words in Italian: duemilioniquattrocentosessantacinquemila, novecento otto (*two million, four hundred sixty-five thousand, nine hundred and eight*).

The numbers milione and miliardo require the preposition di in front of a noun, as in un milione di dollari (*one million dollars*).

Ⓘ

✎ Work Out 2

Write out the following numbers:

1. *68* _____

2. *281* _____

3. *3,726* _____

4. *43,263* _____

5. *875,974* _____

6. *3,268,957* _____

ANSWER KEY

1. sessantotto; 2. duecentottantuno; 3. tremilasettecentoventisei;
4. quarantatremiladuecentosessantatré; 5. ottocentosettantacinquemilanovecentosettantaquattro;
6. tremilioniduecentosessantottomilanovecentocinquantasette

✎ Drive It Home

Complete the following sentences with the correct form of either andare, dare,
fare, or stare.

1. Franco (andare) _____ sempre al cinema la domenica.

2. Sabato Maria e Luisa (fare) _____ le spese di pomeriggio.

3. Ora ho fretta, perché non (noi andare) _____ al ristorante di sera?

4. Che lavoro (fare) _____ Michele?

5. (Noi fare) _____ così: io (stare) _____ a casa, e tu (andare)

_____ al supermercato.

6. Gli studenti (dare) _____ i compiti al professore.

7. Se sei stanca, perché non (dare) _____ lo zaino a Paolo?

8. Da quando abitano a Firenze (stare) _____ molto bene.

ANSWER KEY
1. va; 2. fanno; 3. andiamo; 4. fa; 5. facciamo, sto, vai; 6. danno; 7. dai; 8. stanno

🔆 Tip!

The use of commas and periods in numbers is completely the opposite in Italian from English. Italian numbers use a period instead of a comma, and indicate decimals with a comma rather than a period. In the previous exercise, for example, 3,268,957.00 would be written as **3.268.957,00** in Italian.

How Did You Do?

Let's see how you did in this lesson. By now, you should know:

☐ essential irregular verbs (Still unsure? Jump back to page 74.)

☐ how to use higher numbers (Still unsure? Jump back to page 77.)

✎ Word Recall

A. Translate the following phrases from English into Italian.

1. *I'm wrong* _____

2. *to shop* _____

3. *I'm sorry* _____

4. *in the morning* _____

5. *I wish!* _____

B. Translate the following phrases from Italian into English.

1. **di notte** _____

2. **ho bisogno di** _____

3. **ho fame** _____

4. **una giornata piena** _____

5. **purtroppo** _____

ANSWER KEY
A. 1. ho torto; 2. fare spese; 3. mi dispiace; 4. di mattina; 5. magari!
B. 1. *at night*; 2. *I need*; 3. *I'm hungry*; 4. *a full day*; 5. *unfortunately*

Lesson 7: Sentences

By the end of this lesson, you should know:

☐ how to ask questions with key question words

☐ idiomatic expressions with **avere** (*to have*) and **fare** (*to do, to make*)

Sentence Builder 1

▶ 7A Sentence Builder 1 (CD4, Track 28)

Come stai?	*How are you?*
Che cosa fai?	*What do you do? (What are you doing?)*
Che lavoro fai?	*What kind of work do you do?*
Quante ore lavori?	*How many hours do you work?*
Dove lavori?	*Where do you work?*
Perché hai fretta?	*Why are you in a hurry?*
Chi va al supermercato oggi?	*Who's going to the supermarket today?*
Di che cosa ha bisogno il direttore?	*What does the director need?*
Quando andiamo al ristorante?	*When are we going to the restaurant?*

| Quanto costa un caffè in Italia? | How much does a (cup of) coffee cost in Italy? |
| Quale ristorante preferisci? | Which restaurant do you prefer? |

Ⓘ

✎ Sentence Practice 1

Fill in the blanks using the word bank.

che cosa, quale, quanto, come, che, quante

1. _____ lavoro fai?

2. Di _____ hai bisogno?

3. _____ stai?

4. _____ costa un caffè in Italia?

5. _____ ore lavori?

6. _____ ristorante preferisci?

ANSWER KEY

1. Che; 2. che cosa; 3. Come; 4. Quanto; 5. Quante; 6. Quale

Grammar Builder 1

▶ 7B Grammar Builder 1 (CD4, Track 29)

QUESTION WORDS

As you can see in the sentences above, some Italian questions begin with question words, also known as interrogatives, just as in English. The important interrogatives in Italian are chi (*who*), che, che cosa (*what*), come (*how*), quando (*when*), dove (*where*), perché (*why*), quanto (*how much/how many*), and quale (*which*). In these types of questions, when the subject is expressed, it is usually placed at the end of the sentence.

Quando arriva Marco?
When does Marco arrive?

Most interrogatives are invariable, meaning they never change form. Quale and quanto, however, are adjectives, so they agree in gender and number with the noun they modify. Treat quale like a regular -e adjective (quale, quali), and quanto like a regular -o adjective (quanto, quanta, quanti, quante).

Quali riviste leggi?
Which magazines do you read?

Quanti libri hai?
How many books do you have?

When you need to use a preposition in a sentence beginning with the question word chi (*who*), the preposition always precedes the question word and is never placed at the end of the sentence.

Con chi vai al cinema?
Who are you going to the movies with?

A chi dai il giornale?
Who are you giving the newspaper to?

Ⅱ

✎ Work Out 1

Each of the following is an answer to a question with an interrogative. Read each answer, and then give the question that would have prompted it.

1. Sto bene, grazie. _____

   _____

2. Ho solo una macchina. _____

   _____

3. Preferisco Venezia. _____

   _____

4. Andiamo al cinema alle 8:00. _____

   _____

5. Ha bisogno di denaro. _____

   _____

6. Studiano a Perugia. _____

   _____

7. Oggi non lavoro perché sto male. _____

   _____

8. Andiamo al ristorante con Luisa. _____

   _____

ANSWER KEY
1. Come stai? 2. Quante macchine hai? 3. Quale città preferisci? 4. Quando andate al cinema? 5. Di che cosa ha bisogno? 6. Dove studiano? 7. Perché non lavori oggi? 8. Con chi andate al ristorante?

Sentence Builder 2

▶ 7C Sentence Builder 2 (CD4, Track 30)

Hanno molta fame.	*They're very hungry.*
Il direttore non ha bisogno di aiuto.	*The director doesn't need any help.*
Purtroppo ho fretta.	*Unfortunately, I'm in a hurry.*
Lei ha torto.	*She's wrong.*
Noi abbiamo ragione.	*We're right.*
Gisella fa la giornalista.	*Gisella is a journalist.*
Facciamo la spesa al supermercato.	*We go grocery shopping at the supermarket.*

Ⅱ

✎ Sentence Practice 2

Fill in the blanks using the word bank.

purtroppo, vanno, bisogno, ha torto, fa, fame

1. Ha ragione Franco? No, _____.

2. Noi abbiamo molta _____. E voi?

3. Che lavoro fa Marisa? Lei _____ la giornalista?

4. Loro _____ al supermercato.

5. Ho _____ di una penna per scrivere una lettera.

6. State a pranzo con noi? No, _____ abbiamo fretta.

ANSWER KEY
1. ha torto; 2. fame; 3. fa; 4. vanno; 5. bisogno; 6. purtroppo

Grammar Builder 2

▶ 7D Grammar Builder 2 (CD4, Track 31)

IDIOMATIC EXPRESSIONS WITH AVERE AND FARE

Avere (*to have*) and fare (*to do, to make*) are two very idiomatic verbs. Avere is used in many expressions that use *to be* in English, such as avere fame (*to be hungry*). Fare is often used in expressions that require *to take* in English, such as fare una fotografia (*to take a picture*). Here is a list of the most common idiomatic expressions that use avere.

avere fame	*to be hungry*
avere sete	*to be thirsty*
avere caldo	*to be hot*
avere freddo	*to be cold*
avere ragione	*to be right*
avere torto	*to be wrong*
avere fretta	*to be in a hurry*
avere sonno	*to be sleepy*
avere bisogno di	*to need*
avere voglia di	*to feel like*
avere paura di	*to be afraid of*

In addition, avere is used to express age in Italian:

Quanti anni hai?
How old are you?

Ho ventitré anni.
I am twenty-three years old.

Idiomatic Expressions with
avere and **fare**

          Verbs with **-isc-**

Now let's look at idiomatic expression using fare.

fare la spesa	*to go grocery shopping*
fare spese	*to shop*
fare la doccia	*to take a shower*
fare il bagno	*to take a bath*
fare colazione	*to have breakfast*
fare una domanda	*to ask a question*
fare una fotografia	*to take a picture*
fare una passeggiata	*to take a walk*
fare una pausa	*to take a break*
fare un viaggio	*to take a trip*

(II)

✎ Work Out 2

Complete with the correct form of either fare or avere.

1. Francesca _____ una passeggiata nel parco.

2. Enrico _____ trentacinque anni.

3. Io _____ una fotografia del monumento.

4. I bambini _____ sempre fame!

5. Renzo e Lucia _____ bisogno di soldi.

6. Noi _____ un viaggio in Italia.

7. Voi _____ ragione, questo ristorante è eccellente.

8. Alle dieci Teresa _____ una pausa per un caffè.

ANSWER KEY:
1. fa; 2. ha; 3. faccio; 4. hanno; 5. hanno; 6. facciamo; 7. avete; 8. fa

✎ Drive It Home

Complete the following questions with the appropriate interrogative.

1. _____ costano queste scarpe?

2. Per favore, chiamami _____ arrivi a casa.

3. _____ film danno al cinema stasera?

4. Io preferisco il vino rosso, e tu _____ preferisci?

5. Giorgio va in vacanza con Luigi. E tu _____ vai?

6. _____ camere ci sono nel tuo appartamento?

7. Io prendo un caffè. Voi _____ prendete?

8. _____ zucchero vuoi nel caffè?

9. _____ anni ha tua madre?

10. _____ compri la frutta, al supermercato?

ANSWER KEY
1. Quanto; 2. quando; 3. Quale; 4. quale; 5. con chi; 6. Quante; 7. che cosa; 8. Quanto; 9. Quanti; 10. Dove

💡 Tip!

Remember that every language is made up of many idiomatic expressions, expressions that have a different meaning than the individual words of which they are composed. For instance, when in American English we want to wish someone good luck in a specific task, we often say: *break a leg!* The equivalent expression in Italian is **in bocca al lupo** (lit., *in the mouth of the wolf*). The answer to this expression is **crepi il lupo**, which broadly means *thank you*, but literally means *may the wolf die.* Poor wolf, but lucky for you.

How Did You Do?

Let's see how you did in this lesson. By now, you should know:

☐ how to ask questions with key question words
(Still unsure? Jump back to page 82.)

☐ idiomatic expressions with avere (*to have*) and fare (*to do, to make*)
(Still unsure? Jump back to page 86.)

✎ Word Recall

A. Translate the following phrases from Italian into English.

1. **Ho fretta.** _____

2. **Facciamo spese.** _____

3. **Ha bisogno di ...** _____

4. **Quando?** _____

5. **Come stai?** _____

B. Translate the following phrases from English into Italian.

1. *We are right.* _____

2. *She is a journalist.* _____

3. *We are hungry.* _____

4. *Where?* _____

5. *How much does it cost?* _____

ANSWER KEY
A. 1. *I'm in a hurry.* 2. *We shop.* 3. *He/she needs ...* 4. *When?* 5. *How are you?*
B. 1. Abbiamo ragione. 2. Lei fa la giornalista. 3. Abbiamo fame. 4. Dove? 5. Quanto costa?

Lesson 8: Conversations

By the end of this lesson, you should know:

☐ how to use -ere verbs

☐ how to use -ire verbs

🔊 Conversation 1

▶ 8A Conversation 1 (CD5, Track 1 - Italian; Track 2 - Italian and English)

Renzo:	Ciao Mariella, come stai?
Mariella:	Sto molto bene, grazie. Ho un nuovo lavoro.
Renzo:	Davvero? Che cosa fai?
Mariella:	Lavoro part-time per una rivista di moda.
Renzo:	Fai la giornalista?
Mariella:	Magari! Faccio un po' di tutto: rispondo al telefono, scrivo lettere a macchina, mando fax, metto in ordine, qualche volta servo anche il caffè al direttore.
Renzo:	Quante ore lavori alla settimana?
Mariella:	Lavoro il lunedì e il mercoledì dalle nove alle due e il venerdì dalle nove a mezzogiorno.
Renzo:	Sono in cerca di lavoro. Per caso il tuo direttore ha bisogno di aiuto il martedì e il giovedì?
Mariella:	Non credo, mi dispiace. Ho molta fame, andiamo a mangiare qualcosa?
Renzo:	Purtroppo vado di fretta, ho un colloquio di lavoro fra mezz'ora.
Mariella:	Peccato! Ciao, Renzo, ti chiamo presto e in bocca al lupo!
Renzo:	Crepi il lupo!

Idiomatic Expressions with
avere and **fare**

Renzo:	*Hi Mariella, how are you?*
Mariella:	*I'm very well, thanks. I have a new job.*
Renzo:	*Really? What do you do?*
Mariella:	*I work part-time for a fashion magazine.*
Renzo:	*Are you a journalist?*
Mariella:	*I wish! I do a bit of everything: I answer the phone, type letters, send faxes, I put things away, and sometimes I even serve coffee to the director.*
Renzo:	*How many hours a week do you work?*
Mariella:	*I work Mondays and Wednesdays, from nine to two, and on Fridays from nine to twelve.*
Renzo:	*I'm looking for a job. Does your director, by any chance, need help on Tuesdays and Thursdays?*
Mariella:	*I don't believe so, I'm sorry. I'm really hungry, should we go and have something to eat?*
Renzo:	*Unfortunately I'm in a hurry, I have a job interview in half an hour.*
Mariella:	*Too bad! Good-bye, Renzo, I'll call you soon, and good luck!*
Renzo:	*Thanks!*

Take It Further

When talking about professions, you have two different ways of expressing what a person does. You can either use the idiomatic expression: fare + definite article + profession, as in **Fai la giornalista?** (*Are you a journalist?*), or you can use the more literal expression: essere + (indefinite article) + profession, as in **No, non sono (una) giornalista.** (*No, I'm not a journalist.*) Note that the indefinite article can be omitted.

✎ Conversation Practice 1

Fill in the blanks with the missing words in the word bank.

ho, come stai?, molto bene, in bocca al lupo, quante ore, ha bisogno di, andiamo, il, mi dispiace, peccato!, faccio, fai

1. Ciao Mariella, _____?

2. Sto _____, grazie. _____ un nuovo lavoro.

3. _____ la giornalista?

4. Magari! _____ un po' di tutto.

5. _____ lavori alla settimana?

6. Per caso il tuo direttore _____ aiuto _____

   martedì e _____ giovedì?

7. Non credo, _____. Ho molta fame, _____ a

   mangiare qualcosa?

8. _____! Ciao, Renzo, ti chiamo presto e _____!

ANSWER KEY
1. come stai; 2. molto bene, Ho; 3. Fai; 4. Faccio; 5. Quante ore; 6. ha bisogno di, il, il; 7. mi dispiace, andiamo; 8. Peccato, in bocca al lupo

Grammar Builder 1

▶ 8B Grammar Builder 1 (CD5, Track 3)

REGULAR -ERE AND -IRE VERBS

Now let's go over the two other regular verb categories in Italian, the **-ere** and **-ire** groups. Recall from Essential Italian that **-ere** and **-ire** verbs have very similar endings; the only difference is in the voi forms, which are -ete for -ere verbs, and -ite for -ire verbs.

	-ERE VERBS	-IRE VERBS
io	-o	-o
tu	-i	-i
lui/lei/Lei	-e	-e
noi	-iamo	-iamo
voi	-ete	-ite
loro/Loro	-ono	-ono

Let's take a closer look with scrivere (*to write*) and dormire (*to sleep*).

io scrivo	*I write*	noi scriviamo	*we write*
tu scrivi	*you write*	voi scrivete	*you (pl.) write*
lui/lei/Lei scrive	*he/she writes, you (fml.) write*	loro/Loro scrivono	*they write, you (fml. pl.) write*

io dormo	*I sleep*	noi dormiamo	*we sleep*
tu dormi	*you sleep*	voi dormite	*you (pl.) sleep*
lui/lei/Lei dorme	*he/she sleeps, you (fml.) sleep*	loro/Loro dormono	*they sleep, you (fml. pl.) sleep*

Here are a few more common -ere verbs.

chiedere	*to ask*
chiudere	*to close*
correre	*to run*
credere	*to believe*
leggere	*to read*
mettere	*to put*
perdere	*to lose*

prendere	*to take*
ricevere	*to receive*
rispondere (a)	*to answer*
vedere	*to see*
vivere	*to live*

And here are some -ire verbs.

aprire	*to open*
offrire	*to offer*
partire	*to leave*
seguire	*to follow*
sentire	*to hear*
servire	*to serve*

Ⓘ

✎ Work Out 1

Complete the following sentences with the correct form of the verbs given in parentheses.

1. Loro _____ (vivere) in un appartamento elegante.

2. La signora _____ (servire) un caffè molto buono.

3. Noi _____ (rispondere) alla telefonata.

4. Voi _____ (ricevere) molte lettere.

5. Il treno _____ (partire) alle due.

6. Io _____ (aprire) la finestra perché ho caldo.

7. Marisa _____ (chiudere) la porta.

8. **Tu e Giovanni** _____ (leggere) **il giornale tutti i giorni.**

ANSWER KEY
1. vivono; 2. serve; 3. rispondiamo; 4. ricevete; 5. parte; 6. apro; 7. chiude; 8. leggete

🎧 Conversation 2

▶ 8C Conversation 2 (CD5, Track 4 - Italian; Track 5 - Italian and English)

Marco:	Ciao Daniela, andiamo in centro domani a fare spese?
Daniela:	Magari! Ho una giornata terribile e sono già nervosa! Alle sette preparo la colazione e quando tutti hanno finito di mangiare pulisco la cucina. Poi accompagno i bambini a scuola e vado al supermercato a fare la spesa… Ho mille cose da fare!
Marco:	Un momento, non capisco. Perché non porta i bambini a scuola Mario?
Daniela:	Perché deve essere in ospedale alle sette e mezza per visitare un paziente molto malato.
Marco:	E dopo il supermercato?
Daniela:	I bambini hanno invitato due amici a giocare. Così di pomeriggio ci saranno quattro bambini piccoli, adorabili, ma rumorosi, in casa! Di mattina faccio anche una torta per il compleanno di Mario. Compie cinquantaquattro anni! Come vedi ho una giornata piena!
Marco:	Giusto, io sono solo e depresso e tu non sei una vera amica!
Daniela:	Mi dispiace, Marco, ma hai torto! Sono solo un'amica occupata!
Marco:	Hai ragione, scusami! Ho davvero esagerato!

Marco:	_Hello Daniela, are we going shopping in the city, tomorrow?_
Daniela:	_I wish! I have a terrible day and I'm already nervous! At 7:00, I'm going to prepare breakfast, and when everyone is finished eating, I'll clean the kitchen. Then I'll take the kids to school, and I'll go to the supermarket to buy food… I have a thousand things to do._
Marco:	_Wait a second, I don't understand. Why isn't Mario taking the kids to school?_

Daniela: *Because he has a very sick patient, and he's going to see him at the*
            hospital at 7:30.
Marco: *And after the supermarket?*
Daniela: *The kids have invited two friends over to play. So at two in the*
            afternoon, there are going to be four small children, nice but noisy, in
            the house! In the morning, I'm also going to make a cake for Mario's
            birthday. He's going to be fifty-four … as you can see I have a full day!
Marco: *Yes, and I'm lonely and depressed, and you're not a true friend!*
Daniela: *I'm sorry Marco, you're wrong! I'm just a busy friend!*
Marco: *You're right, I'm sorry! I'm really unreasonable!*

Ⓘ

Take It Further

As you've probably noticed, when there are two verbs in a row in Italian, the
second one is in the infinitive:

Desidero andare al cinema.
I want to go to the movies.

Posso parlare italiano.
I can speak Italian.

Certain verbs, however, take either the preposition **a** or **di** in front of the
infinitive.

Finiscono di mangiare.
They finish eating.

Andiamo a fare spese.
We go shopping.

Idiomatic Expressions with
avere and **fare**

You'll become familiar with these verbs as you hear more Italian. It's best to memorize them as you go.

✎ Conversation Practice 2

Fill in the blanks in the following sentences with the missing words in the word bank. If you're unsure of the answer, listen to the conversation on your audio one more time.

Di pomeriggio, quattro bambini, andiamo, hai ragione, mi dispiace, fare le spese, ho mille cose da fare, vedi, non capisco, faccio, hai torto

1. Ciao Daniela, _____ in centro domani a _____ ?

2. Vado al supermercato a fare la spesa… _____ !

3. Un momento, _____ .

4. Così _____ ci saranno _____

   piccoli.

5. Di mattina _____ anche una torta per il compleanno di Mario.

6. Come _____ ho una giornata piena!

7. _____ , Marco, ma _____ ! Sono solo un'amica

   occupata!

8. _____ , scusami! Ho davvero esagerato!

ANSWER KEY
1. andiamo, fare spese; 2. Ho mille cose da fare; 3. non capisco; 4. di pomeriggio, quattro bambini;
5. faccio; 6. vedi; 7. Mi dispiace, hai torto; 8. Hai ragione

Grammar Builder 2

8D Grammar Builder 2 (CD5, Track 6)

VERBS WITH -ISC-

Don't forget that a lot of **-ire** verbs follow a slightly different, yet still regular pattern. These verbs are known as **-isc** verbs, because they insert **-isc-** between the regular stem and the regular ending of the verb, in the **io**, **tu**, **lui/lei/Lei**, and **loro/Loro** subjects.

Here's how it works with the verb **capire** (*to understand*):

io capisco	*I understand*	noi capiamo	*we understand*
tu capisci	*you understand*	voi capite	*you (pl.) understand*
lui/lei/Lei capisce	*he/she understands, you (fml.) understand*	loro/Loro capiscono	*they understand, you (fml. pl.) understand*

Keep in mind your spelling and pronunciation rules. The letter **c** is pronounced "hard" before **a**, **o**, and **u**, so in **capisco** and **capiscono** the **sc** is pronounced like *sk*. But before **i** and **e**, **c** is soft, so **sc** is pronounced like *sh* in **capisci** and **capisce**. Also note that in general, verbs that have only one consonant before the ending **-ire** (**preferire**, *to prefer*; **finire**, *to finish*; **pulire**, *to clean*), will use the **-isc-** conjugation. If there are two or more consonants before **-ire** (**partire**, **offrire**, **aprire**), the conjugation will be regular.

✎ Work Out 2

Complete the following sentences with the correct forms of the -ire verbs in parentheses.

1. A che ora _____ (partire) Susanna?

2. Tu _____ (pulire) la casa tutti i giorni.

3. Noi _____ (preferire) mangiare a casa.

4. Io non _____ (capire) il professore.

5. Quando _____ (servire) il caffè loro?

6. Il negozio _____ (aprire) alle nove.

7. Giovanna _____ (finire) di lavorare alle sei.

8. Lui _____ (seguire) sempre i miei consigli.

ANSWER KEY
1. parte; 2. pulisci; 3. preferiamo; 4. capisco; 5. servono; 6. apre; 7. finisce; 8. segue

✎ Drive It Home

Give the correct form of the verbs indicated for each subject.

1. tu… (leggere, chiedere, partire, mettere, vedere, aprire, dormire,

rispondere) _____

_____

2. loro… (leggere, chiedere, partire, mettere, vedere, aprire, dormire, rispondere)

_____

_____

3. io… (leggere, chiedere, partire, mettere, vedere, aprire, dormire, rispondere)

_____

_____

4. voi… (leggere, chiedere, partire, mettere, vedere, aprire, dormire, rispondere)

_____

_____

5. lui/lei… (leggere, chiedere, partire, mettere, vedere, aprire, dormire, rispondere)

_____

_____

6. noi… (leggere, chiedere, partire, mettere, vedere, aprire, dormire, rispondere)

_____

_____

ANSWER KEY
1. … leggi, chiedi, parti, metti, vedi, apri, dormi, rispondi
2. … leggono, chiedono, partono, mettono, vedono, aprono, dormono, rispondono
3. … leggo, chiedo, parto, metto, vedo, apro, dormo, rispondo
4. … leggete, chiedete, partite, mettete, vedete, aprite, dormite, rispondete
5. … legge, chiede, parte, mette, vede, apre, dorme, risponde
6. … leggiamo, chiediamo, partiamo, mettiamo, vediamo, apriamo, dormiamo, rispondiamo

⚡ Tip!

Now that you've learned the verb **partire**, and the expression **fare un viaggio**, you might be tempted to organize a trip in Italy. A great way to travel within Italy is by train, and you might want to check out the official site of the **Ferrovie dello Stato** (the national railway system), and find out schedules, prices, and news related to traveling by train in Italy and Europe.

How Did You Do?

Let's see how you did in this lesson. By now, you should know:

☐ how to use **-ere** verbs (Still unsure? Jump back to page 92.)

☐ how to use **-ire** verbs (Still unsure? Jump back to page 98.)

✎ Word Recall

Please translate the following phrases into Italian.

1. *I answer the phone.* _____

_____

2. *I work on Mondays and Wednesdays.* _____

_____

3. *a job interview* _____

_____

4. *Break a leg!* _____

_____

5. *Too bad!* _____

_____

6. *Just a moment, I don't understand.* _____

_____

7. *I'm sorry.* _____

_____

8. *You are right.* _____

_____

9. *I write letters.* _____

_____

10. *I bake a cake.* _____

_____

ANSWER KEY

1. **Rispondo al telefono.** 2. **Lavoro il lunedì e il mercoledì.** 3. **un colloquio di lavoro;** 4. **In bocca al lupo!** 5. **Peccato!** 6. **Un momento, non capisco.** 7. **Mi dispiace.** 8. **Hai ragione.** 9. **Scrivo lettere.** 10. **Faccio una torta.**

Don't forget to practice and reinforce what you've learned by visiting **www.livinglanguage.com/ languagelab** for flashcards, games, and quizzes!

Unit 2 Essentials

Vocabulary Essentials

Test your knowledge of the key material in this unit by filling in the blanks in the following charts. Once you've completed these pages, you'll have tested your retention, and you'll have your own reference for the most essential vocabulary.

DESCRIPTIVE WORDS

	terrible
	beautiful
	sick
	small
	big
	ugly
	lonely
	happy
	true
	false

[pg. 67]

NUMBERS

	twenty
	thirty
	forty
	fifty

[pg. 77–78]

	sixty
	seventy
	eighty
	ninety
	one hundred
	one thousand
	million
	billion

[pg. 78]

QUESTION WORDS

	who?
	what?
	how?
	when?
	where?
	why?
	how much, how many?
	which?

[pg. 82–83]

EXPRESSIONS WITH AVERE

	to be hungry
	to be thirsty
	to be hot
	to be cold

[pg. 86]

	to be right
	to be wrong
	to be in a hurry
	to be sleepy
	to need
	to feel like
	to be afraid of

[pg. 86]

EXPRESSIONS WITH FARE

	to go grocery shopping
	to shop
	to take a shower
	to take a bath
	to have breakfast
	to ask a question
	to take a picture
	to take a walk
	to take a break
	to take a trip

[pg. 87]

-ERE VERBS

	to ask
	to close
	to run

[pg. 93]

	to believe
	to read
	to put
	to lose
	to take
	to receive
	to answer
	to see
	to live

[pg. 93–94]

-IRE VERBS

	to open
	to offer
	to leave
	to follow
	to hear
	to serve
	to understand
	to prefer
	to finish
	to clean

[pg. 94, 98]

Intermediate Italian

Don't forget: if you're having a hard time remembering this vocabulary, check out the supplemental flashcards for this unit online, at **www.livinglanguage.com/languagelab**.

Grammar Essentials

Here is a reference of the key grammar that was covered in Unit 2. Make sure you understand the summary and can use all of the grammar in it.

ADJECTIVE FORMS

	SINGULAR	PLURAL
Masculine	piccolo	piccoli
Feminine	piccola	piccole
Masculine/Feminine	felice	felici

VERBS

ANDARE *(TO GO)*			
io vado	*I go*	noi andiamo	*we go*
tu vai	*you go*	voi andate	*you (pl.) go*
lui/lei/Lei va	*he/she goes, you (fml.) go*	loro/Loro vanno	*they go, you (fml. pl.) go*

DARE *(TO GIVE)*			
io do	*I give*	noi diamo	*we give*
tu dai	*you give*	voi date	*you (pl.) give*
lui/lei/Lei dà	*he/she gives, you (fml.) give*	loro/Loro danno	*they give, you (fml. pl.) give*

FARE *(TO DO, TO MAKE)*			
io faccio	*I do/make*	noi facciamo	*we do/make*
tu fai	*you do/make*	voi fate	*you (pl.) do/make*
lui/lei/Lei fa	*he/she does/ makes, you (fml.) do/make*	loro/Loro fanno	*they do/make, you (fml. pl.) do/make*

STARE *(TO STAY)*			
io sto	*I stay*	noi stiamo	*we stay*
tu stai	*you stay*	voi state	*you (pl.) stay*
lui/lei/Lei sta	*he/she stays, you (fml.) stay*	loro/Loro stanno	*they stay, you (fml. pl.) stay*

CONJUGATION OF -ERE AND -IRE VERBS

	-ERE VERBS	-IRE VERBS
io	-o	-(isc)-o
tu	-i	-(isc)-i
lui/lei/Lei	-e	-(isc)-e
noi	-iamo	-iamo
voi	-ete	-ite
loro/Loro	-ono	-(isc)-ono

SCRIVERE *(TO WRITE)*			
io scrivo	*I write*	noi scriviamo	*we write*
tu scrivi	*you write*	voi scrivete	*you (pl.) write*
lui/lei/Lei scrive	*he/she writes, you (fml.) write*	loro/Loro scrivono	*they write, you (fml. pl.) write*

DORMIRE *(TO SLEEP)*			
io dormo	*I sleep*	noi dormiamo	*we sleep*
tu dormi	*you sleep*	voi dormite	*you (pl.) sleep*

DORMIRE *(TO SLEEP)*			
lui/lei/Lei dorme	*he/she sleeps, you (fml.) sleep*	loro/Loro dormono	*they sleep, you (fml. pl.) sleep*

CAPIRE *(TO UNDERSTAND)*			
io capisco	*I understand*	noi capiamo	*we understand*
tu capisci	*you understand*	voi capite	*you (pl.) understand*
lui/lei/Lei capisce	*he/she understands, you (fml.) understand*	loro/Loro capiscono	*they understand, you (fml. pl.) understand*

Unit 2 Quiz

Let's put the most essential Italian words and grammar points you've learned so far to practice in a few exercises. It's important to be sure that you've mastered this material before you move on. Score yourself at the end of the review and see if you need to go back for more practice, or if you're ready to move on to Unit 3.

A. Translate the following sentences.

1. *Franca lives in Milano.* _____

2. *In her apartment there are two bedrooms.* _____

    _____

3. *She works at home.* _____

4. *They visit all the museums, the stores, and the churches of the city.* _____

    _____

B. Fill the blanks translating the nouns or adjectives given in parentheses.

1. *(On Sundays)* _____ mangiano al ristorante.

2. Questa settimana *(he works on Saturday and Sunday)*

    _____.

3. Noi mangiamo *(a lot of pasta)* _____.

4. Maria è *(very cute)* _____.

C. Complete the following sentences with the correct form of the verbs given in parentheses and spell out the numbers.

1. Il professore (dare) _____ 12 esercizi ai suoi studenti.

2. Loro (andare) _____ in ufficio alle 8:25.

3. Noi (stare) _____ a Roma dal 1996.

4. Io (fare) _____ la spesa 4 volte alla settimana.

D. Complete with the correct form of either fare or avere.

1. Loro _____ una passeggiata in città.

2. Giorgio, _____ bisogno di aiuto?

E. Read each answer, and then give the question that would have prompted it.

1. Marco arriva giovedì sera. _____

_____

2. Vado al cinema con Federico. _____

_____

F. Complete the following sentences with the correct forms of the -ere and -ire verbs in parentheses.

1. I negozi (chiudere) _____ alle otto di sera.

2. Quanti giornali alla settimana (leggere) _____ voi?

3. Quando io (finire) _____ di studiare, mangio.

4. Luisa non (capire) _____ l'inglese.

How Did You Do?

Give yourself a point for every correct answer, then use the following key to tell whether you're ready to move on:

0-7 points: It's probably a good idea to go back through the lesson again. You may be moving too quickly, or there may be too much "down time" between your contact with Italian. Remember that it's better to spend 30 minutes with Italian three or four times a week than it is to spend two or three hours just once a week. Find a pace that's comfortable for you, and spread your contact hours out as much as you can.

8-12 points: You would benefit from a review before moving on. Go back and spend a little more time on the specific points that gave you trouble. Reread the Grammar Builder sections that were difficult, and do the work out one more time. Don't forget about the online supplemental practice material, either. Go to **www.livinglanguage.com/languagelab** for games and quizzes that will reinforce the material from this unit.

13-17 points: Good job! There are just a few points that you might consider reviewing before moving on. If you haven't worked with the games and quizzes on **www.livinglanguage.com/languagelab**, please give them a try.

18-20 points: Great! You're ready to move on to the next unit.

 **points**

Unit 3:
Talking About Other People

In this unit, you'll learn how to speak about **i tuoi amici** (*your friends*), **la tua famiglia** (*your family*), and anything else that belongs to you or to them. By the end of this unit, you'll know:

- ☐ useful words to talk about people you know
- ☐ prepositions
- ☐ vocabulary related to the family
- ☐ the difference between **conoscere** and **sapere** (*to know*)
- ☐ how to express possession
- ☐ how to say *must, can,* and *want*
- ☐ more irregular **-ere** and **-ire** verbs
- ☐ how to talk about people and things
- ☐ possessive adjectives like *my, your,* and *our*
- ☐ possessive pronouns like *mine, yours,* and *ours*

Lesson 9: Words

By the end of this lesson, you'll know:

☐ useful words to talk about people you know

☐ prepositions

☐ vocabulary related to the family

☐ the difference between conoscere and sapere (*to know*)

Word Builder 1

▶ 9A Word Builder 1 (CD5, Track 7)

amico	*(male) friend*
amica	*(female) friend*
viene	*he/she comes*
dici	*you say*
possiamo	*we can*
voglio	*I want*
sai	*you know*
coppia	*couple*
chiaro	*clear*
insieme	*together*
solo	*only, lonely, alone*
posto	*place*

⏸

✎ Word Practice 1

Match the English in the right column with the Italian in the left.

1. **solo**		a. *I want*
2. **voglio**		b. *place*
3. **possiamo**		c. *clear*
4. **coppia**		d. *he/she comes*
5. **posto**		e. *alone*
6. **dici**		f. *couple*
7. **chiaro**		g. *we can*
8. **viene**		h. *you say*

ANSWER KEY
1. e; 2. a; 3. g; 4. f; 5. b; 6. h; 7. c; 8. d

Grammar Builder 1
▶ 9B Grammar Builder 1 (CD5, Track 8)

PREPOSITIONS

Let's take a look at Italian prepositions.

di	*of, from*
a	*at, to, in*
da	*from*
in	*at, to, in*
con	*with*
su	*on, about*
per	*for*
tra/fra (either spelling)	*between, among*

Il libro è su un tavolo in soggiorno.
The book is on a table in the living room.

Vado al cinema con Luisa.
I go to the movies with Luisa.

Lavoro per tre ore.
I (will) work for three hours.

✎ Work Out 1

Complete each sentence with the appropriate preposition:

1. **Noi andiamo _____ Italia d'estate.**

2. **Lui fa una passeggiata _____ Maria.**

3. **Io lavoro _____ il Dottor Romagnoli.**

4. **Loro vanno _____ Roma _____ studiare italiano.**

5. **Il treno arriva _____ Milano alle sette e trenta.**

6. **Voi finite _____ studiare alle cinque.**

ANSWER KEY
1. in; 2. con; 3. per; 4. a, a; 5. a; 6. di

Word Builder 2

In Lesson 2 of *Essential Italian,* you learned basic vocabulary related to the family. Let's review and add a few more words.

▶ 9C Word Builder 2 (CD5, Track 9)

Prepositions Followed by
Definite Articles

Possessive Pronouns like
Mine, Yours, and *Ours*

famiglia	*family*
padre	*father*
madre	*mother*
genitori	*parents*
parenti	*relatives*
fratello	*brother*
sorella	*sister*
fratelli/sorelle	*siblings (brothers/sisters)*
moglie	*wife*
marito	*husband*
figlio	*son*
figlia	*daughter*
cugino/cugina	*cousin (m./f.)*
zia	*aunt*
zio	*uncle*
conoscere	*to know, to meet (for the first time), to get/be acquainted*
sapere	*to know (a fact), to know how*

✎ Word Practice 2

A. Translate the following words from Italian into English.

1. **cugino** _____

2. **figlio** _____

3. **fratello** _____

4. **marito** _____

B. Translate the following words from English into Italian.

1. *uncle* _____

2. *mother* _____

3. *sister* _____

4. *wife* _____

ANSWER KEY
A. 1. *cousin*; 2. *son*; 3. *brother*; 4. *husband*
B. 1. zio; 2. madre; 3. sorella; 4. moglie

Grammar Builder 2

▶ 9D Grammar Builder 2 (CD5, Track 10)

CONOSCERE **AND** SAPERE *(TO KNOW)*

In Italian, there are two separate verbs used to express *to know*: **conoscere** and
sapere. They have slightly different meanings and are not interchangeable.

Conoscere means to be familiar or acquainted with a person, thing, or place.

Conosci mia cugina?
Do you know my cousin?

Io non conosco bene Roma.
I don't know Rome well.

Sapere is an irregular verb, and it's conjugated as follows:

SAPERE *(TO KNOW A FACT, TO KNOW HOW TO DO SOMETHING)* – PRESENT			
io so	*I know*	**noi sappiamo**	*we know*

SAPERE *(TO KNOW A FACT, TO KNOW HOW TO DO SOMETHING)* – PRESENT			
tu sai	*you know*	**voi sapete**	*you (pl.) know*
lui/lei/Lei sa	*he/she knows, you (fml.) know*	**loro/Loro sanno**	*they know, you (fml. pl.) know*

Sapere means *to know a fact* or *to know how to do something*. When **sapere** is used with the latter meaning, it is always followed by a verb in the infinitive form.

Sai che domani arriva mio fratello da Firenze?
Do you know that tomorrow, my brother is arriving from Florence?

Il bambino sa suonare il piano molto bene.
The child can play the piano very well.

🖊 Work Out 2

Choose either the conjugated form of **sapere** or **conoscere** appropriately.

1. **Noi conosciamo/sappiamo un buon ristorante.** _____

2. **Lui conosce/sa cucinare molto bene.** _____

3. **Voi conoscete/sapete mio padre?** _____

4. **Io conosco/so che lui non risponde mai al telefono.** _____

5. **Tu conosci/sai suonare la chitarra?** _____

6. **Io non conosco/so parlare cinese.** _____

ANSWER KEY
1. **conosciamo**; 2. **sa**; 3. **conoscete**; 4. **so**; 5. **sai**; 6. **so**

conoscere and **sapere**
(*to know*)

✎ Drive It Home

Fill in the appropriate prepositions and the appropriate forms of **conoscere** or **sapere**.

1. **Tu** (*to know*) _____ **Firenze?**

2. **Noi andiamo** _____ **Roma domani.**

3. **Lui** (*to know how*) _____ **parlare l'italiano molto bene.**

4. **Mio fratello arriva stasera** _____ **mia madre.**

5. **A Natale compro i regali** _____ **i miei genitori.**

6. **Franco non** (*to know how*) _____ **giocare** _____ **tennis.**

7. **Voi** (*to know*) _____ **i suoi cugini.**

8. **A che ora finisci** _____ **lavorare stasera?**

9. **Loro** (*to know*) _____ **che ho trentaquattro anni.**

10. **Tu** (*know*) _____ **chi sono queste sigarette?**

ANSWER KEY
1. conosci; 2. a; 3. sa; 4. con; 5. per; 6. sa, a; 7. conoscete; 8. di; 9. sanno; 10. sai, di

💡 Tip!

Italian is a language rich in proverbs, those sayings that convey accepted popular wisdom. Many proverbs refer to the family, such as: **Tra moglie e marito non mettere il dito.** It translates literally as *don't put your finger between wife and husband,* meaning *don't interfere in marital affairs.* The equivalent to the English *you can't have your cake and eat it too* is much more salacious in Italian: **Non puoi avere la botte piena e la moglie ubriaca,** or *you can't have the wine cask full, and your wife drunk.*

How Did You Do?

Let's see how you did in this lesson. By now, you should know:

☐ useful words to talk about people you know (Still unsure? Jump back to page 114.)

☐ prepositions (Still unsure? Jump back to page 115.)

☐ vocabulary related to the family (Still unsure? Jump back to page 117.)

☐ the difference between **conoscere** and **sapere** (*to know*) (Still unsure? Jump back to page 118.)

✎ Word Recall

Translate the following nouns and verbs into Italian.

1. *brother* _____

2. *to know how* _____

3. *son* _____

4. *I want* _____

5. *alone* _____

6. *wife* _____

7. *together* _____

8. *we can* _____

9. *friend* _____

10. *parents* _____

ANSWER KEY
1. fratello; 2. sapere; 3. figlio; 4. voglio; 5. solo; 6. moglie; 7. insieme; 8. possiamo; 9. amico/a; 10. genitori

Lesson 10: Phrases

By the end of this lesson, you'll know:

☐ how to express possession

☐ how to say *must*, *can*, and *want*

Phrase Builder 1

▶ 10A Phrase Builder 1 (CD5, Track 11)

Di chi è?	Whose is it?
È di …	It belongs to/it is …
l'amico di Claudia	Claudia's friend
Ma come!	How's it possible!/How can this be!
venire a trovare	to come visit
andare a trovare	to go visit
fare un giro	to go for a walk or a ride
tutti gli anni	every year
d'estate	in the summer
in/d'autunno	in the fall
d'inverno	in the winter
in primavera	in the spring

✎ Phrase Practice 1

Match the Italian and English versions of the following phrases:

1. l'amico di Claudia
2. venire a trovare
3. tutti gli anni
4. d'inverno
5. di chi è?
6. Ma come!
7. fare un giro
8. in primavera

a. *to come visit*
b. *whose is it?*
c. *to go for a walk*
d. *Claudia's friend*
e. *in the spring*
f. *in the winter*
g. *How can this be!*
h. *every year*

ANSWER KEY
1. d.; 2. a; 3. h; 4. f; 5. b; 6. g; 7. c; 8. e

Grammar Builder 1

▶ 10B Grammar Builder 1 (CD5, Track 12)

THE PREPOSITION DI

The preposition **di** (*of*) is used to express possession in Italian. Note the difference in structure between the Italian and the English:

Lorenzo è l'amico di Claudia.
Lorenzo is Claudia's friend.

Sono le sorelle di Michele.
They are Michele's sisters.

Di chi sono quelle riviste?
Whose magazines are those?

⑪

Take It Further

Please note that the preposition **di** is also used in the expressions **d'estate** (*in the summer*) and **d'inverno** (*in the winter*), while with **primavera** (*spring*) we use the preposition **in**. **Autunno** (*fall*) can take either **in** (in autunno) or **di** (d'autunno).

✎ Work Out 1

Translate the following sentences into Italian.

1. *Whose book is it?* _____

_____

2. *It's Giorgio's book.* _____

_____

3. *Mirella's sister is cute.* _____

_____

4. *Paola's brother is nervous.* _____

_____

5. *Alessandro's house is noisy.* _____

_____

6. *In the summer, I'm going to Giulia's house.* _____

_____

7. **ANSWER KEY**

   1. Di chi è il libro? 2. È il libro di Giorgio. 3. La sorella di Mirella è carina. 4. Il fratello di Paola è nervoso. 5. La casa di Alessandro è rumorosa. 6. D'estate vado a casa di Giulia.

Phrase Builder 2

▶ 10C Phrase Builder 2 (CD5, Track 13)

posso	*I can*
vuoi	*you want*
Ti voglio bene.	*I care about you, I love you.*
Siamo in sette.	*There're seven of us.*
eccetto la mia	*except for mine*
mi chiamo	*my name is*
si chiama	*his/her name is*
si chiamano	*their names are*
È sposato/è sposata.	*He/she is married.*
neanche	*not even*

✎ Phrase Practice 2

A. Translate the following Italian phrases into English.

1. È sposato. _____

2. Ti voglio bene. _____

3. si chiama _____

4. neanche _____

B. Translate the following English phrases into Italian.

1. *my name is* _____

2. *I can* _____

3. *you want* _____

4. *There are seven of us.* _____

ANSWER KEY
A. 1. *He is married.* 2. *I love you.* 3. *his/her name is;* 4. *not even*
B. 1. **mi chiamo**; 2. **posso**; 3. **vuoi**; 4. **Siamo in sette.**

Grammar Builder 2
(▶) 10D Grammar Builder 2 (CD5, Track 14)

MUST, CAN, AND WANT

We are now going to learn three important irregular verbs of the **-ere** group: the modal verbs **dovere** (*must, to have to*); **potere** (*can, to be able to*); and **volere** (*to want*). When these verbs are followed by another verb, the second verb will be in the infinitive form.

DOVERE *(MUST, TO HAVE TO)* – PRESENT			
io devo	*I must*	**noi dobbiamo**	*we must*
tu devi	*you must*	**voi dovete**	*you (pl.) must*
lui/lei/Lei deve	*he/she must, you (fml.) must*	**loro/Loro devono**	*they must, you (fml. pl.) must*

POTERE *(CAN, TO BE ABLE TO)* – PRESENT			
io posso	*I can*	**noi possiamo**	*we can*
tu puoi	*you can*	**voi potete**	*you (pl.) can*
lui/lei/Lei può	*he/she can, you (fml.) can*	**loro/Loro possono**	*they can, you (fml. pl.) can*

VOLERE *(TO WANT)* – PRESENT			
io voglio	*I want*	**noi vogliamo**	*we want*
tu vuoi	*you want*	**voi volete**	*you (pl.) want*

VOLERE *(TO WANT)* – PRESENT			
lui/lei/Lei vuole	*he, she wants, you (fml.) want*	loro/Loro vogliono	*they want, you (fml. pl.) want*

Oggi Luigi deve studiare per un esame.
Today, Luigi must study for an exam.

Potete venire a cena a casa mia domani sera?
Can you come to my house for dinner, tomorrow night?

Noi vogliamo andare a trovare i nostri amici.
We want to go visit our friends.

✎ Work Out 2

Insert the correct form of the verb in parentheses.

1. **Loro** _____ **(volere) comprare una macchina nuova.**

2. **Tu** _____ **(dovere) preparare la cena.**

3. **Io non** _____ **(potere) venire con te a fare spese.**

4. **Sofia** _____ **(volere) cercare un nuovo lavoro.**

5. **Tu e Caterina** _____ **(dovere) leggere il giornale.**

6. **Tu ed io** _____ **(potere) guardare la TV.**

ANSWER KEY
1. vogliono; 2. devi; 3. posso; 4. vuole; 5. dovete; 6. possiamo

✎ Drive It Home

Fill in the appropriate prepositions and the forms of the verbs indicated in parentheses.

1. Mi dispiace ma io non *(can)* _____ venire.

2. Domani io *(to have to)* _____ lavorare tutto il giorno.

3. *(Whose)* _____ è questo cappello?

4. Questo è il numero _____ telefono _____ Maria.

5. Tu *(to want)* _____ qualcosa da mangiare?

6. Loro *(to want)* _____ andare in vacanza al mare.

7. Paolo non *(can)* _____ scrivere la lettera, non ha la penna e neanche

   gli occhiali.

8. Voi *(to have to)* _____ ancora comprare i regali di Natale?

9. Il fratello _____ Carlo è un amico _____ mia sorella.

10. La nostra macchina è rotta così *(to have to)* _____ prendere il treno.

11. Io *(to want)* _____ mangiare le lasagne _____ Lucia.

12. *(You can)* _____ venire al cinema con me?

ANSWER KEY
1. posso; 2. devo; 3. Di chi; 4. di, di; 5. vuoi; 6. vogliono; 7. può; 8. dovete; 9. di, di; 10. dobbiamo;
11. voglio, di; 12. Puoi

Tip!

There are words in Italian for *stepmother* (**la matrigna**), *stepfather* (**il patrigno**), *stepbrother* (**il fratellastro**), *stepsister* (**la sorellastra**), *stepson* (**il figliastro**), and *stepdaughter* (**la figliastra**). However, they have historically negative connotations (there was no divorce in Italy until relatively recently) and are avoided as much as possible. So instead of using **matrigna** and **patrigno**, **la moglie di mio padre** (*my father's wife*) and **il marito di mia madre** (*my mother's husband*) are preferred. Simply **fratello** and **sorella** are used instead of **fratellastro** and **sorellastra**; and **il figlio/la figlia di mio marito** (or **di mia moglie**), or **adottivo/a** meaning *my husband's son/daughter* (or *my wife's son/daughter*), or *adopted son/daughter* are used instead of **figliastro** and **figliastra**.

How Did You Do?

Let's see how you did in this lesson. By now, you should know:

☐ how to express possession (Still unsure? Jump back to page 123.)

☐ how to say *must*, *can*, and *want* (Still unsure? Jump back to page 126.)

✎ Word Recall

Translate the following phrases into Italian.

1. *I love you.* _____

2. *not even* _____

3. *every year* _____

4. *to go for a walk* _____

5. *in the summer* _____

6. *in the fall* _____

7. *Giorgio's friend* _____

8. *Whose is it?* _____

9. *He is married.* _____

10. *her name is* _____

ANSWER KEY
1. **Ti amo.** 2. **neanche**; 3. **tutti gli anni**; 4. **fare un giro**; 5. **d'estate**; 6. **in autunno**; 7. **l'amico di Giorgio**;
8. **Di chi è?** 9. **Lui è sposato.** 10. **lei si chiama**

Lesson 11: Sentences

By the end of this lesson, you should know:

☐ more irregular -**ere** and -**ire** verbs

☐ how to talk about people and things

Sentence Builder 1

▶ 11A Sentence Builder 1 (CD5, Track 15)

Di chi è quella Ferrari rossa?	*Whose red Ferrari is it?*
È di Lorenzo, l'amico di Claudia.	*It's Lorenzo's, Claudia's friend.*
Claudia è la mia amica.	*Claudia is my friend.*
Lei dice che è solo un amico.	*She says (that) he's just a friend.*
Sembrano una coppia.	*They look like a couple.*
La sua macchina è bellissima.	*His car is very beautiful.*
Possiamo fare un giro?	*Can we go for a ride?*
Ci sono solo due posti.	*It's a two-seater (car).*

✎ Sentence Practice 1

Translate the following sentences into Italian.

1. *They look like a couple.* _____

_____

2. *Claudia is my friend.* _____

_____

3. *His car is very beautiful.* _____

_____

4. *Can we go for a ride?* _____

_____

5. *Whose red Ferrari is it?* _____

_____

6. *She says (that) he's just a friend.* _____

_____

7. **ANSWER KEY**

   1. Sembrano una coppia. 2. Claudia è la mia amica. 3. La sua macchina è bellissima. 4. Possiamo fare un giro? 5. Di chi è quella Ferrari rossa? 6. Lei dice che è solo un amico.

Grammar Builder 1

▶ 11B Grammar Builder 1 (CD5, Track 16)

IRREGULAR -ERE AND -IRE VERBS

In addition to the irregular **-ere** verbs we have already learned, **sapere**, **dovere**, **potere**, and **volere**, the verb **bere** (*to drink*) has an irregular conjugation.

BERE *(TO DRINK)* – PRESENT			
io bevo	*I drink*	noi beviamo	*we drink*
tu bevi	*you drink*	voi bevete	*you (pl.) drink*
lui/lei/Lei beve	*he/she drinks, you (fml.) drink*	loro/Loro bevono	*they drink, you (fml. pl.) drink*

Note that the conjugation of **bere** includes the stem **bev-** followed by the regular **-ere** endings.

Now we'll learn three important irregular verbs of the **-ire** group: **dire** (*to say, to tell*), **uscire** (*to go out*), and **venire** (*to come*).

DIRE *(TO SAY, TO TELL)* – PRESENT			
io dico	*I say/tell*	noi diciamo	*we say/tell*
tu dici	*you say/tell*	voi dite	*you (pl.) say/tell*
lui/lei/Lei dice	*he/she says/tells, you (fml.) say/tell*	loro/Loro dicono	*they say/tell, you (fml. pl.) say/tell*

USCIRE *(TO GO OUT)* – PRESENT			
io esco	*I go out*	noi usciamo	*we go out*
tu esci	*you go out*	voi uscite	*you (pl.) go out*
lui/lei/Lei esce	*he/she goes out, you (fml.) go out*	loro/Loro escono	*they go out, you (fml. pl.) go out*

VENIRE *(TO COME)* – PRESENT			
io vengo	*I come*	noi veniamo	*we come*
tu vieni	*you come*	voi venite	*you (pl.) come*
lui/lei/Lei viene	*he/she comes, you (fml.) come*	loro/Loro vengono	*they come, you (fml. pl.) come*

Tu dici molte bugie.
You tell many lies.

Loro escono spesso.
They go out often.

Lui viene a trovarci raramente.
He rarely comes to visit us.

⏸

✎ Work Out 1

Complete with the correct forms of either **dire**, **uscire**, or **venire**.

1. Quando noi _____ con loro, di solito andiamo al cinema.

2. Mio cugino _____ a trovare la mia famiglia in primavera.

3. Loro non _____ mai che cosa fanno.

4. La mattina io _____ alle sette per andare in ufficio.

5. (Tu) _____ a casa mia stasera? Ho una sorpresa!

6. Voglio _____ a Mario dove vado domani.

7. Vuoi _____ domani sera? Ho voglia di andare a teatro.

ANSWER KEY
1. usciamo; 2. viene; 3. dicono; 4. esco; 5. vieni; 6. dire; 7. uscire

Sentence Builder 2

▶ 11C Sentence Builder 2 (CD5, Track 17)

Posso conoscere la tua famiglia?	*Can I meet your family?*
La mia famiglia è molto numerosa.	*My family is very big.*
Mi parli di tuo padre e (di) tua madre?	*Would you tell me about your father and mother?*
Non so niente dei tuoi fratelli.	*I don't know anything about your siblings.*
Siamo in sette.	*There are seven of us.*
Non esistono più famiglie così grandi.	*Such big families no longer exist/are rare, nowadays.*
I miei fratelli si chiamano Marco e Giulio.	*My brothers' names are Marco and Giulio.*
Sua moglie si chiama Manuela.	*His wife's name is Manuela.*
I loro bambini si chiamano Andrea e Fabrizio.	*Their children's names are Andrea and Fabrizio.*

⏸

✎ Sentence Practice 2

Match the following sentences.

1. **Non esistono più famiglie così grandi.**   a. *His wife's name is Manuela.*

2. **I loro bambini si chiamano Andrea e Fabrizio.**   b. *My brothers' names are Marco and Giulio.*

3. **Sua moglie si chiama Manuela.**   c. *There are seven of us.*

4. I miei fratelli si chiamano Marco e Giulio.

d. *Such big families are rare, nowadays.*

5. Siamo in sette.

e. *Their children's names are Andrea and Fabrizio.*

6. Posso conoscere la tua famiglia?

f. *I don't know anything about your siblings.*

7. La mia famiglia è molto numerosa.

g. *Can I meet your family?*

8. Non so niente dei tuoi fratelli.

h. *My family is very big.*

ANSWER KEY
1. d; 2. e; 3. a; 4. b; 5. c; 6. g; 7. h; 8. f

Grammar Builder 2

▶ 11D Grammar Builder 2 (CD5, Track 18)

PREPOSITIONS FOLLOWED BY DEFINITE ARTICLES

In Lesson 9 of this unit you learned about Italian prepositions. When followed by a definite article, the prepositions **di**, **a**, **da**, **in**, and **su** contract with the article and form a single word. In this process, the following spelling changes occur:

the preposition **in** takes the stem **ne-**
the preposition **di** takes the stem **de-**
the article **il** drops the **i**
every article beginning with **l** doubles the **l**.

	IL	LO	LA	L'	I	GLI	LE
di	del	dello	della	dell'	dei	degli	delle
a	al	allo	alla	all'	ai	agli	alle
da	dal	dallo	dalla	dall'	dai	dagli	dalle
in	nel	nello	nella	nell'	nei	negli	nelle
su	sul	sullo	sulla	sull'	sui	sugli	sulle

di + l' > dell' → È la macchina dell'amico di Claudia.
It's Claudia's friend's car.

in + la > nella → La famiglia cena nella sala da pranzo.
The family is having dinner in the dining room.

a + il > al → Ho fatto la spesa al mercato.
I bought groceries at the market.

su + gli > sugli → I libri sono sugli scaffali.
The books are on the shelves.

⒨

✎ Work Out 2

Merge the given preposition with the appropriate definite article in the following sentences.

1. La macchina di Filippo è (in) _____ garage.

2. Gi amici di Rodolfo vanno (a) _____ cinema stasera.

3. Gli studenti rispondono (a) _____ domande (di) _____ professore.

4. Marco ritorna (da) _____ ufficio alle sette.

5. Ci sono molti libri (su) _____ tavolo.

6. I figli (di) _____ amica di Giuseppe sono molto bravi a scuola.

ANSWER KEY
1. nel; 2. al; 3. alle, del; 4. dall'; 5. sul; 6. dell'

✎ Drive It Home

Fill in the contractions with prepositions and definite articles and the appropriate forms of the verbs indicated in parentheses.

1. **Quando io (uscire) _____ con Franca andiamo spesso (a) _____ cinema.**

2. **Voi (venire) _____ con noi (a) _____ farmacia.**

3. **Lui (dire) _____ (a) _____ sua amica cosa fare.**

4. **Loro (uscire) _____ (da) _____ ufficio (a) _____ cinque.**

5. **Laura (bere) _____ il vino (di) _____ amici di Giulio.**

6. **Loro (dire) _____ che il bar è lontano (da) _____ stazione.**

7. **Aspetta! (venire) _____ anch'io.**

8. **Noi (venire) _____ con la macchina (di) _____ fratello di Mario.**

9. **Lui (dire) _____ che il giornale è (su) _____ tavolo (in) _____ altra camera.**

10. **Tu non (sapere) _____ quello che (tu dire) _____!**

11. **Noi (dovere) _____ mettere la macchina (in) _____ garage.**

12. **Questi libri (dovere) _____ essere (di) _____ studenti che (venire) _____ di mattina.**

ANSWER KEY
1. esco, al; 2. venite, alla; 3. dice, alla; 4. escono, dall', alle; 5. beve, degli; 6. dicono, dalla; 7. vengo;
8. veniamo, del; 9. dice, sul, nella; 10. sai, dici; 11. dobbiamo, nel; 12. devono, degli, vengono

How Did You Do?

Let's see how you did in this lesson. By now, you should know:

☐ more irregular **-ere** and **-ire** verbs (Still unsure? Jump back to page 132.)

☐ how to speak about people and things (Still unsure? Jump back to page 135.)

✎ Word Recall

Translate the following sentences into Italian.

1. *My family is very big.* _____

   _____

2. *His car is very beautiful.* _____

   _____

3. *Can we go for a ride?* _____

   _____

4. *Claudia is my friend.* _____

   _____

5. *Whose is the red car?* _____

   _____

6. *His wife's name is Daniela.* _____

   _____

7. *Her husband's name is Ettore.* _____

   _____

8. *Their brothers' names are Frank and Peter.* _____

_____

9. *Can I meet your father?* _____

_____

10. *I don't know anything about your family.* _____

_____

ANSWER KEY

1. **La mia famiglia è molto numerosa.** 2. **La sua macchina è bellissima.** 3. **Possiamo fare un giro?**
4. **Claudia è la mia amica.** 5. **Di chi è questa macchina rossa?** 6. **Sua moglie si chiama Daniela.** 7. **Suo marito si chiama Ettore.** 8. **I suoi fratelli si chiamano Frank e Peter.** 9. **Posso conoscere tuo padre?**
10. **Non so nulla della tua famiglia.**

Lesson 12: Conversations

By the end of this lesson, you'll know:

☐ possessive adjectives like *my, your,* and *our*

☐ possessive pronouns like *mine, yours,* and *ours*

🎧 Conversation 1

▶ 12A Conversation 1 (CD5, Track 19 - Italian; Track 20 - Italian and English)

Stefano:	**Cristina, di chi è quella Ferrari rossa parcheggiata davanti al tuo ufficio?**
Cristina:	**È di Lorenzo, l'amico di Claudia.**
Stefano:	**Scusa ma chi è Claudia?**
Cristina:	**Ma come, non ricordi? Claudia è la mia amica di Palermo. Viene a trovarmi tutti gli anni d'estate. E quest'anno è con Lorenzo, il suo amico, o forse il suo ragazzo.**

conoscere and sapere	Must, Can, and Want
(to know)	

Stefano:	Perché dici "forse il suo ragazzo"? Non lo sai se è il suo ragazzo o no?
Cristina:	Non è chiaro. Claudia dice che è solo un amico, ma quando sono insieme sembrano una coppia.
Stefano:	Beh, non è importante se Lorenzo è il suo amico o il suo ragazzo, ma la sua macchina è bellissima. Possiamo andare tutti insieme a fare un giro sulla Ferrari?
Cristina:	La tua idea è interessante, ma nella Ferrari ci sono solo due posti.

Stefano:	Cristina, that red Ferrari parked in front of your office, who does it belong to?
Cristina:	It's Lorenzo's, Claudia's friend.
Stefano:	Wait, who's Claudia? (lit., Excuse me, and who's Claudia?)
Cristina:	What! You don't remember? Claudia is that friend of mine from Palermo. She comes to visit me every year in the summer. And this year she's with Lorenzo, her friend, or perhaps her boyfriend.
Stefano:	Why do you say "perhaps her boyfriend"? Don't you know if he's her boyfriend or not?
Cristina:	It's not clear. Claudia says that he's just a friend, but when they're together they look like a couple.
Stefano:	Well, it doesn't matter (lit., it's not important) if Lorenzo is her friend or her boyfriend, but his car is very beautiful. Can we all go together and take a ride in the Ferrari?
Cristina:	Your idea is interesting, but there're only two seats in a Ferrari.

Prepositions Followed by
Definite Articles

Possessive Pronouns like
Mine, Yours, and *Ours*

Take It Further

Ma come! (*How come!, How can it be!*) is a very common exclamation in Italian, which shows surprise and disappointment.

Andare (or **venire**) **a trovare** is an idiomatic expression that means *to go* (or *to come*) *and visit someone.*

Lo so, and **non lo so**, translate to English as *I know* and *I don't know.*

✎ Conversation Practice 1

Fill in the blanks in the following sentences with the missing words in the word bank. If you're unsure of the answer, listen to the conversation on your audio one more time.

viene, dici, sembrano, lo sai, ma come, possiamo, di, chi, tutti gli anni, due posti, al tuo, fare un giro, chi

1. _____ a trovarmi _____ d'estate.

2. _____, non ricordi?

3. Cristina, _____ è quella Ferrari rossa parcheggiata davanti _____ ufficio?

4. Scusa ma _____ è Claudia?

5. Perché _____ "forse il suo ragazzo"? Non _____ se è il suo ragazzo o no?

6. Quando sono insieme _____ una coppia.

7. _____ andare tutti insieme a _____ sulla

Ferrari?

8. Nella Ferrari ci sono solo _____ .

ANSWER KEY

1. Viene, tutti gli anni; 2. Ma come; 3. di chi, al tuo; 4. chi; 5. dici, lo sai; 6. sembrano; 7. Possiamo, fare un giro; 8. due posti

Grammar Builder 1

▶ 12B Grammar Builder 1 (CD5, Track 21)

POSSESSIVE ADJECTIVES LIKE *MY, YOUR,* AND *OUR*

Let's take a look at Italian possessive adjectives, words equivalent to *my, his, her,* etc., in English.

	MASCULINE Singular	FEMININE Singular	MASCULINE Plural	FEMININE Plural
my	il mio	la mia	i miei	le mie
your (infml.)	il tuo	la tua	i tuoi	le tue
his/her/its, your (fml.)*	il suo	la sua	i suoi	le sue
our	il nostro	la nostra	i nostri	le nostre
your (pl.)	il vostro	la vostra	i vostri	le vostre
their, your (fml. pl.)**	il loro	la loro	i loro	le loro

* When your is used in the formal form it's written with a capital S-: il Suo, la Sua, i Suoi, le Sue.

** When your (pl.) is used in the formal form it's written with a capital **L-**: **il Loro, la Loro, i Loro, le Loro.**

Italian possessive adjectives agree in gender and number with what is possessed and not the possessor (except for **loro** which is invariable). Note that because of this, there is no difference in Italian between *his* or *her.*

Possessive adjectives are always preceded by the definite article, and less often by the indefinite **article** (**un mio amico**, *a friend of mine*). As an exception, the definite article does not precede the possessive adjectives before singular nouns denoting members of the family (**suo padre, mia sorella, vostro zio**).

Differently from the other Italian adjectives, the possessive adjectives are always used in front of the noun they modify, except when we need to express a special emphasis, as in exclamations: **Mamma mia!**, or poetic expressions and songs: **O sole mio!** Also in these cases the article will not be used.

Claudia è la mia amica.
Claudia is my friend.

La sua macchina è bellissima.
His/her car is very beautiful.

Il suo amico è simpatico.
His/her friend is nice.

Mi puoi parlare di tuo padre?
Can you speak to me about your father?

Mia sorella si chiama Franca.
My sister's name is Franca.

Note that the definite article is used in front of plural nouns denoting members of the family.

I miei fratelli abitano a Torino.
My brothers live in Torino.

✎ Work Out 1

Translate the possessive adjective given in parentheses. Insert the definite article when appropriate.

1. *(My)* _____ amica Cristina viene a trovarmi domani.

2. *(Their)* _____ casa è bellissima.

3. *(His)* _____ cugine abitano a Toronto.

4. *(His)* _____ sorella non è sposata.

5. *(Her)* _____ figli studiano in una scuola privata.

6. *(Your)* _____ lavoro è interessante, ma stressante.

7. *(Our)* _____ vicini di casa sono inglesi.

8. *(Your pl.)* _____ genitori arrivano domani.

ANSWER KEY
1. La mia; 2. La loro; 3. Le sue; 4. Sua; 5. I suoi; 6. Il tuo; 7. I nostri; 8. I vostri

❝ Conversation 2

▷ 12C Conversation 2 (CD5, Track 22 - Italian; Track 23 - Italian and English)

Luca:	**Mi presenti la tua famiglia?**
Elisabetta:	**Sei sicuro che vuoi?**
Luca:	**Perché no? Ti voglio bene e voglio conoscerli tutti.**

Elisabetta:	Va bene, ma lo sai, la mia famiglia è molto numerosa.
Luca:	Mi hai raccontato molto di tuo padre e tua madre, ma non so quasi niente dei tuoi fratelli.
Elisabetta:	Beh, sai che siamo in sette, quattro femmine e tre maschi.
Luca:	Lo so, è davvero difficile immaginare una famiglia così numerosa. Non esistono più famiglie con tanti figli!
Elisabetta:	Eccetto la mia! Allora, i miei fratelli si chiamano Marco, Giulio e Francesco. Mio fratello Francesco è sposato. Sua moglie si chiama Manuela, e loro non hanno bambini. Le mie sorelle si chiamano Carla, Rossella e Silvana. Rossella è sposata, e suo marito si chiama Giovanni. Loro hanno due bambini che si chiamano Andrea e Fabrizio. Carla è fidanzata e il suo fidanzato si chiama …
Luca:	Basta così! Non ricordo già più neanche un nome!

Luca:	Can I meet your family?
Elisabetta:	Are you sure you want to?
Luca:	Why not? I care about you, and I want to meet all of them.
Elisabetta:	All right, but you know, my family is very large.
Luca:	You told me a lot about your father and mother, but I know almost nothing about your siblings.
Elisabetta:	Well, you know there are seven of us (lit., we're seven), four girls and three boys.
Luca:	I know, and it's really difficult to imagine such a large family. Families with a lot of children don't exist any longer.
Elisabetta:	Except for mine. So, my brothers' names are Marco, Giulio, and Francesco. My brother Francesco is married. His wife's name is Manuela, and they don't have any children. My sisters' names are Carla, Rossella, and Silvana. Rossella is married, and her husband's name is Giovanni. They have two children whose names are Andrea and Fabrizio. Carla is engaged and her fiancée's name is …
Luca:	That's enough! Already I can't remember any names!

Take It Further

The expression **ti voglio bene** is literally translated as *I want goodness for you.*
It is used to express love toward members of the family or friends and lovers,
whereas the expression **ti amo** would only be used between lovers.

Note that we use the article in front of **il suo fidanzato** because he is not a family
member yet.

The expression **mi hai raccontato**... (*you told me about* ...) is in the past tense,
which we will learn in the next unit!

✎ Conversation Practice 2

Unscramble the following sentences.

1. **famiglia/la/presenti/tua/mi/?** _____

   _____

2. **ma/mia/numerosa/sai/la/famiglia/è/lo/molto/.** _____

   _____

3. **i/miei/chiamano/fratelli/Marco/Giulio/e/si/Francesco/.** _____

   _____

4. **Manuela/si/sua/chiama/moglie/.** _____

   _____

5. **bambini/hanno/due/loro/.** _____

   _____

6. neanche/non/ricordo/già/un/più/nome/! _____

_____

ANSWER KEY
1. **Mi presenti la tua famiglia?** 2. **Ma lo sai, la mia famiglia è molto numerosa.** 3. **I miei fratelli si chiamano Marco, Giulio e Francesco.** 4. **Sua moglie si chiama Manuela.** 5. **Loro hanno due bambini.** 6. **Non ricordo già più neanche un nome!**

Grammar Builder 2

▶ 12D Grammar Builder 2 (CD5, Track 24)

POSSESSIVE PRONOUNS LIKE *MINE, YOURS,* AND *OURS*

The Italian possessive pronouns have exactly the same forms as the possessive adjectives, and they're always preceded by the definite articles, even with singular nouns indicating members of the family.

Mia sorella fa l'insegnante e la tua fa l'impiegata.
My sister is a teacher, and yours is an office employee.

La sua casa è grande, ma la loro è piccola.
His/her house is big, but theirs is small.

I miei parenti vivono in Italia, ma i suoi vivono in Argentina.
My relatives live in Italy, but his/hers live in Argentina.

⧐

✎ Work Out 2

Translate the following sentences into Italian.

1. *My brother works every day, and yours works part-time.* _____

   _____

2. *His mother teaches, and mine doesn't work.* _____

   _____

3. *Their house is old, but ours is new.* _____

   _____

4. *Her job is stressful, buy yours is easy.* _____

   _____

5. *I know your (pl.) sister; do you know mine?* _____

   _____

ANSWER KEY
1. Mio fratello lavora tutti i giorni e il tuo lavora part-time. 2. Sua madre fa l'insegnante e la mia
non lavora. 3. La loro casa è vecchia, ma la nostra è nuova. 4. Il suo lavoro è stressante, ma il tuo è
facile. 5. Conosco vostra sorella; conoscete la mia (or le mie)?

✎ Drive It Home

Fill in the blanks with the appropriate possessive adjectives or pronouns.

1. (*My*) _____ sigarette sono sul tavolo, dove sono (*yours pl.*)

   _____ .

2. (*Their*) _____ cane si chiama Ugo e (*hers*) _____ si chiama

   Stordo.

3. *(My)* _____ scarpe sono molto comode, e *(yours)* _____?

4. *(Our)* _____ amici italiani ci hanno presentato *(their)* _____

amici.

5. *(Your)* _____ macchina è più veloce della *(mine)* _____.

6. *(Her)* _____ giacca è rossa e *(his)* _____ è azzurra.

ANSWER KEY
1. Le mie, le vostre; 2. Il loro, il suo; 3. Le mie, le tue; 4. I nostri, i loro; 5. La tua, mia; 6. La sua, la sua

☀ Tip!

Although the contemporary Italian family does not look anything like the large patriarchal family of the past, one thing has not changed: food is still the center of the Italian family life. If you want to learn more about Italian food, there are plenty of websites, including ones with great recipes, that you can explore, both in English and in Italian. Search for key words like *Italian food*, *Italian cuisine*, or **cucina italiana**.

How Did You Do?

Let's see how you did in this lesson. By now, you should know:

☐ possessive adjectives like *my*, *your*, and *our* (Still unsure? Jump back to page 142.)

☐ possessive pronouns like *mine*, *yours*, and *ours* (Still unsure? Jump back to page 147.)

✎ Word Recall

Please translate the following sentences into Italian.

1. *Are you sure you want to?* _____

_____

2. *I care about you.* _____

_____

3. *My family is very large.* _____

_____

4. *You told me a lot about your father.* _____

_____

5. *What! You don't remember?* _____

_____

6. *She comes to visit me every year.* _____

7. *Claudia says that he's just a friend.* _____

_____

8. *Who does that red Ferrari belong to?* _____

_____

ANSWER KEY

1. **Sei sicuro che vuoi?** 2. **Ti voglio bene.** 3. **La mia famiglia è molto numerosa.** 4. **Mi hai raccontato molto di tuo padre.** 5. **Ma come! Non ricordi?** 6. **Lei viene a trovarmi tutti gli anni.** 7. **Claudia dice che è solo un amico.** 8. **Di chi è quella Ferrari rossa?**

Don't forget to practice and reinforce what you've learned by visiting **www.livinglanguage.com/ languagelab** for flashcards, games, and quizzes!

Unit 3 Essentials

Vocabulary Essentials

Test your knowledge of the key material in this unit by filling in the blanks in the following charts. Once you've completed these pages, you'll have tested your retention, and you'll have your own reference for the most essential vocabulary.

FAMILY

	family
	father
	mother
	parents
	relatives
	brother
	sister
	siblings (brothers/sisters)
	wife
	husband
	son
	daughter
	cousin (m./f.)
	aunt
	uncle

[pg. 117]

VERBS

	to know, to meet (for the first time), to get/be acquainted
	to know (a fact), to know how
	have to, must
	to want to
	can
	to say, to tell

[pg. 118, 126, 132]

EXPRESSIONS OF TIME

	every year
	in the summer
	in the fall
	in the winter
	in the spring

[pg. 122]

PREPOSITIONS

	of, from
	at, to, in
	from
	at, to, in
	with
	on, about
	for
	between, among

[pg. 115]

Intermediate Italian

Don't forget: if you're having a hard time remembering this vocabulary, check out the supplemental flashcards for this unit online, at **www.livinglanguage.com/languagelab**.

Grammar Essentials

Here is a reference of the key grammar that was covered in Unit 3. Make sure you understand the summary and can use all of the grammar in it.

CONTRACTIONS WITH PREPOSITIONS

	IL	LO	LA	L'	I	GLI	LE
di	del	dello	della	dell'	dei	degli	delle
a	al	allo	alla	all'	ai	agli	alle
da	dal	dallo	dalla	dall'	dai	dagli	dalle
in	nel	nello	nella	nell'	nei	negli	nelle
su	sul	sullo	sulla	sull'	sui	sugli	sulle

POSSESSIVES

	MASCULINE SINGULAR	FEMININE SINGULAR	MASCULINE PLURAL	FEMININE PLURAL
my	il mio	la mia	i miei	le mie
your	il tuo	la tua	i tuoi	le tue
his/her/its, your (fml.)*	il suo	la sua	i suoi	le sue
our	il nostro	la nostra	i nostri	le nostre
your (pl.)	il vostro	la vostra	i vostri	le vostre
their, your (fml. pl.)**	il loro	la loro	i loro	le loro

* When *your* is used in the formal form it's written with a capital S-: il Suo, la Sua, i Suoi, le Sue.
** When *your (pl.)* is used in the formal form it's written with a capital L-: il Loro, la Loro, i Loro, le Loro.

VERBS

DOVERE *(MUST, TO HAVE TO)* – PRESENT

io devo	*I must*	noi dobbiamo	*we must*
tu devi	*you must*	voi dovete	*you (pl.) must*
lui/lei/Lei deve	*he/ she must, you (fml.) must*	loro/Loro devono	*they must, you (fml. pl.) must*

POTERE *(CAN, TO BE ABLE TO)* – PRESENT

io posso	*I can*	noi possiamo	*we can*
tu puoi	*you can*	voi potete	*you (pl.) can*
lui/lei/Lei può	*he/she can, you (fml.) can*	loro/Loro possono	*they can, you (fml. pl.) can*

VOLERE *(TO WANT)* – PRESENT

io voglio	*I want*	noi vogliamo	*we want*
tu vuoi	*you want*	voi volete	*you (pl.) want*
lui/lei/Lei vuole	*he/she wants, you (fml.) want*	loro/Loro vogliono	*they want, you (fml. pl.) want*

SAPERE *(TO KNOW A FACT, TO KNOW HOW TO DO SOMETHING)* – PRESENT

io so	*I know*	noi sappiamo	*we know*
tu sai	*you know*	voi sapete	*you (pl.) know*
lui/lei/Lei sa	*he, she knows, you (fml.) know*	loro/Loro sanno	*they know, you (fml. pl.) know*

BERE *(TO DRINK)* – PRESENT

io bevo	*I drink*	noi beviamo	*we drink*
tu bevi	*you drink*	voi bevete	*you (pl.) drink*
lui/lei/Lei beve	*he/she drinks, you (fml.) drink*	loro/Loro bevono	*they drink, you (fml. pl.) drink*

DIRE (TO SAY/TO TELL) – PRESENT

io dico	*I say/I tell*	noi diciamo	*we say/tell*
tu dici	*you say/tell*	voi dite	*you (pl.) say/tell*
lui/lei/Lei dice	*he/she says/tells, you (fml.) say/tell*	loro/Loro dicono	*they say/tell, you (fml. pl.) say/tell*

USCIRE (TO GO OUT) – PRESENT

io esco	*I go out*	noi usciamo	*we go out*
tu esci	*you go out*	voi uscite	*you (pl.) go out*
lui/lei/Lei esce	*he/ she goes out, you (fml.) go out*	loro/Loro escono	*they go out, you (fml. pl.) go out*

VENIRE (TO COME) – PRESENT

io vengo	*I come*	noi veniamo	*we come*
tu vieni	*you come*	voi venite	*you (pl.) come*
lui/lei/Lei viene	*he/she comes, you (fml.) come*	loro/Loro vengono	*they come, you (fml. pl.) come*

Unit 3 Quiz

Let's put the most essential Italian words and grammar points you've learned so far to practice in a few exercises. Score yourself at the end of the review and see if you need to go back for more practice, or if you're ready to move on to Unit 4.

A. Complete each sentence with the appropriate preposition.

1. Noi andiamo _____ Roma.

2. Loro stanno _____ Italia _____ studiare la lingua.

3. Vado _____ Firenze _____ treno.

4. Lei va al cinema _____ Luisa.

B. Fill in the blanks with the appropriate forms of conoscere or sapere.

1. Tu _____ mio fratello?

2. Franca _____ guidare la macchina.

3. Loro _____ Roma molto bene.

4. Voi _____ a che ora arriva l'aereo da Milano?

C. Fill in the blanks with the correct forms of the verbs indicated in parentheses.

1. Mi dispiace, non (can) _____ venire domani.

2. Loro (to have to) _____ lavorare tutto il giorno.

3. Tu (to want) _____ venire al cinema con me?

D. Give the correct form of the verbs indicated for each subject.

1. **tu (bere, dire, venire, uscire)** _____

2. **lei (bere, dire, venire, uscire)** _____

3. **noi (bere, dire, venire, uscire)** _____

E. Merge the given preposition with the appropriate definite article.

1. **Vado a nuotare (in)** _____ **piscina vicino (a)** _____ **chiesa.**

2. **Quando esco (da)** _____ **ristorante vado (a)** _____ **discoteca.**

3. **Il professore parla (a)** _____ **studenti in italiano.**

F. Translate the correct form of the possessive adjectives in agreement to the nouns indicated.

1. **libri** *(my, your, their)* _____

2. **gatto** *(his, our, her)* _____

3. **sorella** *(my, his, your pl.)* _____

ANSWER KEY
A. 1. a; 2. in, per; 3. a, in; 4. con
B. 1. conosci; 2. sa; 3. conoscono; 4. sapete
C. 1. posso; 2. devono; 3. vuoi
D. 1. bevi, dici, vieni, esci; 2. beve, dice, viene, esce; 3. beviamo, diciamo, veniamo, usciamo
E. 1. nella, alla; 2. dal, alla; 3. agli
F. 1. i miei, i tuoi, i loro; 2. il suo, il nostro, il suo; 3. mia, sua, vostra

How Did You Do?

Give yourself a point for every correct answer, then use the following key to tell whether you're ready to move on:

0-7 points: It's probably a good idea to go back through the lesson again. You may be moving too quickly, or there may be too much "down time" between your contact with Italian. Remember that it's better to spend 30 minutes with Italian three or four times a week than it is to spend two or three hours just once a week. Find a pace that's comfortable for you, and spread your contact hours out as much as you can.

8-12 points: You would benefit from a review before moving on. Go back and spend a little more time on the specific points that gave you trouble. Reread the Grammar Builder sections that were difficult, and do the work out one more time. Don't forget about the online supplemental practice material, either. Go to **www.livinglanguage.com/languagelab** for games and quizzes that will reinforce the material from this unit.

13-17 points: Good job! There are just a few points that you might consider reviewing before moving on. If you haven't worked with the games and quizzes on **www.livinglanguage.com/languagelab**, please give them a try.

18-20 points: Great! You're ready to move on to the next unit.

points

Unit 4:
Food

In Unit 4 we're going to learn vocabulary related to food and restaurants, so you'll be ready to read Italian menus when you go out to eat! By the end of this unit, you'll know:

- ☐ key vocabulary related to food
- ☐ how to use the adjectives **buono** (*good*) and **bello** (*beautiful, nice*)
- ☐ key vocabulary for ordering in a restaurant
- ☐ how to say *this* and *that*
- ☐ how to say *some* or *any*
- ☐ how to tell time
- ☐ useful phrases related to grocery shopping
- ☐ how to express a completed action in the past
- ☐ direct object pronouns like *me*, *her*, or *him*
- ☐ how to use direct object pronouns like *me*, *her*, or *him* when talking about the past

Lesson 13: Words

In this lesson, you'll learn:

☐ key vocabulary related to food

☐ how to use the adjectives **buono** (*good*) and **bello** (*beautiful, nice*)

☐ key vocabulary for ordering in a restaurant

☐ how to say *this* and *that*

Word Builder 1

▶ 13A Word Builder 1(CD5, Track 25)

(il) supermercato	*supermarket*
(il) frigorifero	*refrigerator*
vuoto	*empty*
(la) roba	*stuff*
(il) gelato	*ice cream*
(il) vino	*wine*
(la) birra	*beer*
(la) carne	*meat*
(la) fettina	*thin slice*
(il) vitello	*veal*
(la) ricetta	*recipe*
(il) piatto	*plate/dish*
comprare	*to buy*
cucinare	*to cook*
(l')ospite	*guest (m., f.)*

Ⅱ

✎ Word Practice 1

A. Translate the following Italian words into English.

1. **cucinare** _____

2. **birra** _____

3. **carne** _____

4. **supermercato** _____

5. **vitello** _____

B. Translate the following English words into Italian.

1. *refrigerator* _____

2. *recipe* _____

3. *ice cream* _____

4. *plate* _____

5. *guest* _____

ANSWER KEY
A. 1. *to cook*; 2. *beer*; 3. *meat*; 4. *supermarket*; 5. *veal*
B. 1. **frigorifero**; 2. **ricetta**; 3. **gelato**; 4. **piatto**; 5. **ospite**

Grammar Builder 1

▶ 13B Grammar Builder 1 (CD5, Track 26)

ADJECTIVES BUONO AND BELLO

The adjectives buono (*good*) and bello (*beautiful, nice*) usually precede the noun and work differently from typical adjectives. In the singular, the -no ending of buono changes in the same pattern as the indefinite article un/uno/una/un': un buon gelato, un buono studente, una buona ricetta, una buon'amica. The plural forms are always buoni and buone.

The -lo ending of bello changes in the same pattern as the definite articles. Let's see how this works with che bello, which is often used to mean *What a beautiful …* when referring to food.

il piatto	Che bel piatto!	*What a beautiful dish!*
lo spezzatino	Che bello spezzatino!	*What a nice stew!*
la minestra	Che bella minestra!	*What a nice soup!*
l'arancia	Che bell'arancia!	*What a nice orange!*
l'ossobuco	Che bell'ossobuco!	*What a nice osso buco!*
i panini	Che bei panini!	*What nice sandwiches!*
gli zucchini	Che begli zucchini!	*What nice zucchini!*
gli ananas	Che begli ananas!	*What nice pineapples!*
le fragole	Che belle fragole!	*What nice strawberries!*

Loro preparano sempre un bel pranzo.
They always prepare a nice lunch.

Che begli spaghetti ci sono sulla tavola!
What nice spaghetti there is on the table!

⏸

✎ Work Out 1

Choose the correct form of the adjective.

1. Mangiano spesso in un (bello/bel/bell') ristorante francese. _____

2. Nel negozio vendono dei (belli/bei/begli) avocado. _____

3. Che (belli/belle/bell') carote! _____

4. È un (buono/buona/buon) cappuccino. _____

5. Sono dei (buoni/buone/buon) tortellini. _____

6. Voglio comprare un (bello/bella/bell') arrosto. _____

ANSWER KEY
1. bel; 2. begli; 3. belle; 4. buon; 5. buoni; 6. bell'

Word Builder 2

▶ 13C Word Builder 2 (CD5, Track 27)

ieri	yesterday
sera	evening
(la) trattoria	family style restaurant
(il) primo	first course
(il) secondo	second course
(il) contorno	side dish
(l')arrosto	roast
(la) frutta	fruit
ordinare	to order
(il) conto	bill
pieno	full
soddisfatto	satisfied

(la) colazione	*breakfast*
(il) pranzo	*lunch*
(la) cena	*dinner*

🖊 Word Practice 2

Match the following words.

1. **(il) primo**	a. *yesterday*
2. **(il) conto**	b. *to order*
3. **(la) frutta**	c. *bill*
4. **ieri**	d. *roast*
5. **(la) cena**	e. *first course*
6. **ordinare**	f. *full*
7. **(la) trattoria**	g. *second course*
8. **pieno**	h. *dinner*
9. **(il) secondo**	i. *family style restaurant*
10. **(l')arrosto**	l. *fruit*

ANSWER KEY
1. e; 2. c; 3. l; 4. a; 5. h; 6. b; 7. i; 8. f; 9. g; 10. d

Grammar Builder 2

▶ 13D Grammar Builder 2 (CD5, Track 28)

DEMONSTRATIVE ADJECTIVES QUESTO AND QUELLO

Questo (*this*) and **quello** (*that*) are demonstrative adjectives that always precede the noun. **Questo** has four different forms: **questo, questa** (*this*), and **questi, queste** (*these*). Just as with **bello**, however, the endings of **quello** change in the same pattern as the definite article.

quel formaggio	*that cheese*
quello spezzatino	*that stew*
quella cipolla	*that onion*
quell'avocado	*that avocado*
quell'insalata	*that salad*
quei gamberetti	*those shrimp (lit. those shrimps)*
quegli ananas	*those pineapples*
quegli spaghetti	*that spaghetti (lit. those spaghetti)*
quelle mele	*those apples*

Quanto costa quel pollo?
How much does that chicken cost?

Quei broccoli sono molto freschi.
That broccoli is very fresh. (lit. Those broccoli are very fresh.)

Ⅱ

✎ Work Out 2

Complete with the correct forms of quello.

1. _____ trattoria è buona e non è cara.

2. Come sono _____ tortellini?

3. Quanto costa _____ gelato?

4. Come cucini _____ aragosta?

5. _____ spaghetti sono molto buoni.

ANSWER KEY
1. Quella; 2. quei; 3. quel; 4. quell'; 5. Quegli

✎ Drive It Home

Fill in the blanks making the appropriate agreements, and contractions when needed, with the adjectives indicated in parentheses and the nouns they refer to:

1. *(This)* _____ cappello costa troppo.

2. *(Those)* _____ macchine sono bellissime.

3. *(This)* _____ pasta è così *(good)* _____!

4. Che *(beautiful)* _____ giornata!

5. *(Those)* _____ bambini sono molto carini.

6. *(Those)* _____ studenti sono davvero bravi.

7. *(These)* _____ scarpe sono molto più *(beautiful)* _____ di *(those)*

   _____.

8. *(These)* _____ fagioli non sono buoni, posso provare *(those)*

_____ zucchini?

9. **Non voglio comprare** *(that)* _____ **ombrello, è troppo grande.**

10. **Mia madre prepara un** *(good)* _____ **caffè.**

ANSWER KEY
1. **Questo**; 2. **Quelle**; 3. **Questa, buona**; 4. **bella**; 5. **Quei**; 6. **Quegli**; 7. **Queste, belle, quelle**; 8. **Questi, quegli**; 9. **quell'**; 10. **buon**

🔦 Tip!

Hungry for a nice **spezzatino**? Or perhaps some **ossobuco**? If you look up "recipe for spezzatino", or "recipe for osso buco," on the internet, you will be surprised how many recipes you'll find! The choice is yours. **Buon appetito!**

How Did You Do?

Let's see how you did in this lesson. By now, you should know:

☐ key vocabulary related to food (Still unsure? Jump back to page 160.)

☐ how to use the adjectives **buono** *(good)* and **bello** *(beautiful, nice)* (Still unsure? Jump back to page 162.)

☐ key vocabulary for ordering in a restaurant (Still unsure? Jump back to page 163.)

☐ how to say *this* and *that* (Still unsure? Jump back to page 165.)

✎ Word Recall

A. Translate the following words into English.

1. **il vino** _____

2. **il piatto** _____

3. la carne _____

4. il frigorifero _____

5. la cena _____

B. Translate the following words and phrases into Italian.

1. *first course* _____

2. *side dish* _____

3. *bill* _____

4. *breakfast* _____

5. *lunch* _____

> **ANSWER KEY**
> A. 1. *wine*; 2. *dish*; 3. *meat*; 4. *refrigerator*; 5. *dinner*
> B. 1. **il primo**; 2. **il contorno**; 3. **il conto**; 4. **la colazione**; 5. **il pranzo**

Lesson 14: Phrases

By the end of this lesson, you'll know:

☐ how to say *some* or *any*

☐ how to tell time

Phrase Builder 1

▶ 14A Phrase Builder 1 (CD5, Track 29)

del gelato	some ice cream
della birra	some beer

degli spaghetti	some spaghetti
d'accordo	all right
se insisti	if you insist
che tipo di pasta?	what kind of pasta?
due giorni fa	two days ago
un sacco di roba	a bunch/lot of stuff
meglio	better, the best
stasera (questa sera)	tonight

✎ Phrase Practice 1

Match the following words and phrases.

1. **degli spaghetti**   a. *all right*

2. **un sacco di roba**   b. *better*

3. **d'accordo**   c. *some spaghetti*

4. **due giorni fa**   d. *tonight*

5. **meglio**   e. *a lot of stuff*

6. **stasera**   f. *some ice cream*

7. **del gelato**   g. *what kind of pasta?*

8. **che tipo di pasta?**   h. *two days ago*

ANSWER KEY

1. c; 2. e; 3. a; 4. h; 5. b; 6. d; 7. f; 8. g

Grammar Builder 1

▷ 14B Grammar Builder 1 (CD5, Track 30)

EXPRESSING *SOME* OR *ANY*

The preposition **di** + article is used idiomatically to express the partitive *some* or *any*.

Per favore, compra del latte e della pasta.
Please, buy some milk and some pasta.

Ieri ho mangiato delle penne alla vodka.
Yesterday, I ate (some) penne with vodka sauce.

Qualche and **alcuni/e** also express the partitive in Italian. **Qualche** can only be used with nouns in the singular form, although it always has a plural meaning. **Alcuni/e** is only used with nouns in the plural form.

Ho bisogno di alcune braciole di maiale.
I need some pork chops.

Puoi sbucciare qualche mela, per favore?
Can you please peel some apples?

⏸

✎ Work Out 1

Choose the appropriate partitive.

1. **Loro mangiano della/qualche/alcune mele tutti i giorni.** _____

2. **Stasera cucinano delle/qualche/alcune bistecche.** _____

3. Domani invitiamo degli/qualche/alcuni amico a cena. _____

4. Hai comprato del/qualche/alcuni caffè? _____

5. In questa città ci sono dei/qualche/alcuni ristoranti buoni. _____

ANSWER KEY
1. alcune; 2. delle; 3. qualche; 4. del; 5. dei

Phrase Builder 2

▶ 14C Phrase Builder 2 (CD5, Track 31)

ieri sera	last night
davvero	really
lasagne alla bolognese	lasagna Bolognese style
spaghetti alla carbonara	spaghetti carbonara style
per primo	as first course
di secondo	as second course
di contorno	as side dish
per finire	to end, to finish
un conto salato	an expensive bill
ho ordinato	I ordered
ho mangiato	I ate

⏸

✎ Phrase Practice 2

A. Translate the following Italian phrases into English.

1. per finire _____

2. di secondo _____

3. **ho ordinato** _____

4. **un conto salato** _____

B. Translate the following English phrases into Italian.

1. *lasagna Bolognese style* _____

2. *I ate* _____

3. *as side dish* _____

4. *really* _____

ANSWER KEY
A. 1. *to finish*; 2. *as a second course*; 3. *I ordered;* 4. *an expensive bill*
B. 1. **lasagne alla bolognese**; 2. **ho mangiato**; 3. **di contorno**; 4. **davvero**

Grammar Builder 2
▶ 14D Grammar Builder 2 (CD5, Track 32)

TELLING TIME

In Lesson 9 of *Essential Italian* you learned how to tell time. Let's review and add some more vocabulary!

There are two interchangeable ways to ask what time it is in Italian: **Che ora è?** and **Che ore sono?** The answer, according to the time we are asked is:

È mezzogiorno.
It's noon.

È mezzanotte.
It's midnight.

Notice that there is no article in front of the time in the above two cases. Note that the article does appear before **una** as **l'**.

È l'una.
It's one o'clock.

For the rest of the hours we use the article **le** (**le** refers to the word **ore** [hours, f. pl.] even though it is omitted: **sono le (ore) due.**

Sono le due.
It's two o'clock.

Sono le tre.
It's three o'clock.

Sono le quattro.
It's four o'clock.

Minutes are expressed after the hour and are introduced by **e**: for instance, **sono le tre e dieci** (*it's 3:10*). *It's 3:15* can be expressed by either: **sono le tre e quindici**, or **sono le tre e un quarto** (more commonly used). *It's 3:30* can be expressed by either: **sono le tre e trenta**, or **sono le tre e mezza** (more commonly used). *It's 3:45* can be expressed by either **sono le tre e quarantacinque, sono le tre e tre quarti, manca un quarto alle quattro**, or **sono le quattro meno un quarto** (more commonly used).

To indicate a.m. or p.m., Italians use **di mattina** (*in the morning*), **di pomeriggio** (*in the afternoon*), **di sera** (*in the evening*), and **di notte** (*at night*) whenever it's not clear by the context.

Finally, to indicate that an action occurs at a certain time, the preposition **a** is used and contracts with the article.

A che ora pranzate?
At what time do you have lunch?

Pranziamo sempre alle due.
We always have lunch at 2:00 p.m.

🖊 Work Out 2

Express what time it is in Italian.

1. *It's 8:15.* _____

2. *It's 9:25.* _____

3. *It's 10:30.* _____

4. *It's 11:45.* _____

5. *It's 12 p.m.* _____

6. *It's 12 a.m.* _____

7. *It's 1:20.* _____

ANSWER KEY

1. Sono le otto e un quarto. 2. Sono le nove e venticinque. 3. Sono le dieci e trenta (sono le dieci e mezza). 4. Sono le undici e quarantacinque (sono le undici e tre quarti) (sono le dodici meno un quarto). 5. Sono le dodici (è mezzogiorno). 6. Sono le ventiquattro (è mezzanotte). 7. È l'una e venti.

✎ Drive It Home

Fill in the blanks using the appropriate Italian equivalent of *some* and *any* and spell out numbers and time expressions:

1. A colazione mangio sempre (*some*) _____ cereali.

2. (*What time*) _____ ritorni a casa di solito?

3. Quando bevo un caffè uso sempre (*some*) _____ zucchero.

4. La banca apre (*at 8:30*) _____.

5. Vuoi (*some*) _____ vino rosso con la carne?

6. Ora vado al supermercato e compro (*some*) _____ mele e (*some*)
_____ zucchini.

7. (*Some*) _____ volta finisco di lavorare (*at 6:30*) _____
_____ di sera.

8. (*What time*) _____ è?

9. Di contorno vorrei (*some*) _____ patatine e (*some*) _____ insalata.

10. Franco dice che arriva (*at 12:30 p.m.*) _____
e Luigi (*at 12:45*) _____.

ANSWER KEY
1. dei; 2. A che ora; 3. dello; 4. alle otto e mezza; 5. del; 6. delle, degli; 7. Qualche, alle sei e mezza;
8. Che ora; 9. delle, dell'; 10. a mezzogiorno e mezza, all'una meno un quarto

🌐 Culture Note

While in America there are no well defined times for meals, Italians always follow a very strict schedule. Breakfast typically takes place between 7:00 and 9:00. Lunch is between 1:00 and 2:00, and dinner between 7:30 and 8:30. In southern Italy lunch and dinner are usually later. Restaurants will close between lunch and dinner, but if you get hungry during those hours, you can always go to a café to have **uno spuntino** (*a snack*).

How Did You Do?

Let's see how you did in this lesson. By now, you should know:

☐ how to say *some* or *any* (Still unsure? Jump back to page 170.)

☐ how to tell time (Still unsure? Jump back to page 172.)

✎ Word Recall

Translate the following phrases into Italian.

1. *some spaghetti* _____

2. *last night* _____

3. *what kind of pasta* _____

4. *tonight* _____

5. *spaghetti carbonara style* _____

6. *all right* _____

7. *I ordered* _____

8. *an expensive bill* _____

9. *some beer* _____

10. *as side dish* _____

ANSWER KEY
1. **degli spaghetti**; 2. **ieri sera**; 3. **che tipo di pasta**; 4. **stasera**; 5. **spaghetti alla carbonara**;
6. **d'accordo**; 7. **ho ordinato**; 8. **un conto salato**; 9. **della birra**; 10. **di contorno**

Lesson 15: Sentences

By the end of this lesson, you'll know:

☐ useful phrases related to grocery shopping

☐ how to express a completed action in the past

Sentence Builder 1

▶ 15A Sentence Builder 1 (CD6, Track 1)

Puoi andare al supermercato a fare la spesa?	Can you go grocery shopping at the supermarket?
Di che cosa abbiamo bisogno?	What do we need?
Ho fatto la spesa due giorni fa.	I went grocery shopping two days ago.
Ho comprato un sacco di roba.	I bought a bunch/lot of stuff.
Hai portato a casa solo del gelato.	You brought home only ice cream.
Compra delle fettine di vitello.	Buy some thin veal slices.
Abbiamo già mangiato carne ieri.	We already ate meat yesterday.
È il piatto che so cucinare meglio.	It's the dish that I know how to cook the best.

Ⅱ

✎ Sentence Practice 1

A. Translate the following sentences into English.

1. **Ho comprato un sacco di roba.** _____

_____

2. **Puoi andare al supermercato a fare la spesa?** _____

_____

3. **Ho fatto la spesa due giorni fa.** _____

_____

B. Translate the following sentences into Italian.

1. *What do we need?* _____

_____

2. *Buy some thin veal slices.* _____

_____

3. *We already ate meat yesterday.* _____

_____

ANSWER KEY
A. 1. *I bought a bunch/lot of stuff.* 2. *Can you go grocery shopping at the supermarket?* 3. *I went grocery shopping two days ago.*
B. 1. **Di che cosa abbiamo bisogno?** 2. **Compra delle fettine di vitello.** 3. **Abbiamo già mangiato carne ieri.**

Grammar Builder 1
▶ 15B Grammar Builder 1 (CD6, Track 2)

THE PRESENT PERFECT

The present perfect (**passato prossimo**) is used to indicate a completed action in the past. **Ho mangiato**, for example, translates into English as *I have eaten, I ate*, or *I did eat*. With the majority of verbs, this tense is formed with the present tense of the auxiliary verb **avere**, followed by the past participle of the main verb.

Regular past participles are formed by dropping the infinitive ending (-are, -ere, or -ire), and replacing it respectively with -ato, -uto, or -ito

INFINITIVE	PAST PARTICIPLE
mangiare	mangiato
ricevere	ricevuto
dormire	dormito

Here is the passato prossimo of these verbs:

MANGIARE *(TO EAT)* – PRESENT PERFECT			
io ho mangiato	*I ate/have eaten*	noi abbiamo mangiato	*we ate/have eaten*
tu hai mangiato	*you ate/have eaten*	voi avete mangiato	*you (pl.) ate/have eaten*
lui/lei/Lei ha mangiato	*he/ she ate/has eaten, you (fml.) ate/have eaten*	loro/Loro hanno mangiato	*they ate/have eaten, you (fml. pl.) ate/have eaten*

RICEVERE *(TO RECEIVE)* – PRESENT PERFECT			
io ho ricevuto	*I received/have received*	noi abbiamo ricevuto	*we received/have received*
tu hai ricevuto	*you received/have received*	voi avete ricevuto	*you (pl.) received/ have received*
lui/lei/Lei ha ricevuto	*he/she received/ has received, you (fml.) received/ have received*	loro/Loro hanno ricevuto	*they received/have received, you (fml. pl.) received/have received*

DORMIRE *(TO SLEEP)* – PRESENT PERFECT			
io ho dormito	*I slept/have slept*	**noi abbiamo dormito**	*we slept/have slept*
tu hai dormito	*you slept/have slept*	**voi avete dormito**	*you (pl.) slept/have slept*
lui/lei/Lei ha dormito	*he/she slept/has slept, you (fml.) slept/have slept*	**loro/Loro hanno dormito**	*they slept/have slept, you (fml. pl.) slept/have slept*

Ieri abbiamo comprato delle mele.
Yesterday, we bought some apples.

Loro hanno servito un caffè molto buono.
They served (a) very good coffee.

Very few verbs in the **-are** and **-ire** groups have irregular past participles. Many verbs in the **-ere** group, however, do have irregular past participles. Here are some of the most common irregular past participles.

fare	fatto	*to do, to make*
chiedere	chiesto	*to ask*
chiudere	chiuso	*to close*
correre	corso	*to run*
leggere	letto	*to read*
mettere	messo	*to put*
perdere	perso	*to lose*
prendere	preso	*to take, to have*
rispondere	risposto	*to answer*
scrivere	scritto	*to write*
vedere	visto	*to see*

aprire	aperto	*to open*
dire	detto	*to say, to tell*

Che cosa hai preso di primo?
What did you have as a first course?

Il cameriere ha risposto a tutte le nostre domande.
The waiter answered all our questions.

Hai messo le posate in tavola?
Did you put the silverware on the table?

Common time expressions used in the past include: **ieri** (*yesterday*), **fa** (*ago*), and the adjective **scorso/a** (*last*).

Ieri il bambino ha detto una bugia.
Yesterday, the child told a lie.

Abbiamo comprato la nostra casa sei anni fa.
We bought our house six years ago.

L'anno scorso hanno aperto un ristorante italiano vicino a casa mia.
Last year, they opened an Italian restaurant near my house.

The adverbs of time, **sempre** (*always*), **mai** (*never*), **già** (*already*), and **ancora** (*yet*) are inserted between the auxiliary and the past participle. **Mai** means *never* when it is used by itself in exclamations (**mai!**) and in negative sentences, otherwise it means *ever*. **Ancora**, when used in positive sentences, means *again* or *still*.

Non ho ancora fatto la spesa.
I haven't shopped for groceries yet.

Abbiamo già finito di cenare.
We have already finished having dinner.

Hai mai mangiato in questo ristorante?
Have you ever eaten in this restaurant?

ⓘ

✎ Work Out 1

Complete the following sentences with the correct form of the past tense.

1. Ieri lui _____ (portare) la sua ragazza al ristorante.

2. La settimana scorsa noi _____ (vedere) un
   film interessante.

3. Tre anni fa io _____ (lavorare) in America per sei mesi.

4. (Voi) _____ (mettere) i piatti in tavola?

5. Lei non _____ (leggere) quel libro di Eco.

6. Tu _____ (scrivere) una lettera ai tuoi cugini?

7. Loro _____ (cucinare) un'ottima cena.

8. Ieri Marco ed io _____ (studiare) insieme.

ANSWER KEY
1. ha portato; 2. abbiamo visto; 3. ho lavorato; 4. avete messo; 5. ha letto; 6. hai scritto; 7. hanno
cucinato; 8. abbiamo studiato

Sentence Builder 2

▶ 15C Sentence Builder 2 (CD6, Track3)

Ieri sera siamo andati a mangiare in un buon ristorante.	*Last night, we went to eat in a good restaurant.*
Che cosa avete mangiato?	*What did you eat?*
Maria ha ordinato dell'arrosto.	*Maria ordered some roast.*
Ci hanno portato delle verdure alla griglia.	*They brought us some grilled vegetables.*
Avete preso della frutta?	*Did you have any fruit?*
Sì, abbiamo ordinato delle mele.	*Yes, we ordered some apples.*
Siete stati soddisfatti?	*Were you satisfied?*
È stata una bella cena.	*It was a nice dinner.*

⏸

✎ Sentence Practice 2

A. Translate the following sentences into English.

1. Che cosa avete mangiato? _____

   _____

2. È stata una bella cena. _____

   _____

3. Avete preso della frutta? _____

   _____

B. Translate the following sentences into Italian.

1. *Maria ordered some roast.* _____

_____

2. *Yes, we ordered some apples.* _____

_____

3. *Last night, we went to eat in a good restaurant.* _____

_____

ANSWER KEY
1. *What did you eat?* 2. *It was a nice dinner.* 3. *Did you have any fruit?*
B. 1. Maria ha ordinato dell'arrosto. 2. Sì abbiamo ordinato delle mele. 3. Ieri sera siamo andati a
mangiare in un buon ristorante.

Grammar Builder 2
▶ 15D Grammar Builder 2 (CD6, Track 4)

THE PRESENT PERFECT WITH ESSERE + PAST PARTICIPLE

While the majority of verbs form the **passato prossimo** with the auxiliary **avere**,
some verbs use the present tense of **essere** + past participle. When a verb is
conjugated with **avere**, the past participle usually remains unchanged. (There's
one case where it doesn't, but we'll come back to that later.) When a verb is
conjugated with **essere**, however, the past participle agrees in gender and number
with the subject of the verb.

ANDARE *(TO GO)* – PRESENT PERFECT			
io sono andato/a	*I went*	**noi siamo andati/e**	*we went*
tu sei andato/a	*you went*	**voi siete andati/e**	*you (pl.) went*
lui è andato, lei è andata	*he went, she went*	**loro sono andati/e**	*they went*

The Present Perfect with
essere + Past Participle

Direct Object Pronouns in
the Present Perfect

ANDARE *(TO GO)* – PRESENT PERFECT			
Lei è andato/a	*you (fml.) went*	Loro sono andati/e	*you (fml. pl.) went*

Verbs conjugated with essere include: verbs indicating movement from a place to another, such as andare (*to go*), venire (*to come*), uscire (*to go out*), entrare (*to come in*), arrivare (*to arrive*), partire (*to leave*), ritornare (*to return*), etc., as well as verbs that indicate absence of movement, such as stare (*to stay*), restare (*to stay*), rimanere (*to remain*), etc.

Il treno è arrivato con mezz'ora di ritardo.
The train arrived half an hour late.

Un mese fa siamo andati in Italia.
A month ago we went to Italy.

Other verbs that are conjugated with essere are verbs indicating a physical or psychological change of state, such as nascere (*to be born*), morire (*to die*), ingrassare (*to gain weight*), dimagrire (*to lose weight*), invecchiare (*to grow old*), succedere (*to happen*), etc.

Quando sono andata in Italia sono ingrassata un chilo.
When I went to Italy, I gained a kilo.

Suo padre è invecchiato molto.
His/her father aged a lot.

Note that **essere** is conjugated with **essere** in the past, and that **essere** and **stare** share the same past participle, **stato**. Also note that the following verbs have an irregular past participle.

rimanere	rimasto	*to remain*
morire	morto	*to die*
nascere	nato	*to be born*
succedere	successo	*to happen*
venire	venuto	*to come*

La festa è stata molto bella.
It was a very nice party.

L'anno scorso i miei amici italiani sono venuti a trovarmi.
Last year, my Italian friends came to see me.

I miei genitori sono nati in Germania.
My parents were born in Germany.

In compound tenses, the modal verbs **dovere**, **potere**, and **volere** use the auxiliary normally used by the infinitive that follows them. However, in modern spoken Italian, **avere** is often used in all cases.

Ieri siamo dovuti andare a lavorare presto.
Yesterday, we had to go to work early.

La settimana scorsa abbiamo dovuto pulire la casa.
Last week, we had to clean the house.

Ⅱ

✎ Work Out 2

Complete the following sentences with the correct form of the past tense. Pay attention to the auxiliary avere or essere.

1. Quando _____ (arrivare) Marta?

2. Ieri sera noi _____ (uscire) e _____

   (vedere) una bella commedia.

3. L'anno scorso le ragazze _____ (andare) a Roma e

   _____ (visitare) il Colosseo.

4. Un mese fa io _____ (ritornare) in Italia perché

   mio padre _____ (compiere) 80 anni.

5. Ieri Luisa _____ (rimanere) a casa.

6. La settimana scorsa noi _____ (potere) uscire con

   gli amici.

7. L'anno scorso loro _____ (dovere) visitare i

   nostri parenti.

   ANSWER KEY
   1. è arrivata; 2. siamo usciti/e, abbiamo visto; 3. sono andate, hanno visitato; 4. sono ritornato/a, ha compiuto; 5. è rimasta; 6. siamo potuti/e; 7. hanno dovuto

✎ Drive It Home

Translate the verbs indicated in parentheses in the passato prossimo.

1. Ieri sera io (andare) _____ al supermercato e (comprare)

   _____ della carne.

2. **Paolo e Lucia (arrivare)** _____ **sabato scorso.**

3. **Voi (visitare)** _____ **il Colosseo quando (andare)**

   _____ **a Roma?**

4. **Io (mangiare)** _____ **moltissimo in vacanza. (io**

   ingrassare) _____ **tre chili.**

5. **Dove (comprare)** _____ **quelle scarpe?**

6. **Tu (venire)** _____ **in metro o (prendere)** _____

   l'autobus?

7. **Quando Lucia (arrivare)** _____ **a casa, (cucinare)**

   _____ **degli spaghetti.**

8. **Noi (arrivare)** _____ **al ristorante e (bere)**

   _____ **un aperitivo prima di mangiare.**

9. **Franca (rimanere)** _____ **a casa. Io (uscire)**

   _____ **con Gina.**

10. **Quest'anno non (vedere)** _____ **ancora un bel film.**

ANSWER KEY

1. sono andato/a, ho comprato; 2. sono arrivati; 3. avete visitato, siete andati/e; 4. ho mangiato, Sono ingrassato/a; 5. avete comprato; 6. sei venuto/a, hai preso; 7. è arrivata, ha cucinato; 8. siamo arrivati/e, abbiamo bevuto; 9. è rimasta, sono uscito/a; 10. ho visto

How Did You Do?

Let's see how you did in this lesson. By now, you should know:

☐ useful phrases related to grocery shopping (Still unsure? Jump back to page 177.)

The Present Perfect with
essere + Past Participle

Direct Object Pronouns in
the Present Perfect

☐ how to express a completed action in the past
(Still unsure? Jump back to page 178.)

✎ Word Recall

Translate the following sentences into Italian:

1. *What did you eat?* _____

    _____

2. *Maria ordered some roast.* _____

    _____

3. *Did you have any fruit?* _____

    _____

4. *Were you satisfied?* _____

    _____

5. *We ate some grilled vegetables.* _____

    _____

6. *I bought a lot of stuff.* _____

    _____

7. *We already ate meat yesterday.* _____

    _____

8. *I went grocery shopping two days ago.* _____

    _____

9. *It is the dish I can cook the best.* _____

    _____

10. *What do we need?* _____

_____

ANSWER KEY

1. Che cosa avete mangiato? 2. Maria ha ordinato dell'arrosto. 3. Avete preso della frutta? 4. Siete stati soddisfatti? 5. Abbiamo mangiato delle verdure alla griglia. 6. Ho comprato un sacco di roba. 7. Abbiamo già mangiato carne ieri. 8. Sono andato a fare la spesa due giorni fa. 9. È il piatto che cucino meglio. 10. Di che cosa abbiamo bisogno?

Lesson 16: Conversations

By the end of this lesson, you should know:

☐ direct object pronouns like *me, her,* or *him*

☐ how to use direct object pronouns like *me, her,* or *him* when talking about the past

Conversation 1

▶ 16A Conversation 1 (CD6, Track 5 - Italian; Track 6 - Italian and English)

Alessia:	Giorgio, puoi andare al supermercato a fare la spesa?
Giorgio:	D'accordo, di che cosa abbiamo bisogno?
Alessia:	Di tutto! Il frigorifero è vuoto!
Giorgio:	Ma come! Ho fatto la spesa due giorni fa e ho comprato un sacco di roba.
Alessia:	No, hai portato a casa solo del gelato, del vino e della birra!
Giorgio:	Non è vero, ma se insisti… Allora, che tipo di pasta devo prendere?
Alessia:	Compra degli spaghetti e delle penne.
Giorgio:	E che carne vuoi?
Alessia:	Compra delle fettine di vitello per fare delle scaloppine.
Giorgio:	Ma le abbiamo già mangiate ieri!

Alessia:	**Sì, ma abbiamo ospiti stasera ed è il piatto che so cucinare meglio!**

Alessia:	*Giorgio, can you go to the supermarket and buy food?*
Giorgio:	*All right, what do we need?*
Alessia:	*Everything! The refrigerator is empty!*
Giorgio:	*What do you mean! I bought groceries two days ago and I bought a lot of stuff.*
Alessia:	*No, you only brought home ice cream, wine, and beer.*
Giorgio:	*It's not true, but if you insist… So, what kind of pasta do I have to get?*
Alessia:	*Buy some spaghetti and some penne.*
Giorgio:	*And which meat do you want?*
Alessia:	*Buy some thin slices of veal to make scaloppine.*
Giorgio:	*But we ate them yesterday!*
Alessia:	*Yes, but we have guests tonight, and it's the dish that I can cook the best!*

(II)

✎ Conversation Practice 1

Fill in the blanks in the following sentences with the missing words in the word bank. If you're unsure of the answer, listen to the conversation on your audio one more time.

che tipo di, abbiamo bisogno, degli, frigorifero, già, delle, due giorni, comprato

1. **D'accordo, di che cosa** _____ **?**

2. **Compra** _____ **spaghetti e** _____ **penne.**

3. **Ho fatto la spesa** _____ **fa e ho** _____ **un sacco di roba.**

4. **Il** _____ **è vuoto!**

5. Allora, _____ pasta devo prendere?

6. Ma le abbiamo _____ mangiate ieri!

ANSWER KEY
1. abbiamo bisogno; 2. degli, delle; 3. due giorni, comprato; 4. frigorifero; 5. che tipo di; 6. già

Grammar Builder 1
▶ 16B Grammar Builder 1 (CD6, Track 7)

DIRECT OBJECT PRONOUNS

A direct object indicates the direct recipient(s) of the action of the verb. It is not introduced by a preposition, and it answers the question *what?* or *whom?* For example, in the sentence **Stefania compra il pane tutti i giorni** (*Stefania buys bread every day*), **il pane** is the direct object. In Italian, just as in English, a direct object noun can be replaced by a direct object pronoun. But in Italian, this pronoun is generally placed immediately before the verb. Let's take a look at the Italian direct object pronouns:

mi	*me*
ti	*you*
lo	*him, it*
la	*her, it*
La	*you (fml.)*
ci	*us*
vi	*you (pl.)*
li	*them (m.)*
le	*them (f.)*

"Mangi spesso la pasta?" "Sì, la mangio tutti i giorni."
"Do you eat pasta often?" "Yes, I eat it every day."

The Present Perfect with
essere + Past Participle

"Vedi Paolo stasera?" "No, lo vedo domani."
"Are you seeing Paolo tonight?" "No, I'll see him tomorrow."

Ci chiamano una volta alla settimana.
They call us once a week.

When the verb is in the infinitive form, the object pronoun is attached to the end of the infinitive, after dropping its final **-e**. However, with the modal verbs **potere, dovere** or **volere**, the object pronoun can be placed either before the conjugated modal verb or attached to the infinitive.

"Quando posso invitarti a cena?" (or **"Quando ti posso invitare a cena?"**)
"When can I invite you (home) for dinner?"

Note that the following verbs take a noun or a pronoun after a preposition in English, but in Italian they take the noun as a direct object or its pronoun without a preposition: **ascoltare** (*to listen to*); **aspettare** (*to wait for*); **cercare** (*to look for*); **guardare** (*to look at*) and **pagare** (*to pay for*).

"Ascolti molto la musica?" "Sì, l'ascolto sempre."
"Do you listen to music a lot?" "Yes, I listen to it all the time."

Lui è sempre in ritardo e io lo devo sempre aspettare.
He's always late, and I always have to wait for him.

Ⓟ

✎ Work Out 1

Answer the following questions using the appropriate pronouns.

1. **Mangi spesso la carne? Sì,** _____.

2. Ci porti al ristorante domani? Sì, _____

_____.

3. Vuoi ordinare il dolce? No, _____.

4. Posso pagare il conto? No, _____.

5. Mi chiami più tardi? Sì, _____.

6. Per favore, cucini gli spaghetti? Sì, _____.

ANSWER KEY
1. la mangio spesso; 2. vi porto al ristorante domani; 3. non lo voglio ordinare, (non voglio ordinarlo); 4. non puoi pagarlo, (non lo puoi pagare); 5. ti chiamo più tardi; 6. li cucino

❝ Conversation 2

▶ 16C Conversation 2 (CD6, Track 8 - Italian; Track 9 - Italian and English)

Fabio:	**Ieri sera Maria ed io siamo andati a mangiare in un buon ristorante italiano.**
Lucia:	**Davvero? Cosa avete mangiato?**
Fabio:	**Per primo io ho mangiato delle buone lasagne alla bolognese e Maria degli spaghetti alla carbonara.**
Lucia:	**E di secondo?**
Fabio:	**Maria ha ordinato dell'arrosto di vitello ed io ho preso della carne alla brace. E di contorno ci hanno portato delle verdure alla griglia.**
Lucia:	**E per finire avete preso della frutta?**
Fabio:	**Sì, l'abbiamo ordinata, ma non l'abbiamo mangiata perché eravamo troppo pieni.**
Lucia:	**Siete rimasti soddisfatti?**
Fabio:	**Sì, è stata una bella cena, ma abbiamo pagato anche un bel conto salato!**

The Present Perfect with
essere + Past Participle

Fabio: *Last night, Maria and I went to eat in a good Italian restaurant.*

Lucia: *Really? What did you eat?*

Fabio: *As a first course I ate some good lasagna Bolognese, and Maria had some spaghetti carbonara.*

Lucia: *And as a second course?*

Fabio: *Maria ordered some veal roast, and I had some grilled meat. And as a side dish we were served grilled vegetables.*

Lucia: *And to finish, did you have any fruit?*

Fabio: *Yes, we ordered some, but we didn't eat it because we were too full.*

Lucia: *Were you satisfied with your dinner?*

Fabio: *Yes, it was a plentiful dinner, but we paid quite a bill as well!*

Take It Further

In Italian the preposition a + article is used idiomatically to express how, or in what style, a food is cooked. Note the four examples in the dialogue above: lasagne alla bolognese, spaghetti alla carbonara, carne alla brace, and verdure alla griglia.

Also note that lasagne, like every kind of pasta, is plural in Italian.

✎ Conversation Practice 2

Unscramble the following sentences.

1. **Maria/ed/io/a/mangiare/in/un/buon/siamo/ristorante/ieri/sera/italiano/
andati/.** _____

_____

2. **Di/delle/hanno/verdure/contorno/ci/portato/.** _____

_____

3. **Maria/ha/vitello/ordinato/dell'/arrosto/di/.** _____

_____

4. **Siete/soddisfatti/rimasti/?** _____

_____

5. **Cosa/mangiato/avete/?** _____

_____

6. **E/preso/per/della/frutta/finire/avete/?** _____

_____

ANSWER KEY

1. Ieri sera Maria ed io siamo andati a mangiare in un buon ristorante italiano. 2. Di contorno ci hanno portato delle verdure. 3. Maria ha ordinato dell'arrosto di vitello. 4. Siete rimasti soddisfatti? 5. Cosa avete mangiato? 6. E per finire avete preso della frutta?

Grammar Builder 2

▶ 16D Grammar Builder 2 (CD6, Track 10)

DIRECT OBJECT PRONOUNS IN THE PRESENT PERFECT

When direct object pronouns are used in a sentence in the **passato prossimo**, they are placed right in front of the verb **avere**, and the past participle agrees in gender and number with the pronoun. The pronouns **lo** and **la** drop the final vowel in front of the present forms of **avere**.

"Daniela, hai finito la frutta?" "Sì, l'ho finita."
"Daniela, did you finish your fruit?" "Yes, I did."

Abbiamo ordinato due gelati, ma non li abbiamo mangiati.
We ordered two ice creams, but we didn't eat them.

In the first example above, finito becomes finita, to agree with la (la frutta) and
in the second, mangiato becomes mangiati, to agree with li (due gelati).

Ⓘ

✎ Work Out 2

Answer the following questions using the appropriate direct object pronouns. Pay
attention to the past participle.

1. **Hai visto Teresa ieri? Sì,** _____.

2. **Avete comprato le pere? No,** _____

     _____.

3. **Giuseppe ha mangiato i fusilli? Sì,** _____.

4. **Loro hanno cucinato le braciole di maiale? Sì,** _____

     _____.

5. **Franca ha apparecchiato la tavola? No,** _____.

6. **Hai pulito gli zucchini? Sì,** _____.

ANSWER KEY
1. l'ho vista; 2. non le abbiamo comprate; 3. li ha mangiati; 4. le hanno cucinate; 5. non l'ha
apparecchiata; 6. li ho puliti

✎ Drive It Home

Answer the following questions using the direct object pronouns and the verbs appropriately.

1. **Leggi il giornale tutti i giorni? Sì** _____.

2. **Guardi la televisione di notte? No, non** _____ **mai.**

3. **Hai visto tua madre ieri? Sì,** _____.

4. **Cucini spesso gli spaghetti? Sì,** _____ **sempre.**

5. **Hai fatto i compiti ieri? No, non** _____.

6. **Hanno preso il treno per venire a scuola? No, non** _____
_____, **sono venuti in macchina.**

7. **Hai portato fuori il cane ieri? No, non** _____.

8. **Hai salutato i tuoi fratelli prima di andare via? Sì,** _____
_____ **tutti.**

9. **Hai assaggiato il vino che ha portato Giorgio? Sì,** _____
_____.

10. **Prendi la macchina per andare in chiesa domani? No, non** _____
_____, **vado in bicicletta.**

ANSWER KEY
1. lo leggo; 2. la guardo; 3. l'ho vista; 4. li cucino; 5. li ho fatti; 6. l'hanno preso; 7. l'ho portato; 8. li ho salutati; 9. l'ho assaggiato; 10. la prendo

🌐 Culture Note

As you saw in the dialogue, an Italian meal consists of different courses. It begins with an antipasto, which could be affettati misti (*mixed cold cuts*), prosciutto e melone (*prosciutto and melon*), or many other options. The **primo** (*first course*) consists of **pasta**, **risotto**, or **minestra** (*soup*). The **secondo** is a dish of meat or fish, accompanied by the **contorno** of vegetables (ordered separately). **L'insalata** (*salad*) is served as **contorno** or after the **secondo**, never at the beginning of the meal. Finally, the meal ends with **il dolce**, which may consist of just plain fruit.

How Did You Do?

Let's see how you did in this lesson. By now, you should know:

☐ direct object pronouns like *me*, *her*, or *him* (Still unsure? Jump back to page 192.)

☐ how to use direct object pronouns like *me*, *her*, or *him* when talking about the past (Still unsure? Jump back to page 196.)

✎ Word Recall

Translate the following sentences into Italian.

1. *Can you go to the supermarket and buy food?* _____

_____

2. *I bought groceries two days ago.* _____

_____

3. *Buy some spaghetti and some penne.* _____

_____

4. *All right, what do we need?* _____

_____

5. *It's the dish that I can cook the best!* _____

_____

6. *As a first course I ate some good lasagna Bolognese.* _____

_____

7. *Were you satisfied?* _____

_____

8. *What did you eat?* _____

_____

9. *Maria ordered some veal roast.* _____

_____

10. *It was a plentiful dinner.* _____

_____

ANSWER KEY

1. Puoi andare al supermercato a fare la spesa? 2. Ho fatto la spesa due giorni fa. 3. Compra degli spaghetti e delle penne. 4. D'accordo, di che cosa abbiamo bisogno? 5. È il piatto che so cucinare meglio. 6. Per primo ho mangiato delle buone lasagne alla bolognese. 7. Siete rimasti soddisfatti? 8. Cosa avete mangiato? 9. Maria ha ordinato dell'arrosto di vitello. 10. È stata una bella cena.

Don't forget to practice and reinforce what you've learned by visiting **www.livinglanguage.com/languagelab** for flashcards, games, and quizzes!

Unit 4 Essentials

Vocabulary Essentials

Test your knowledge of the key material in this unit by filling in the blanks in the following charts. Once you've completed these pages, you'll have tested your retention, and you'll have your own reference for the most essential vocabulary.

FOOD

	ice cream
	wine
	beer
	meat
	veal
	recipe
	plate, dish

[Pg. 160]

AT A RESTAURANT

	family style restaurant
	first course
	second course
	side dish
	roast
	fruit
	bill

[Pg. 163]

	full
	satisfied

[Pg. 163]

MEALS

	breakfast
	lunch
	dinner

[Pg. 164]

DISHES

	lasagna Bolognese style
	spaghetti carbonara style

[Pg. 171]

AT THE GROCERY STORE

	Can you go grocery shopping at the supermarket?
	What do we need?
	I bought a bunch/lot of stuff.
	Buy some thin veal slices.

[Pg. 177]

VERBS

	to buy
	to cook
	to order

[Pg. 160, 163]

TELLING TIME

	It's noon.
	It's midnight.
	It's one o'clock.
	It's two o'clock.
	It's a quarter after three.
	It's half past three.
	It's a quarter to four.
	in the morning
	in the afternoon
	in the evening
	at night

[Pg. 172–173]

Don't forget: if you're having a hard time remembering this vocabulary, check out the supplemental flashcards for this unit online, at **www.livinglanguage.com/languagelab**.

Grammar Essentials

Here is a reference of the key grammar that was covered in Unit 4. Make sure you understand the summary and can use all of the grammar in it.

THE ADJECTIVES BUONO AND BELLO

The adjectives **buono** (*good*) and **bello** (*beautiful, nice*) usually precede the noun.

MASCULINE	
buon	in front of a consonant or vowel
buono	in front of s + consonant, z-, ps-, gn-

FEMININE	
buona	in front of a consonant
buon'	in front of a vowel

Plural:

MASCULINE	FEMININE
buoni	buone

THE DEMONSTRATIVE ADJECTIVES QUESTO AND QUELLO

Questo (*this*) and **quello** (*that*) always precede the noun.

THIS		THESE	
questo	questa	questi	queste

MASCULINE	
quel	in front of a consonant
quello	in front of s + consonant, z-, ps-, gn-
quell'	in front of a vowel

FEMININE	
quella	in front of a consonant
quell'	in front of a vowel

EXPRESSING *SOME*

The preposition **di** + article is used idiomatically to express the partitive some or any.

di + il	del
di + la	della
di + gli	degli

Qualche can only be used with nouns in the singular form, although it always has a plural meaning.

Alcuni/e is only used with nouns in the plural form.

DIRECT OBJECT PRONOUNS

mi	*me*
ti	*you*
lo	*him, it*
la	*her, it*
La	*you (fml.)*
ci	*us*
vi	*you (pl.)*
li	*them (m.)*
le	*them (f.)*

THE PRESENT PERFECT

The present perfect:

- indicates a completed action in the past.

- is formed with the present tense of the auxiliary verb **avere** or **essere**, followed by the past participle of the main verb.

Regular past participles are formed by dropping the infinitive ending (**-are**, **-ere**, or **-ire**), and replacing it respectively with **-ato**, **-uto**, or **-ito**.

THE PAST PARTICIPLE WITH AVERE

When a verb is conjugated with avere, the past participle usually remains unchanged.

MANGIARE *(TO EAT)* – PRESENT PERFECT			
io ho mangiato	*I ate/have eaten*	**noi abbiamo mangiato**	*we ate/have eaten*
tu hai mangiato	*you ate/have eaten*	**voi avete mangiato**	*you (pl.) ate/have eaten*
lui/lei/Lei ha mangiato	*he/she ate/has eaten, you (fml.) ate/have eaten*	**loro/Loro hanno mangiato**	*they ate/have eaten, you (fml. pl.) ate/have eaten*

RICEVERE *(TO RECEIVE)* – PRESENT PERFECT			
io ho ricevuto	*I received/have received*	**noi abbiamo ricevuto**	*we received/have received*
tu hai ricevuto	*you received/have received*	**voi avete ricevuto**	*you (pl.) received/have received*
lui/lei/Lei ha ricevuto	*he/she received/has received, you (fml.) received/have received*	**loro/Loro hanno ricevuto**	*they received/have received, you (fml. pl.) received/have received*

DORMIRE *(TO SLEEP)* – PRESENT PERFECT			
io ho dormito	*I slept/have slept*	**noi abbiamo dormito**	*we slept/have slept*
tu hai dormito	*you slept/have slept*	**voi avete dormito**	*you (pl.) slept/have slept*
lui/lei/Lei ha dormito	*he/she slept/has slept, you (fml.) slept/have slept*	**loro/Loro hanno dormito**	*they slept/have slept, you (fml. pl.) slept/have slept*

Intermediate Italian

COMMON IRREGULAR PAST PARTICIPLES AVERE		
fare	fatto	to do, to make
chiedere	chiesto	to ask
chiudere	chiuso	to close
correre	corso	to run
leggere	letto	to read
mettere	messo	to put
perdere	perso	to lose
prendere	preso	to take, to have
rispondere	risposto	to answer
scrivere	scritto	to write
vedere	visto	to see
aprire	aperto	to open
dire	detto	to say, to tell

COMMON IRREGULAR PAST PARTICIPLES (ESSERE)

When a verb is conjugated with essere, the past participle agrees in gender and number with the subject of the verb.

ANDARE *(TO GO)* – PRESENT PERFECT			
io sono andato/a	*I went*	noi siamo andati/e	*we went*
tu sei andato/a	*you went*	voi siete andati/e	*you (pl.) went*
lui/lei è andato/a	*he/she went*	loro sono andati/e	*they went*
Lei è andato/a	*you (fml.) went*	Loro sono andati/e	*you (fml. pl.) went*

COMMON IRREGULAR PAST PARTICIPLES ESSERE		
rimanere	rimasto	*to remain*
morire	morto	*to die*
nascere	nato	*to be born*
succedere	successo	*to happen*
venire	venuto	*to come*

Unit 4 Quiz

Let's put the most essential Italian words and grammar points you've learned so far to practice in a few exercises. It's important to be sure that you've mastered this material before you move on. Score yourself at the end of the review and see if you need to go back for more practice, or if you're ready to move on to Unit 5.

A. Choose the correct form of the adjective.

1. Nel negozio vendono dei (belli/bei/begli) cappelli. _____

2. Che (belli/belle/bell') scarpe! _____

3. Loro vogliono comprare una (bello/bella/bell') macchina. _____

B. Complete with the correct forms of quello.

1. _____ casa è molto bella.

2. Come sono _____ spinaci?

3. Quanto costa _____ ombrello?

C. Choose the appropriate partitive.

1. Hai comprato del/qualche/alcuni vino per pranzo? _____

2. Domani compro dello/qualche/alcune spumante per la festa. _____

3. La settimana prossima vanno a trovare degli/qualche/alcuni amico. _____

D. Spell out in Italian what time it is.

1. *It's 6:15* _____

2. *It's 9:55* _____

3. *It's 1:30* _____

E. Complete the following sentences with the correct form of the past tense.

1. L'anno scorso lei _____ (lavorare) in un

ristorante per due mesi.

2. Ieri io _____ (scrivere) una lettera a mia madre.

3. Sabato scorso Marco ed io _____ (ballare) alla

discoteca tutta la notte.

F. Complete the following sentences with the correct form of the past tense. Pay attention to the auxiliary avere or essere.

1. Ieri sera noi _____ (andare) al cinema e

_____ (vedere) un film italiano.

2. Un mese fa loro _____ (ritornare) in Italia e

_____ (conoscere) molti nuovi amici.

3. Ieri Franca non _____ (potere) andare al mare perché

_____ (dovere) studiare tutto il giorno.

G. Answer the following questions using the appropriate direct object pronouns. Pay attention to the verbs' tenses.

1. Fai i compiti stasera? No, stasera non _____

perché _____ già _____ ieri.

2. **Hai già mangiato l'insalata? No, non** _____ **ancora** _____

_____ **quando finisco il primo.**

How Did You Do?

Give yourself a point for every correct answer, then use the following key to tell whether you're ready to move on:

0-7 points: It's probably a good idea to go back through the lesson again. You may be moving too quickly, or there may be too much "down time" between your contact with Italian. Remember that it's better to spend 30 minutes with Italian three or four times a week than it is to spend two or three hours just once a week. Find a pace that's comfortable for you, and spread your contact hours out as much as you can.

8-12 points: You would benefit from a review before moving on. Go back and spend a little more time on the specific points that gave you trouble. Reread the Grammar Builder sections that were difficult, and do the work out one more time. Don't forget about the online supplemental practice material, either. Go to **www.livinglanguage.com/languagelab** for games and quizzes that will reinforce the material from this unit.

13-17 points: Good job! There are just a few points that you might consider reviewing before moving on. If you haven't worked with the games and quizzes on **www.livinglanguage.com/languagelab** please give them a try.

18-20 points: Great! You're ready to move on to the next unit.

points

ANSWER KEY

A. 1. **bei**; 2. **belle**; 3. **bella**
B. 1. **Quella**; 2. **quegli**; 3. **quell'**
C. 1. **del**; 2. **dello**; 3. **qualche**
D. 1. **Sono le sei e un quarto**; 2. **Sono le dieci meno cinque**; 3. **è l'una e mezza**
E. 1. **ha lavorato**; 2. **ho scritto**; 3. **abbiamo ballato**
F. 1. **siamo andati, abbiamo visto**; 2. **sono ritornati, hanno conosciuto**; 3. **è potuta, ha dovuto**
G. 1. **li faccio, li ho, fatti**; 2. **l'ho, mangiata, la mangio**

Unit 5:
Shopping

In this unit, you will learn everything you need to have a wonderful shopping experience in Italy! By the end of this unit, you'll know:

☐ key vocabulary related to clothing

☐ how to express something you're doing

☐ the months of the year

☐ how to say *to me, to you, to them*

☐ how to say *I enjoy myself*

☐ how to express likes and dislikes

☐ how to describe habitual actions in the past

☐ how to talk about the future

☐ how to use the preposition *from*

☐ expressions of quantity

Lesson 17: Words

By the end of this lesson, you'll know:

☐ key vocabulary related to clothing

☐ how to express something you're doing

☐ the months of the year

☐ how to say *to me, to you, to them*

Word Builder 1

▶ 17A Word Builder 1 (CD6, Track 11)

(il) negozio d'abbigliamento	*clothing store*
(la) giacca	*jacket*
(i) pantaloni	*pants*
(l')abito	*suit*
(la) camicia	*shirt*
(la) cravatta	*tie*
(il) vestito	*dress*
(la) scarpa	*shoe*
(la) borsa	*purse*
(il) cappello	*hat*
bianco	*white*
rosso	*red*
nero	*black*
grigio	*gray*
giallo	*yellow*

✎ Word Practice 1

A. Translate the following nouns and adjectives into English.

1. (il) vestito _____

2. la) borsa _____

3. (la) cravatta _____

4. (il) negozio d'abbigliamento _____

5. rosso _____

B. Translate the following nouns and adjectives into Italian.

1. *jacket* _____

2. *black* _____

3. *shoe* _____

4. *shirt* _____

5. *pants* _____

ANSWER KEY
A. 1. *suit*; 2. *purse*; 3. *tie*; 4. *clothing store*; 5. *red*
B. 1. **(la) giacca**; 2. **nero**; 3. **(la) scarpa**; 4. **(la) camicia**; 5. **(i) pantaloni**

Grammar Builder 1

▶ 17B Grammar Builder 1 (CD6, Track 12)

THE GERUND

As we have already learned, in Italian the present indicative can be used to express a habitual action in the present: **pranzo sempre all'una** (*I always have lunch at one*), but also an action in progress: **in questo momento guardo la TV** (*I'm watching TV right now*). An action in progress, however, can also be expressed with the progressive form, which is constructed with the present tense of the verb **stare** + gerund, and is the equivalent of the English *to be doing something*. The Italian gerund is formed by adding **-ando** to the stem of verbs belonging to the first conjugation, and **-endo** to the stem of verbs belonging to the second and third conjugation: **parl-ando, scriv-endo; dorm-endo.** So the sentence **in questo momento guardo la TV** can also be expressed with (**in questo momento**) **sto guardando la TV.** There are a few irregular gerunds: **bere → bevendo, dire → dicendo,** and **fare → facendo.**

Cosa stai facendo qui?
What are you doing here?

Sto cercando un paio di scarpe eleganti.
I'm looking for an elegant pair of shoes.

Stanno leggendo il giornale.
They're reading the paper.

Ⓘ

✎ Work Out 1

Restate the following sentences in the present progressive.

Example: **Maria parla con Teresa → Maria sta parlando con Teresa.**

1. **Noi compriamo una casa nuova.** _____

   _____

2. **Tu scrivi una lettera.** _____

   _____

3. **Loro giocano a tennis.** _____

   _____

4. **Io lavoro molto.** _____

_____

5. **Voi imparate l'italiano.** _____

_____

6. **Lei segue un corso di storia dell'arte.** _____

_____

ANSWER KEY

1. Noi stiamo comprando una casa nuova. 2. Tu stai scrivendo una lettera. 3. Loro stanno giocando a tennis. 4. Io sto lavorando molto. 5. Voi state imparando l'italiano. 6. Lei sta seguendo un corso di storia dell'arte.

Word Builder 2

▶ 17C Word Builder 2 (CD6, Track 13)

(la) camicetta	blouse
(il) maglione	sweater
(il) maglioncino	light sweater
(la) gonna	skirt
convinto	convinced
indossare	to wear
(il) mese	month
gennaio	January
febbraio	February
marzo	March
aprile	April
maggio	May
giugno	June
luglio	July

agosto	*August*
settembre	*September*
ottobre	*October*
novembre	*November*
dicembre	*December*

Word Practice 2

Match the following words:

1. **agosto**	a. *May*
2. **(la) gonna**	b. *convinced*
3. **maggio**	c. *blouse*
4. **(il) maglioncino**	d. *shirt*
5. **(la) camicetta**	e. *April*
6. **luglio**	f. *skirt*
7. **convinto**	g. *light sweater*
8. **dicembre**	h. *July*
9. **(la) camicia**	i. *sweater*
10. **aprile**	l. *August*
11. **(il) maglione**	m. *January*
12. **gennaio**	n. *December*

ANSWER KEY

1. l; 2. f; 3. a; 4. g; 5. c; 6. h; 7. b; 8. n; 9. d; 10. e; 11. i; 12. m

Grammar Builder 2

▶ 17D Grammar Builder 2 (CD6, Track 14)

INDIRECT OBJECT PRONOUNS

An indirect object indicates the indirect recipient(s) of the action of the verb. As a noun, it is introduced by the preposition **a**, and it answers the question *to whom?* or *for whom?* In the sentence **Maria scrive una lettera a sua madre** (*Maria writes a letter to her mother*), **a sua madre** is the indirect object (while **una lettera** is the direct object). An indirect object noun can be replaced by an indirect object pronoun, which does not need the preposition **a,** and is generally placed immediately before the verb. While a direct object pronoun can refer to both a thing or a person, an indirect object pronoun can only refer to a person. When indirect object pronouns are used in the **passato prossimo** the ending of the verb's past participle is unaffected by the pronouns. Let's take a look at the Italian indirect object pronouns:

mi	*to me*
ti	*to you*
gli	*to him*
le	*to her*
Le	*to you (fml.)*
ci	*to us*
vi	*to you (pl.)*
gli	*to them*

The rules governing the position of the indirect object pronoun are exactly the same as those for the direct object pronoun (Unit 4, Lesson 16).

Certain verbs, such as **telefonare** (*to telephone*), **insegnare** (*to teach*), **interessare** (*to interest*), **rispondere** (*to answer*), **mandare** (*to send*), and **spedire** (*to send*) take an indirect object pronoun in Italian, but a direct object pronoun in English.

"Hai parlato al direttore?" "Sì, gli ho parlato."
"Did you speak to the director?" "Yes, I spoke to him."

Perché non ci telefonate stasera?
Why don't you call us tonight?

"Hai risposto a Silvana?" "No, non le ho ancora risposto."
"Did you answer Silvana?" "No, I didn't answer her yet."

La prossima settimana è il compleanno di Giulio e devo mandargli un regalo.
Next week is Giulio's birthday and I have to send him a gift.

✎ Work Out 2

Answer the following questions replacing the underlined words with the appropriate pronouns:

1. **Hai scritto** *a tua cugina*?

   Sì, _____.

2. **Avete telefonato** *a Roberto*?

   No, _____.

3. **Hai parlato** *ai tuoi amici*?

   Sì, _____.

4. *Vi* **hanno spedito il pacco?**

   No, _____.

5. **Hai raccontato la favola** *alle bambine*?

   Sì, _____.

ANSWER KEY
1. le ho scritto; 2. non gli abbiamo telefonato; 3. gli ho parlato; 4. non ci hanno spedito il pacco;
5. gli ho raccontato la favola

✎ Drive It Home

A. Restate the following sentences in the present progressive:

1. Che cosa scrivi? _____

2. Ora bevo il caffè. _____

3. Gino va all'ufficio di fretta. _____

4. Loro non possono venire ora perché mangiano la frutta. _____

5. Noi leggiamo lo stesso libro. _____

B. Restate the following sentences using the appropriate indirect object pronouns
   instead of the nouns:

1. Vado al cinema da solo perché a Marco e a Luisa non interessa. _____

   _____

2. Non hai ancora telefonato a Lucia? _____

   _____

3. Quando mandi i regali ai bambini? _____

   _____

4. Ho insegnato a mio marito un sacco di parole italiane. _____

   _____

5. Avete detto a Franca di venire presto? _____

   _____

ANSWER KEY

A. 1. stai scrivendo; 2. sto bevendo; 3. sta andando; 4. stanno mangiando; 5. stiamo leggendo

B. 1. Vado al cinema da solo perché non gli interessa. 2. Non le hai ancora telefonato? 3. Quando gli mandi i regali? 4. Gli ho insegnato un sacco di parole italiane. 5. Le avete detto di venire presto?

⊕ Culture Note

If you're going on a shopping spree in Italy, make sure you really like or need what you buy, because it is almost impossible to return any merchandise after you walk out of a store. Very few stores will give you a store credit, but none will return your money!

How Did You Do?

Let's see how you did in this lesson. By now, you should know:

☐ key vocabulary related to clothing (Still unsure? Jump back to page 213.)

☐ how to express something you're doing (Still unsure? Jump back to page 214.)

☐ the months of the year (Still unsure? Jump back to page 216.)

☐ how to say *to me, to you, to them* (Still unsure? Jump back to page 218.)

✎ Word Recall

A. Translate the following words into English.

1. bianco _____

2. la cravatta _____

3. febbraio _____

4. il negozio di abbigliamento _____

5. indossare _____

6. il maglione _____

B. Translate the following words into Italian.

1. *dress* _____

2. *shoe* _____

3. *month* _____

4. *blouse* _____

5. *pants* _____

6. *convinced* _____

ANSWER KEY
A. 1. *white*; 2. *tie*; 3. *February*; 4. *clothing store*; 5. *to wear*; 6. *sweater*
B. 1. **(il) vestito**; 2. **(la) scarpa**; 3. **(il) mese**; 4. **(la) camicetta**; 5. **(i) pantaloni**; 6. **convinto**

Lesson 18: Phrases

By the end of this lesson, you'll know:

☐ how to say *I enjoy myself*

☐ how to express likes and dislikes

Phrase Builder 1
▶ 18A Phrase Builder 1 (CD6, Track 15)

Si sposa.	*He/she is getting married.*
si mette	*he/she wears/puts on*
si chiama …	*his/her name is …*
a proposito di …	*speaking of …*
Che sorpresa!	*What a surprise!*

da Bang Bang	at Bang Bang's
Mi sembra bello.	It seems nice to me.
Come mi sta?	How do I look?
di velluto a coste	made out of corduroy
di pelle	made out of leather

✎ Phrase Practice 1

Match the following expressions:

1. **Che sorpresa!**
2. **Mi sembra bello.**
3. **Si sposa.**
4. **Come mi sta?**
5. **di pelle**
6. **a proposito di …**
7. **si mette**
8. **si chiama …**

a. *How do I look?*
b. *made out of leather*
c. *It seems nice to me.*
d. *he/she puts on*
e. *his/her name is …*
f. *What a surprise!*
g. *He/she is getting married.*
h. *speaking of …*

ANSWER KEY
1. f; 2. c; 3. g; 4. a; 5. b; 6. h; 7. d; 8. e

Grammar Builder 1

▷ 18B Grammar Builder 1 (CD6, Track 16)

REFLEXIVE VERBS

Reflexive verbs, whose infinitives are recognizable by their **-si** ending, are verbs in which the action refers back to the subject (as in *I enjoy myself*). You have already learned the verb **chiamarsi** (*to be named*). Italian uses reflexive verbs more often than English, which prefers prepositional sentences (i.e., *to wake up, to get* up, etc.) to express the same idea. Reflexive verbs are conjugated just like non-reflexive verbs, but are preceded by the reflexive pronoun as follows:

ALZARSI (TO GET UP)	METTERSI (TO PUT ON)	DIVERTIRSI (TO ENJOY ONESELF)	PULIRSI (TO CLEAN ONESELF)
io mi alzo	io mi metto	io mi diverto	io mi pulisco
tu ti alzi	tu ti metti	tu ti diverti	tu ti pulisci
lui si alza	lui si mette	lui si diverte	lui si pulisce
lei/Lei si alza	lei/Lei si mette	lei/Lei si diverte	lei/Lei si pulisce
noi ci alziamo	noi ci mettiamo	noi ci divertiamo	noi ci puliamo
voi vi alzate	voi vi mettete	voi vi divertite	voi vi pulite
loro/Loro si alzano	loro/Loro si mettono	loro/Loro si divertono	loro/Loro si puliscono

Here's a list of some more common reflexive verbs:

addormentarsi	to fall asleep
annoiarsi	to get bored
fermarsi	to stop
lavarsi	to wash up
preoccuparsi	to worry
prepararsi	to get ready
sentirsi	to feel
svegliarsi	to wake up
vestirsi	to get dressed

Perché ti preoccupi sempre così tanto?
Why do you always worry so much?

A che ora vi svegliate la mattina?
At what time do you wake up in the morning?

Quando lo vedo mi fermo sempre per salutarlo.
When I see him I always stop to say hi.

In the past (**passato prossimo**) reflexive verbs are always conjugated with **essere**.

Claudia, ti sei divertita ieri sera alla festa?
Claudia, did you enjoy yourself at the party last night?

Ieri ci siamo alzati molto tardi.
Yesterday, we got up very late.

Ⓘ

✎ Work Out 1

Complete the following sentences with the present or past tenses of the verbs in parentheses.

1. **Tutte le mattine lui** _____ **(svegliarsi) alle sei e mezza.**

2. **Ieri io** _____ **(annoiarsi) molto a teatro.**

3. **Oggi noi non** _____ **(sentirsi) molto bene.**

4. **Ieri sera tu** _____ **(addormentarsi)**

   davanti alla TV.

5. **Voi** _____ **(lavarsi) sempre prima di andare a letto.**

6. **La settimana scorsa loro** _____ **(mettersi) un vestito**

   da sera per andare alla festa.

ANSWER KEY
1. si sveglia; 2. mi sono annoiato/a; 3. ci sentiamo; 4. ti sei addormentato/a; 5. vi lavate; 6. si sono messe

Phrase Builder 2

18C Phrase Builder 2 (CD6, Track 17)

Posso esserLe utile?	*How can I help you? (fml.) (lit., Can I be useful to you?), Can I assist you?*
di seta	*made out of silk*
di cachemire	*made out of cashmere*
Le faccio vedere.	*I'll show you. (fml.)*
Le piace?	*Do you like it? (fml.)*
Mi piace.	*I like it.*
le mezze stagioni	*half seasons (spring and fall)*
Ci penso.	*I (will) think about it.*
fra qualche giorno	*in a few days*
chiedere (un) consiglio	*to ask for advice*

Phrase Practice 2

A. Translate the following phrases and sentences into English.

1. Le faccio vedere. _____

2. Mi piace. _____

3. fra qualche giorno _____

4. chiedere (un) consiglio _____

B. Translate the following phrases and sentences into Italian.

1. *Do you like it?* _____

2. *I'll think about it.* _____

3. *made out of silk* _____

4. *half seasons* _____

ANSWER KEY
A. 1. *I'll show you.* 2. *I like it.* 3. *in a few days*; 4. *to ask for advice*
B. 1. **Le piace?** 2. **Ci penso.** 3. **di seta**; 4. **le mezze stagioni**

Grammar Builder 2
▷ 18D Grammar Builder 2 (CD6, Track 18)

EXPRESSING LIKES AND DISLIKES

Although **piacere** and *to like* have the same meaning, they have very different structures. The verb **piacere** can be literally translated as *to be pleasing to* or *to appeal to*. So when you want to express the English *Cristina likes this dress* in Italian, you need to rephrase it as *this dress is appealing to Cristina*. In this structure, what is liked (*the dress*) constitutes the subject of the sentence, while the person who likes (*Cristina*) is the indirect object. So the sentence would be rendered in Italian as **il vestito piace a Cristina**. If the subject of the sentence (what is liked) is a plural noun, then the verb **piacere** will be in the plural form **piacciono**. Although the word order is flexible, the most typical construction is: indirect object + **piacere** + what is liked:

A Maria piace quella borsa.
Maria likes that purse.

Alla signora Panzacchi piacciono le scarpe rosse.
Mrs. Panzacchi likes red shoes.

Gli piacciono i vestiti di Armani.
He likes Armani suits.

If what is liked is an action expressed in the infinitive, the verb **piacere** will be in the third person singular.

Gli piace svegliarsi presto la mattina.
He likes to wake up early in the morning.

Non ci piace fare spese al centro commerciale.
We don't like shopping at the mall.

The verb **piacere** is conjugated with **essere** in the past. As with all other verbs conjugated with **essere**, the past participle has to agree with the subject of the sentence, which with **piacere** is the entity that is liked.

Mi è piaciuta la festa di ieri sera.
I liked the party last night.

Gli sono piaciute le cravatte che gli hai comprato.
He liked the ties you bought for him.

The verb **dispiacere**, which has the same structure of **piacere**, means *to be sorry* or *to mind*. The negative form of **piacere** is used to express dislike.

Le dispiace farmi vedere quella giacca?
Would you mind showing me that jacket?

Non ci piace quella gonna.
We don't like that skirt.

Ⓜ

✎ Work Out 2

Form sentences following the example, and then replace the indirect object with a pronoun:

Giorgio/comprare vestiti → **A Giorgio piace comprare vestiti** → **Gli piace comprare vestiti.**

1. **Luigi/la pasta.** _____

   _____

2. **I bambini/le favole.** _____

   _____

3. **Le ragazze/fare spese.** _____

   _____

4. **La signora Piccoli/i vestiti eleganti.** _____

   _____

5. **Noi/le vacanze.** _____

   _____

6. **Lui/imparare le lingue straniere.** _____

   _____

ANSWER KEY

1. **A Luigi piace la pasta/gli piace la pasta. 2. Ai bambini piacciono le favole/gli piacciono le favole. 3. Alle ragazze piace fare spese/gli piace fare spese. 4. Alla signora Piccoli piacciono i vestiti eleganti/le piacciono i vestiti eleganti. 5. A noi piacciono le vacanze/ci piacciono le vacanze. 6. A lui piace imparare le lingue straniere/gli piace imparare le lingue straniere.**

✎ Drive It Home

A. Complete the following sentences translating the verbs indicated in the present and in the **passato prossimo**.

1. Marco (mettersi) _____ l'impermeabile.

2. I bambini (divertirsi) _____

   _____ con i loro amici.

3. Maria e Lucia (lavarsi) _____ i

   denti prima di andare a letto.

4. Noi (alzarsi) _____ molto presto.

5. A che ora (svegliarsi) _____

   _____ voi?

B. Translate the following sentences and turn them in the **passato prossimo**.

1. *I like the movie.* _____

   _____

2. *They like the book very much.* _____

   _____

3. *We don't like my mother's ravioli.* _____

   _____

4. *Do you like to eat at the restaurant?* _____

   _____

5. *Do they like to come back home early after work?* _____

_____

ANSWER KEY

A. 1. si mette/si è messo; 2. si divertono/si sono divertiti; 3. si lavano/si sono lavate; 4. ci alziamo/ci siamo alzati/e; 5. vi svegliate/vi siete svegliati/e

B. 1. Mi piace il film./Mi è piaciuto il film. 2. Gli piace moltissimo il libro./Gli è piaciuto moltissimo il libro. 3. Non ci piacciono i ravioli di mia madre./Non ci sono piaciuti i ravioli di mia madre. 4. Ti piace mangiare al ristorante?/Ti è piaciuto mangiare al ristorante? 5. Gli piace ritornare a casa presto dopo il lavoro?/Gli è piaciuto ritornare a casa presto dopo il lavoro?

🔆 Tip!

Are you interested in fashion? Would you like to know what the latest trends are? Search online for **moda autunno-inverno**, or **moda primavera-estate**, and you will find all you need to know about fashion for the coming season.

How Did You Do?

Let's see how you did in this lesson. By now, you should know:

☐ how to say *I enjoy myself* (Still unsure? Jump back to page 223.)

☐ how to express likes and dislikes (Still unsure? Jump back to page 227.)

✎ Word Recall

A. Translate the following words into English.

1. **il cappello** _____

2. **grigio** _____

3. **la camicia** _____

4. **giallo** _____

5. **il maglione** _____

6. **il mese** _____

B. Translate the following words into Italian.

1. *purse* _____

2. *suit* _____

3. *to wear* _____

4. *May* _____

5. *skirt* _____

6. *light sweater* _____

ANSWER KEY
A. 1. *hat*; 2. *gray*; 3. *shirt*; 4. *yellow*; 5. *sweater*; 6. *month*
B. 1. la borsa; 2. l'abito; 3. indossare; 4. maggio; 5. la gonna; 6. il maglioncino

Lesson 19: Sentences

By the end of this lesson, you'll know:

☐ how to describe habitual actions in the past

☐ how to talk about the future

Sentence Builder 1

▶ 19A Sentence Builder 1 (CD6, Track 19)

Sto cercando un vestito.	*I'm looking for a dress.*
Mia sorella si sposa il mese prossimo.	*My sister is getting married next month.*
Sto cominciando a preoccuparmi.	*I'm beginning to worry.*
Anche lui frequentava il nostro liceo.	*He also used to attend our high school.*
Era due anni avanti.	*He was two years ahead (of us).*
Aveva i capelli lunghi.	*He had long hair.*
Portava una giacca di pelle.	*He used to wear a leather jacket.*
Guidava una motocicletta rossa.	*He used to drive a red motorbike.*

⓫

✎ Sentence Practice 1

Translate the following sentences from English into Italian:

1. *I'm beginning to worry.* _____

   _____

2. *He used to wear a leather jacket.* _____

   _____

3. *He also used to attend our high school.* _____

   _____

4. *I'm looking for a dress.* _____

   _____

5. *He had long hair.* _____

_____

6. *He used to drive a red motorbike.* _____

_____

ANSWER KEY

1. Sto cominciando a preoccuparmi. 2. Portava una giacca di pelle. 3. Anche lui frequentava il nostro liceo. 4. Sto cercando un vestito. 5. Aveva i capelli lunghi. 6. Guidava una motocicletta rossa.

Grammar Builder 1

▶ 19B Grammar Builder 1 (CD6, Track 20)

THE IMPERFECT TENSE

The imperfect is a simple (not compound) past tense used to describe habitual actions in the past (what we used to do), actions in progress in the past (what we were doing), and general circumstances in the past. The imperfect is formed by dropping the final -re of the infinitive, and by adding the following endings: -vo, -vi, -va, -vamo, -vate, -vano.

PARLARE (TO SPEAK)	VEDERE (TO SEE)	DORMIRE (TO SLEEP)	FINIRE (TO FINISH)
io parlavo	io vedevo	io dormivo	io finivo
tu parlavi	tu vedevi	tu dormivi	tu finivi
lui parlava	lui vedeva	lui dormiva	lui finiva
lei/Lei parlava	lei/Lei vedeva	lei/Lei dormiva	lei/Lei finiva
noi parlavamo	noi vedevamo	noi dormivamo	noi finivamo
voi parlavate	voi vedevate	voi dormivate	voi finivate
loro/Loro parlavano	loro/Loro vedevano	loro/Loro dormivano	loro/Loro finivano

The verb **essere** is irregular in the imperfect: **ero, eri, era, eravamo, eravate, erano**.

The following verbs have irregular stems, but regular endings: **bere: beve-; dire: dice-; fare: face-**.

Quando ero giovane portavo sempre vestiti sportivi.
When I was young I always used to dress casual.

Che cosa cercavi ieri al centro commerciale?
What were you looking for at the mall, yesterday?

Le modelle alla sfilata (di moda) erano troppo magre.
The models at the (fashion) show were too thin/skinny.

Ⅱ

✎ Work Out 1

Put the following sentences in the imperfect tense.

1. **Facciamo spesso spese in quella boutique.** _____

_____

2. **Quel vestito costa troppo.** _____

_____

3. **Mi piace indossare scarpe comode.** _____

_____

4. **Quella ragazza porta sempre gonne corte.** _____

_____

5. La signora Giordani è molto elegante. _____

_____

6. Bevete sempre spumante. _____

_____

7. Lui dice spesso bugie. _____

_____

ANSWER KEY

1. Facevamo spesso spese in quella boutique. 2. Quel vestito costava troppo. 3. Mi piaceva indossare scarpe comode. 4. Quella ragazza portava sempre gonne corte. 5. La signora Giordani era molto elegante. 6. Bevevate sempre spumante. 7. Lui diceva spesso bugie.

Sentence Builder 2

▶ 19C Sentence Builder 2 (CD6, Track21)

Sto cercando una camicetta di seta.	I'm looking for a silk blouse.
Sta arrivando la primavera.	Spring is coming.
Le faccio vedere i maglioncini che abbiamo.	I'll show you the light sweaters we have.
Le piace questo maglioncino?	Do you like this light sweater?
Ci devo pensare.	I'll think about it.
Tornerò fra qualche giorno.	I'll come back in a few days.
Forse fra qualche giorno non lo troverà più.	Perhaps, in a few days, you will not find it anymore.
Chiederò consiglio a mio marito.	I'll ask my husband for advice./I'll discuss it with my husband.

✎ Sentence Practice 2

A. Translate the following sentences into English.

1. **Le piace questo maglioncino?** _____

   _____

2. **Sta arrivando la primavera.** _____

   _____

3. **Ci devo pensare.** _____

   _____

B. Translate the following sentences into Italian.

1. *I'll come back in a few days.* _____

   _____

2. *I'm looking for a silk blouse.* _____

   _____

3. *I'll ask my husband for advice.* _____

   _____

ANSWER KEY

A. 1. *Do you like this light sweater?* 2. *Spring is coming.* 3. *I'll think about it.*

B. 1. **Tornerò fra qualche giorno.** 2. **Sto cercando una camicetta di seta.** 3. **Chiederò consiglio a mio marito.**

Grammar Builder 2

▶ 19D Grammar Builder 2 (CD6, Track 22)

THE FUTURE TENSE

The future tense is formed by dropping the final -e from the infinitive, and adding the endings -ò, -ai, -à, -emo, -ete, -anno. In verbs of the first conjugation, the -a of the infinitive ending changes to -e:

PARLARE (TO SPEAK)	RICEVERE (TO RECEIVE)	DORMIRE (TO SLEEP)	FINIRE (TO FINISH)
io parlerò	io riceverò	io dormirò	io finirò
tu parlerai	tu riceverai	tu dormirai	tu finirai
lui parlerà	lui riceverà	lui dormirà	lui finirà
lei/Lei parlerà	lei/Lei riceverà	lei/Lei dormirà	lei/Lei finirà
noi parleremo	noi riceveremo	noi dormiremo	noi finiremo
voi parlerete	voi riceverete	voi dormirete	voi finirete
loro/Loro parleranno	loro/Loro riceveranno	loro/Loro dormiranno	loro/Loro finiranno

Several common verbs that have irregular stems in the future are: venire → verr-; volere → vorr-; bere → berr-, etc. Other irregular stems are formed by dropping both vowels from the infinitive ending: andare → andr-; avere → avr-; cadere → cadr-; dovere → dovr-; potere → potr-; sapere → sapr-; vedere → vedr-. The future stem of essere is sar-.

La prossima settimana comprerò un vestito da sera.
Next week, I'll buy an evening gown.

L'estate prossima loro andranno in Europa.
Next summer, they will go to Europe.

Se verrete in campagna vedrete molti animali.
If you come to the country you'll (be able to) see many animals.

Since Italians these days commonly use the present tense to talk about the future, when the future tense is used it has a bit of more emphatic and assertive quality than the present tense. In addition to indicating future actions, the future tense is used idiomatically to express the idea of probability of a present situation.

"Che taglia porta Maria?" "Porterà una 44."
"What size does Maria wear?" "She probably wears a 44."

"Quanti anni ha Giulio?" "Avrà 38 anni."
"How old is Giulio?" "He's probably 38."

Ⅱ

✎ Work Out 2

Change the following sentences from the present to the future.

1. **Domani lei va a fare compere al centro commerciale.** _____

   _____

2. **Non so se domani volete andare in centro.** _____

   _____

3. **Per rilassarmi questo weekend leggo un libro nuovo.** _____

   _____

4. **Stasera non guardiamo la TV.** _____

   _____

5. **Loro arrivano domani.** _____

_____

6. **Il bambino partecipa a una gara sportiva.** _____

_____

ANSWER KEY
1. Domani lei andrà a fare compere al centro commerciale. 2. Non so se domani vorrete andare in centro. 3. Per rilassarmi questo weekend leggerò un libro nuovo. 4. Stasera non guarderemo la TV. 5. Loro arriveranno domani. 6. Il bambino parteciperà a una gara sportiva.

✎ Drive It Home

A. Fill in the blanks with the appropriate form of the imperfect tense.

1. **Quando io (essere)** _____ **piccolo d'estate (andare)** _____ **al mare tutte le domeniche.**

2. **Mentre lei (cucinare)** _____ **io (guardare)** _____ **la televisione.**

3. **Quando i bambini (avere)** _____ **cinque anni (sapere)** _____ **già leggere.**

4. **Quando noi (essere)** _____ **in Italia (mangiare)** _____ **sempre al ristorante.**

5. **Voi (avere)** _____ **molti amici quando (abitare)** _____ **all'estero?**

B. Fill in the blanks with the appropriate form of the future tense.

1. **La settimana prossima loro (partire)** _____ **per Boston.**

2. **Martedì Giorgio (venire)** _____ **a trovarci.**

3. L'anno prossimo io (andare) _____ finalmente in Italia.

4. Domani noi (mangiare) _____ di sicuro al ristorante.

5. Sono certo/a che il film ti (piacere) _____.

ANSWER KEY

A. 1. ero, andavo; 2. cucinava, guardavo; 3. avevano, sapevano; 4. eravamo, mangiavamo; 5. avevate, abitavate

B. 1. partiranno; 2. verrà; 3. andrò; 4. mangeremo; 5. piacerà

💡 Tip!

Most likely, when you're in Italy, you'll want to buy some clothes and shoes. Here is a very useful chart comparing American sizes (le taglie americane) with those of many European countries. Buone spese!

LADIES								
Coats, Dresses, Suits								
Europe	36	38	40	42	44	46		
America	8	10	12	14	16	18		
Sweaters, Blouses								
Europe	40	42	44	46	48	50	52	
America	32	34	36	38	40	42	44	
Stockings								
Europe	35	36	37	38	39	40	41	
America	8	8½	9	9½	10	10½	11	
Shoes								
Europe	34	35	36	37	38	39	40	41
America	3½	4	4½	5	6	7	8½	9

MEN								
Coats, Suits								
Europe	44	46	48	50	52	54	56	58
America	34	36	38	40	42	44	46	48
Shirts								
Europe	37	38	39	40	41	42	43	44
America	14½	15	15½	16	16½	17	17½	18
Shoes								
Europe	39	40	41	42	43	44	45	46
America	6	7	8	9	10	11	12	13
Underwear								
Europe	3	4	5	6	7	8		
America	XS	S	M	L	XL	XXL		
Socks								
Europe	39	40	41	42	43	44	45	46
America	9½	10	10½	11	11½	12	12½	13

How Did You Do?

Let's see how you did in this lesson. By now, you should know:

☐ how to describe habitual actions in the past (Still unsure? Jump back to page 234.)

☐ how to talk about the future (Still unsure? Jump back to page 238.)

✎ Word Recall

A. Translate the following phrases and sentences into English.

1. **Lui frequentava il nostro liceo.** _____

   _____

2. **Tornerò fra qualche giorno.** _____

   _____

3. **Sto cercando un vestito.** _____

   _____

4. **una camicetta di seta** _____

   _____

5. **Si sposa il mese prossimo.** _____

   _____

6. **Chiederò consiglio a mio marito.** _____

   _____

B. Translate the following sentences into Italian.

1. *Do you like this light sweater?* _____

   _____

2. *Spring is coming.* _____

   _____

3. *He had long hair.* _____

   _____

4. *I'll think about it.* _____

_____

5. *I'm beginning to worry.* _____

_____

6. *He used to drive a red motorbike.* _____

_____

ANSWER KEY

A. 1. *He used to attend our high school.* 2. *I'll come back in a few days.* 3. *I'm looking for a dress.* 4. *a silk blouse;* 5. *He/She is getting married next month.* 6. *I'll ask my husband for advice.*

B. 1. Le piace questo maglioncino?. 2. Sta arrivando la primavera. 3. Aveva i capelli lunghi. 4. Ci devo pensare. 5. Sto cominciando a preoccuparmi. 6. Guidava una motocicletta rossa.

Lesson 20: Conversations

By the end of this lesson, you'll know:

☐ how to use the preposition *from*

☐ expressions of quantity

Conversation 1

▷ 20A Conversation 1 (CD6, Track 23 - Italian; Track 24 - Italian and English)

Gianni:	Ciao Lucia, che sorpresa! Che cosa stai facendo qui?
Lucia:	Sto cercando un abito da cerimonia. Mia sorella si sposa il mese prossimo e devo andare al suo matrimonio.
Gianni:	Che bello! Non conosco il suo fidanzato, come si chiama?

Lucia: **Luca Zanetti, sei sicuro che non lo conosci? Anche lui frequentava il nostro liceo, ma era due anni avanti. Aveva i capelli molto lunghi, portava sempre una giacca di pelle nera, dei pantaloni di velluto a coste grigi e guidava una motocicletta rossa enorme. Adesso è diventato un medico famoso e si mette sempre abiti, camicie e cravatte di Armani!**

Gianni: **Sì, lo ricordo vagamente… ma a proposito di vestiti, hai idea di cosa metterti per il matrimonio?**

Lucia: **Non lo so, sto cominciando a preoccuparmi perché non ho ancora trovato nulla. Sono andata da Bang Bang, da Alexander e da Carnini, in tutti i migliori negozi d'abbigliamento e non ho visto un vestito che mi piace!**

Gianni: **Guarda questo, Lucia, mi sembra molto bello!**

Lucia: **Hai ragione, lo provo. Hai tempo di guardare come mi sta?**

Gianni: **Certamente e poi ti accompagno a cercare gli accessori. Devi assolutamente coordinare scarpe, borsa e cappello per essere veramente elegante.**

Gianni: *Hi Lucia, what a surprise! What are you doing here?*

Lucia: *I'm looking for a formal dress. My sister is getting married next month, and I must go to her wedding.*

Gianni: *How nice! I don't know her fiancé, what's his name?*

Lucia: *Luca Zanetti, are you sure you don't know him? He also attended our high school, but he was two years ahead. He used to have very long hair, was always wearing a black leather jacket, a pair of gray corduroy pants, and was driving an enormous red motorbike. Now he's become a famous doctor and always wears Armani suits, shirts, and ties!*

Gianni: *Yes, I vaguely remember him… but speaking of clothes, do you know what you want to wear for the wedding?*

Lucia:	I don't know, I'm beginning to worry because I haven't found anything yet. I went to Bang Bang's, Alexander's, and Carnini's, all the best clothing stores, and I haven't seen a dress I like!
Gianni:	Look at this one, Lucia, it seems very beautiful to me!
Lucia:	You're right. I'll try it. Do you have time to look at how it fits me?
Gianni:	Certainly, and then I'll take you to look for accessories. You absolutely must find the perfect shoes, purse, and hat to be truly elegant.

Notes:

Liceo. In Italy there are various types of high schools. Students who expect to continue studying at the university will attend a liceo, while other students may prefer to go to one of the professional schools, or **istituti tecnici**, where they will be trained for a technical job.

Una giacca di pelle. To express what material an object is made of, Italian uses the preposition **di** + material. Other examples are: **una camicia di lino** (*a linen shirt*), **un tavolo di legno** (*a wooden table*), etc.

Una motocicletta rossa. Remember that colors are adjectives, and in Italian they agree in gender and number with the noun they modify. A few exceptions are foreign words, such as **blu** and **beige**, and colors that refer to the name of a flower: **viola** (*purple*); **rosa** (*pink*); **fucsia** (*fuchsia*), etc. These colors are invariable.

✎ Conversation Practice 1

Fill in the blanks in the following sentences with the missing words in the word bank. If you're unsure of the answer, listen to the conversation on your audio one more time.

come si chiama, sto cominciando, guidava, mi piace, si sposa, frequentava, devo andare, di pelle nera, come mi sta

1. Mia sorella _____ il mese prossimo e _____

   al suo matrimonio.

2. _____ una motocicletta rossa enorme.

3. Non ho visto un vestito che _____.

4. Non conosco il suo fidanzato, _____?

5. _____ a preoccuparmi.

6. Lui _____ il nostro liceo.

7. Portava sempre una giacca _____.

8. Hai tempo di guardare _____?

ANSWER KEY
1. si sposa, devo andare; 2. Guidava; 3. mi piace; 4. come si chiama; 5. Sto cominciando;
6. frequentava; 7. di pelle nera; 8. come mi sta

Grammar Builder 1

▶ 20B Grammar Builder 1 (CD6, Track 25)

THE PREPOSITION DA

The preposition **da** literally means *from*.

Gli studenti tornano da scuola alle tre.
Students come back from school at 3:00 p.m.

Il treno da Milano arriva a Roma alle dodici e trenta.
The train from Milan arrives in Rome at 12:30 p.m.

Da, however, is also used idiomatically to express at somebody's house, store, office, or place in general.

Stasera ceniamo da Giorgio.
Tonight, we are having dinner at Giorgio's.

Domani vado dal dottore.
Tomorrow, I'm going to the doctor's.

Compro i vestiti da Bang Bang.
I buy my clothes at Bang Bang's.

✎ Work Out 1

Complete the following sentences using one of the following prepositions as appropriate: di, a, da, in.

1. **Partiamo _____ New York alle sette di sera e arriviamo _____ Roma alle nove di mattina.**

2. **Ogni anno andiamo _____ Italia per due mesi.**

3. **Perché non andiamo a mangiare _____ Tonino?**

4. **Domenica non saremo _____ casa perché andiamo _____ vacanza.**

5. **"_____ chi è questo libro?" "È _____ Mirella."**

ANSWER KEY
1. da, a; 2. in; 3. da; 4. a, in; 5. Di, di

🎧 Conversation 2

▶ 20C Conversation 2 (CD6, Track 26 - Italian; Track 27 - Italian and English)

Commesso: Buon giorno signora, benvenuta da Carnini, posso esserLe utile?

Signora Ricci: Sì, grazie, sto cercando una camicetta di seta da indossare con questa gonna.

Commesso: La gonna è molto bella, ma è un po' sportiva. Ha pensato di indossarla con un maglioncino di cachemire invece che con una camicetta? Se vuole Le faccio vedere i maglioncini che abbiamo. Ecco, guardi, Le piace questo?

Signora Ricci: Sì, mi piace molto, ma ormai siamo in aprile e forse il cachemire fa un po' troppo caldo.

Commesso: Signora, quando i maglioncini sono arrivati, ho parlato al direttore del negozio e gli ho detto la stessa cosa, ma lui mi ha risposto che sono di cachemire e seta, sono molto leggeri e adatti per le mezze stagioni.

Signora Ricci: È molto bello, ma ho già molti maglioncini. Ci penserò e se decido di comprarlo tornerò fra qualche giorno.

Commesso: Signora, forse fra qualche giorno non lo troverà più. Questo è l'ultimo che abbiamo.

Signora Ricci: Mi dispiace, ma non sono convinta. Chiederò consiglio a mio marito, e tornerò domani.

Salesperson: *Good day Madam, welcome to Carnini's. Can I help you?*

Signora Ricci: *Yes, thanks. I'm looking for a silk blouse to wear with this skirt.*

Salesperson: *Your skirt is very beautiful, but a bit casual. Have you thought about wearing it with a light, cashmere sweater rather than a blouse? If you'd like, I can show you the light sweaters we have. Look, do you like this one?*

Signora Ricci: *Yes, I like it a lot, but we are already in April and perhaps cashmere is a bit too warm.*

Salesperson:	*Madam, I spoke to the store manager as soon as we got the light sweaters, and I told him the same thing, but he answered that these silk and cashmere sweaters are very light, perfect for spring or fall weather.*
Signora Ricci:	*It's very beautiful, but I already have many light sweaters. I'll think about it and, if I decide to buy it, I will come back in a few days.*
Salesperson:	*Madam, perhaps in a few days you will not find it anymore. This is the last one we have left.*
Signora Ricci:	*I'm sorry, but I'm not sure. I will ask my husband for advice, and I'll come back tomorrow.*

Notes:

Le faccio vedere i maglioncini. Fare vedere (*to show*), literally means *to make* or *let someone see something.*

Ho pensato di indossare la gonna. The verb **pensare** is followed by the preposition **di** + infinitive to convey the idea of thinking about doing something. It is followed by the preposition **a** + pronoun when it means to think about something or someone, as in: **penso sempre ai miei figli** (*I always think about my children*).

✎ Conversation Practice 2

Unscramble the following sentences.

1. cachemire/lui/sono/mi/ha/risposto/che/di/e/seta/. _____

   _____

2. ha/un/maglioncino/di/indossarla/con/pensato/? _____

   _____

The Future Tense   Adjective/Adverbs **molto**, **poco**, and **troppo**

3. non/mi/dispiace/,/ma/convinta/sono/. _____

_____

4. sto/una/di/seta/cercando/camicetta/. _____

_____

5. la/bella/è/molto/gonna/. _____

_____

6. questo/che/è/l'ultimo/abbiamo/. _____

_____

7. ho/maglioncini/già/molti/. _____

_____

8. piace/Le/questo/? _____

_____

ANSWER KEY

1. Lui mi ha risposto che sono di cachemire e seta. 2. Ha pensato di indossarla con un maglioncino? 3. Mi dispiace, ma non sono convinta. 4. Sto cercando una camicetta di seta. 5. La gonna è molto bella. 6. Questo è l'ultimo che abbiamo. 7. Ho già molti maglioncini. 8. Le piace questo?

Grammar Builder 2

▶ 20D Grammar Builder 2 (CD6, Track 28)

ADJECTIVES/ADVERBS MOLTO, POCO, AND TROPPO

Remember that molto (*much, a lot*) can be used both as an adjective and as an adverb. As an adjective it modifies a noun, and it agrees with that noun in gender and number.

Ho comprato molte scarpe.
I bought many (pairs of) shoes.

Mangio sempre molta verdura.
I always eat a lot of vegetables.

As an adverb, it modifies a verb, an adjective, or another adverb, and is always invariable.

Questa camicia è molto bella.
This shirt is very beautiful.

Lui gioca molto a tennis.
He plays tennis a lot.

Voi vestite molto elegantemente.
You dress very elegantly.

Poco (*few, little*), and **troppo** (*too much*) work exactly the same way.

Lei ha poche borse.
She has few purses.

Loro dormono troppo.
They sleep too much.

⏸

✎ Work Out 2

Complete with the correct form of molto.

1. Compriamo _____ vestiti.

2. Loro _____.

3. È una ragazza _____ intelligente.

4. Noi abbiamo _____ amiche.

5. Correte _____ velocemente.

6. Mangio _____ pasta.

ANSWER KEY
1. molti; 2. molto; 3. molto; 4. molte; 5. molto; 6. molta

✎ Drive It Home

A. Complete the following sentences using the appropriate preposition (di, a, da, in).

1. Ieri ho studiato _____ cinque _____ sette e mezza.

2. Sono uscito _____ ristorante e sono andato _____ cinema.

3. Penso _____ andare _____ dottore domani.

4. Penso spesso _____ quella ragazza _____ Roma.

5. Domani rimango _____ casa fino _____ sette.

B. Complete with the correct form of **molto**, **poco**, or **troppo** according to the suggestions in parentheses.

1. **Lei ha conosciuto** *(many)* _____ **persone alla festa.**

2. **Ho un gran mal di stomaco perché ho mangiato** *(too much)* _____ .

3. **Ci sono** *(too many)* _____ **macchine e** *(too few)* _____

   biciclette in questa città.

4. **Il volume della televisione è** *(too)* _____ **basso, non sento nulla.**

5. **Questo libro è** *(little)* _____ **conosciuto, ma è** *(very)* _____

   interessante.

   ANSWER KEY
   A. 1. dalle, alle; 2. dal, al; 3. di, dal; 4. a, di; 5. a, alle
   B. 1. molte; 2. troppo; 3. troppe, troppo poche; 4. troppo; 5. poco, molto

☀ Tip!

Although traditionally Italians have always shopped in small stores and boutiques, in recent years, **centri commerciali** *(malls)*, **supermercati** *(supermarkets)*, and outlet stores have become ubiquitous, and Italians enjoy the longer hours, with an **orario continuato** *(open all day, not closed during lunch break)*, and the cheaper prices offered by these stores.

How Did You Do?

Let's see how you did in this lesson. By now, you should know:

☐ how to use the preposition *from* (Still unsure? Jump back to page 246.)

☐ expressions of quantity (Still unsure? Jump back to page 251.)

✎ Word Recall

A. Translate the following sentences into English.

1. **Ciao Lucia, che sorpresa!** _____

_____

2. **Ci penserò.** _____

_____

3. **Devo andare al suo matrimonio.** _____

_____

4. **Che cosa stai facendo qui?** _____

_____

5. **Se decido di comprarlo tornerò.** _____

_____

6. **Forse il cachemire fa un po' troppo caldo.** _____

_____

B. Translate the following sentences into Italian.

1. *I'm looking for a formal dress.* _____

_____

2. *I spoke to the store manager and I told him the same thing.* _____

_____

3. *I haven't seen a dress I like!* _____

_____

4. *Madam, perhaps in a few days you will not find it anymore.* _____

_____

Don't forget to practice and reinforce what you've learned by visiting **www.livinglanguage.com/languagelab** for flashcards, games, and quizzes!

Unit 5 Essentials

Vocabulary Essentials

Test your knowledge of the key material in this unit by filling in the blanks in the following charts. Once you've completed these pages, you'll have tested your retention, and you'll have your own reference for the most essential vocabulary.

CLOTHING

	clothing store
	jacket
	pants
	suit
	shirt
	tie
	dress
	shoe
	purse
	hat
	blouse
	sweater
	light sweater
	skirt
	to wear

[Pg. 213, 216]

COLORS

	white
	red
	black
	gray
	yellow

[Pg. 213]

MONTHS OF THE YEAR

	month
	January
	February
	March
	April
	May
	June
	July
	August
	September
	October
	November
	December

[Pg. 216–217]

SHOPPING

	How can I help you? (lit., Can I be useful to you?), Can I assist you?
	made out of silk
	made out of cashmere
	I'll show you
	Do you like it?
	I like it.
	half seasons (spring and fall)
	I (will) think about it.
	in a few days
	to ask for advice

[Pg. 226]

EXPRESSIONS OF QUANTITY

	much, a lot
	few, little
	too much

[Pg. 252]

Don't forget: if you're having a hard time remembering this vocabulary, check out the supplemental flashcards for this unit online, at **www.livinglanguage.com/languagelab**.

Grammar Essentials

Here is a reference of the key grammar that was covered in Unit 5. Make sure you understand the summary and can use all of the grammar in it.

THE GERUND

To form the gerund, add **-ando** to the stem of verbs belonging to the first conjugation, and **-endo** to the stem of verbs belonging to the second and third conjugation: **parl-ando**, **scriv-endo**; **dorm-endo**.

IRREGULAR GERUNDS

bere	bevendo
dire	dicendo
fare	facendo

INDIRECT OBJECT PRONOUNS

mi	*to me*
ti	*to you*
gli	*to him*
le	*to her*
Le	*to you (fml.)*
ci	*to us*
vi	*to you (pl.)*
gli	*to them*
Loro	*to you (fml. pl.)*

REFLEXIVE VERBS

Reflexive verbs are conjugated just like non-reflexive verbs, but are preceded by the reflexive pronoun:

ALZARSI (TO GET UP)	METTERSI (TO PUT ON)	DIVERTIRSI (TO ENJOY ONESELF)	PULIRSI (TO CLEAN ONESELF)
io mi alzo	io mi metto	io mi diverto	io mi pulisco
tu ti alzi	tu ti metti	tu ti diverti	tu ti pulisci
lui si alza	lui si mette	lui si diverte	lui si pulisce
lei/Lei si alza	lei/Lei si mette	lei/Lei si diverte	lei/Lei si pulisce
noi ci alziamo	noi ci mettiamo	noi ci divertiamo	noi ci puliamo
voi vi alzate	voi vi mettete	voi vi divertite	voi vi pulite
loro/Loro si alzano	loro/Loro si mettono	loro/Loro si divertono	loro/Loro si puliscono

COMMON REFLEXIVE VERBS

addormentarsi	to fall asleep
annoiarsi	to get bored
fermarsi	to stop
lavarsi	to wash up
preoccuparsi	to worry
prepararsi	to get ready
sentirsi	to feel
svegliarsi	to wake up
vestirsi	to get dressed

THE IMPERFECT TENSE

The imperfect is formed by dropping the final -re of the infinitive, and by adding the following endings:

io -vo	noi -vamo
tu -vi	voi -vate
lui -va	loro -vano

PARLARE	VEDERE	DORMIRE	FINIRE
io parlavo	io vedevo	io dormivo	io finivo
tu parlavi	tu vedevi	tu dormivi	tu finivi
lui parlava	lui vedeva	lui dormiva	lui finiva
lei/Lei parlava	lei/Lei vedeva	lei/Lei dormiva	lei/Lei finiva
noi parlavamo	noi vedevamo	noi dormivamo	noi finivamo
voi parlavate	voi vedevate	voi dormivate	voi finivate
loro/Loro parlavano	loro/Loro vedevano	loro/Loro dormivano	loro/Loro finivano

THE VERB ESSERE IS IRREGULAR IN THE IMPERFECT:

io ero	noi eravamo
tu eri	voi eravate
lui/lei/Lei era	loro/Loro erano

The following verbs have irregular stems, but regular endings:

bere	beve
dire	dice
fare	face

THE FUTURE TENSE

The future tense is formed by dropping the final -e from the infinitive, and adding the endings:

io -ò	noi -emo
tu -ai	voi -ete
lui/lei/Lei -à	loro/Loro -anno

In verbs of the first conjugation, the -a of the infinitive ending changes to -e:

PARLARE	RICEVERE	DORMIRE	FINIRE
io parlerò	io riceverò	io dormirò	io finirò
tu parlerai	tu riceverai	tu dormirai	tu finirai
lui parlerà	lui riceverà	lui dormirà	lui finirà
lei/Lei parlerà	lei/Lei riceverà	lei/Lei dormirà	lei/Lei finirà
noi parleremo	noi riceveremo	noi dormiremo	noi finiremo
voi parlerete	voi riceverete	voi dormirete	voi finirete
loro/Loro parleranno	loro/Loro riceveranno	loro/Loro dormiranno	loro/Loro finiranno

IRREGULAR FUTURE STEMS

venire	verr-
volere	vorr-
bere	berr-
andare	andr-
avere	avr-
cadere	cadr-
dovere	dovr-
potere	potr-
sapere	sapr-
vedere	vedr-
essere	sar-

Unit 5 Quiz

Let's put the most essential Italian words and grammar points you've learned so far to practice in a few exercises. It's important to be sure that you've mastered this material before you move on. Score yourself at the end of the review and see if you need to go back for more practice, or if you're ready to move on to *Advanced Italian*.

A. Restate the following sentences in the present progressive.

1. **Noi mangiamo un gelato.** _____

_____

2. **Tu leggi il giornale.** _____

_____

B. Answer the following questions using the appropriate indirect object pronouns.

1. **Hai parlato al professore? Sì,** _____ .

2. **Avete risposto a Roberto e Giulia? No,** _____

_____ .

3. **Hai spedito la lettera a Franca? Sì,** _____

_____ .

C. Complete the following sentences with the present or past tenses of the verbs in parentheses.

1. Tutte le sere lui _____ (addormentarsi)

   mentre legge.

2. Ieri io _____ (svegliarsi) alle sei e mezza a teatro.

3. Di solito noi _____ (divertirsi) alle feste, ma

   ieri sera _____ (annoiarsi) molto.

D. Replace the indirect object in parentheses with a pronoun and write the appropriate form of the verb piacere.

1. (Ai bambini) _____ i dolci.

2. (A Giovanna) non _____ la pasta ai funghi.

3. (Alle ragazze) _____ andare alla discoteca.

E. Put the following sentences in the imperfect tense.

1. Andiamo in vacanza al mare. _____

   _____

2. Mangiano sempre le stesse cose. _____

   _____

3. D'estate mi piace ritornare a casa presto. _____

   _____

F. Change the following sentences from the present to the future.

1. Domani Paolo va a trovare i suoi amici. _____

   _____

2. **Questo weekend io guardo un film alla televisione.** _____

_____

3. **Arriviamo con il treno delle nove e un quarto.** _____

_____

G. Complete the following sentences using one of the following prepositions as appropriate: di, a, da, in.

1. **Andiamo** _____ **dottore** _____ **autobus e poi ritorniamo**

_____ **casa** _____ **metrò.**

2. **Domenica rimango** _____ **parco fino** _____ **cinque, poi porto i**

bambini _____ **negozio** _____ **giocattoli.**

H. Complete with the correct form of molto.

1. *(Many)* _____ **amici erano** *(very)* _____ **contenti di venire alla**

festa portando *(many)* _____ **bottiglie di vino e** *(a lot of)* _____

regali per il mio compleanno.

ANSWER KEY

A. 1. Noi stiamo mangiando un gelato. 2. Tu stai leggendo il giornale.

B. 1. gli ho parlato. 2. non gli abbiamo risposto. 3. le ho spedito la lettera.

C. 1. si addormenta; 2. mi sono svegliato/a; 3. ci divertiamo, ci siamo annoiati

D. 1. Gli, piacciono; 2. le, piace; 3. Gli, piace

E. 1. Andavamo in vacanza al mare. 2. Mangiavano sempre le stesse cose. 3. D'estate mi piaceva ritornare a casa presto.

F. 1. Domani Paolo andrà a trovare i suoi amici. 2. Questo weekend io guarderò un film alla televisione. 3. Arriveremo con il treno delle nove e un quarto.

G. 1. dal, in, a, in; 2. al, alle, al, di

H. 1. Molti, molto, molte, molti

How Did You Do?

Give yourself a point for every correct answer, then use the following key to tell whether you're ready to move on:

0-7 points: It's probably a good idea to go back through the lesson again. You may be moving too quickly, or there may be too much "down time" between your contact with Italian. Remember that it's better to spend 30 minutes with Italian three or four times a week than it is to spend two or three hours just once a week. Find a pace that's comfortable for you, and spread your contact hours out as much as you can.

8-12 points: You would benefit from a review before moving on. Go back and spend a little more time on the specific points that gave you trouble. Reread the Grammar Builder sections that were difficult, and do the work outs one more time. Don't forget about the online supplemental practice material, either. Go to **www.livinglanguage.com/languagelab** for games and quizzes that will reinforce the material from this unit.

13-17 points: Good job! There are just a few points that you might consider reviewing before moving on. If you haven't worked with the games and quizzes on **www.livinglanguage.com/languagelab**, please give them a try.

18-20 points: Great! You did it! You've come to the end of *Living Language Intermediate Italian!* Feel free to move on to *Advanced Italian*. Of course, you can always come back to review whenever you need to.

points

Pronunciation Guide

Italian pronunciation

Many Italian sounds are like English sounds, though the differences are enough that you need to familiarize yourself with them in order to make yourself understood properly in the Italian language. Some key things to remember:

1. Each vowel is pronounced clearly and crisply.

2. A single consonant is pronounced with the following vowel.

3. Some vowels bear an accent mark, sometimes used to show the accentuated syllable (la città, *the city*), and sometimes merely to distinguish words (e, *and*; è, *is*). An acute accent, on the other hand, gives a more closed pronunciation (perché, *why*).

4. When the accent is on the letter e, it gives it a more open pronunciation (caffè, *coffee*).

5. The apostrophe is used to mark elision, the omission of a vowel. For example, when the word dove (*where*) is combined with è (*is*), the e in dove is dropped: Dov'è? (*Where is?*).

The rest is a matter of listening and repeating, which you should do with each word in this section as you start to learn how the Italian language sounds.

VOWELS

Now that you've looked at the difference between Italian and English on a broad scale, let's get down to the specifics by looking at individual sounds, starting with Italian vowels.

LETTER	PRONUNCIATION	EXAMPLES
a	*ah* in *father*	a, amico, la, lago, pane, parlare
e	*e* in *bent*	era, essere, pera, padre, carne, treno, tre, estate, se
i	*i* in *police, machine, marine*	misura, sì, amica, oggi, piccolo, figlio
o	*o* in *no*	no, poi, ora, sono, corpo, con, otto, come, forma, voce
u	*oo* in *noon*	uno, una, tu, ultimo

There are also several diphthongs in Italian, vowel-and-vowel combinations which create a new sound.

LETTER	PRONUNCIATION	EXAMPLES
ai	*i* in *ripe*	guai
au	*ow* in *now*	auto
ei	*ay* in *say*	sei
eu	*ay* in *say* + *oo* in *noon*	neutro
ia	*ya* in *yarn*	italiano
ie	*ye* in *yet*	miele
io	*yo* in *yodel*	campione
iu	*you*	fiume
oi	*oy* in *boy*	poi

LETTER	PRONUNCIATION	EXAMPLES
ua	*wa* in *wand*	quando
ue	*we* in *wet*	questo
uo	*wa* in *war*	suono
ui	*wee* in *sweet*	guido

1. CONSONANTS

Next, let's take a look at Italian consonants. The consonants b, d, f, k, l, m, n, p, q, t, and v are all pronounced as they are in English. The rest differ slightly, as you'll see below.

LETTER	PRONUNCIATION	EXAMPLES
c	before e or i, *ch* in *church*	cena, cibo
c	before a, o, and u, *k* in *bake*	caffè, conto, cupola
g	before e or i, *j* in *joy*	gente, gita
g	before a, o, or u, *g* in *gold*	gala, gondola, gusto
h	silent	hotel
r	trilled	rumore
s	generally, *s* in *set*	pasta
s	between two vowels, or before b, d, g, l, m, n, r, or v, *z* in *zero*	sbaglio
z	generally, *ts* in *pits*	zucchero, grazie
z	sometimes, *ds* in *toads*	zingaro, zanzara

2. SPECIAL ITALIAN SOUNDS

There are several sound combinations in Italian that appear quite often as exceptions to the above rules, so study them carefully.

CLUSTER	PRONUNCIATION	EXAMPLES
ch	before e or i, *c* in *can*	amiche, chilo

CLUSTER	PRONUNCIATION	EXAMPLES
gh	*g* in *get*	spaghetti, ghiotto
	gh in *ghost*	funghi
gl	before a vowel + consonant, *gl* in *globe*	globo, negligente
gli	*lli* in *scallion*	gli
glia	*lli* in *scallion* + *ah*	famiglia
glie	*lli* in *scallion* + *eh*	moglie
glio	*lli* in *scallion* + *oh*	aglio
gn	*ny* in *canyon*	Bologna
sc	before e or i, *sh* in *fish*	pesce, sci
sc	before a, o, or u, *sc* in *scout*	scala, disco
sch	before e or i, *sk* in *sky*	pesche, fischi

Grammar Summary

1. ARTICLES

a. Definite

	MASCULINE	FEMININE
Singular	**il** (in front of a consonant) **l'** (in front of a vowel) **lo** (in front of s + consonant, z-, ps-, or gn-)	**la** (in front of a consonant) **l'** (in front of a vowel)
Plural	**i** (in front of consonants) **gli** (in front of s + consonant, z-, ps-, gn-, or vowels)	**le** (in front of consonants or vowels)

b. Indefinite

	MASCULINE	FEMININE
Singular	**un** (in front of a consonant or vowel) **uno** (in front of s + consonant, z-, ps-, gn-)	**una** (in front of a consonant) **un'** (in front of a vowel)

2. PLURALS OF NOUNS AND ADJECTIVES

GENDER	SINGULAR ENDING	PLURAL ENDING
Masculine	-o	-i
Masculine/Feminine	-e	-i
Feminine	-a	-e

Some exceptions:

a. A few nouns ending in -o are feminine.

b. Some masculine nouns ending in -o have two plurals, with different meanings for each.

c. Masculine nouns ending in -a form their plural in –i.

SPECIAL CASES

1. Nouns ending in -ca or -ga insert h in the plural in order to keep the "k" and "g" sound in the plural.

2. Nouns ending in -cia or -gia (with unaccented i) form their plural in -ce or -ge if the c or g is double or is preceded by another consonant. Nouns ending in -cia or -gia form their plural in -cie or -gie if c or g is preceded by a vowel or if the i is accented.

3. Nouns ending in -io (without an accent on the i) have a single i in the plural. If the i is accented, the plural has ii.

4. Nouns ending in -co or -go form their plural in -chi or -ghi if the accent falls on the syllable before the last. If the accent falls on the third-to-last syllable, the plural is in -ci or -gi.

5. Nouns in the singular with the accent on the last vowel do not change in the plural.

6. There is no special plural form for:

- Nouns with a written accent on the last vowel.

- Nouns ending in i in the singular, and almost all the nouns in ie.

- Nouns ending in a consonant.

3. **THE PARTITIVE**
    a. di + a form of the definite article il, lo, la, l', i, le, gli
    b. qualche (only with singular nouns)
    c. alcuni, alcune (only in the plural)
    d. un po' di

4. COMPARISON

Equality	(così) ... come	*as ... as*
Equality	tanto ... quanto	*as much/as many as*
Superiority	più ... di or che	*More ... than*
Inferiority	meno ... di or che	*less/fewer ... than*

5. RELATIVE SUPERLATIVE

a. The relative superlative (expressed in English using *the most/the least/the . . . -est of/in*) is formed by placing the appropriate definite article before più or meno followed by the adjective. *Of/in* is translated with di, whether by itself or combined with the definite article.

b. If a clause follows the superlative, the verb is often in the subjunctive form.

c. With the superlative of adverbs, the definite article is often omitted, unless *possibile* is added to the adverb.

6. ABSOLUTE SUPERLATIVE

a. The absolute superlative is formed by dropping the last vowel of the adjective and adding -issimo, -issima, -issimi, -issime.

b. By putting the words molto, troppo, or assai in front of the adjectives.

c. By using a second adjective of almost the same meaning, or by repeating the adjective.

d. By using stra-, arci-, sopra-, super-, extra-.

7. IRREGULAR COMPARATIVES AND SUPERLATIVES

ADJECTIVE	COMPARATIVE	SUPERLATIVE
good: buono(a)	*better:* più buono(a) migliore	*the best:* il più buono buonissimo(a) ottimo(a) il/la migliore
bad: cattivo(a)	*worse:* peggiore più cattivo(a) peggio	*the worst:* il/la più cattivo(a) cattivissimo(a) pessimo(a) il/la peggiore
big/great: grande	*bigger/greater:* maggiore più grande	*the biggest/greatest:* il/la più grande grandissimo(a) massimo(a) il/la maggiore
small/little: piccolo(a)	*smaller/lesser:* minore più piccolo(a)	*the smallest:* il/la più piccolo(a) piccolissimo(a) minimo(a) il/la minore

ADVERB	COMPARATIVE	SUPERLATIVE
well: bene	*better:* meglio (il migliore)	*the best:* il meglio
badly: male	*worse:* peggio (il peggiore)	*the worst:* il peggio

8. DIMINUTIVES AND AUGMENTATIVES

a. The endings -ino, -ina, -ello, -ella, -etto, -etta, -uccio, -uccia imply smallness.

b. The endings -one, -ona, -otta imply largeness or hyperbole.

c. The endings -uccia, -uccio indicate endearment.

d. The endings -accio, -accia, -astro, -astra, -azzo, -azza indicate depreciation.

9. DEMONSTRATIVES

questo, -a, -i, -e	*this, these*
quello, -a, -i, -e	*that, those*

There are also the masculine forms quel, quell', quei, quegli. Here is how they are used:

a. If the article il is used before the noun, use quel.

b. If the article l' is used before the noun, then use quell'.

c. If i is used before the noun, use quei.

d. If gli is used before the noun, use quegli.

Note that the same rules apply to bel, bell', bei, begli, from bello, -a, -i, -e (*beautiful*).

10. POSSESSIVE ADJECTIVES

	MASCULINE SINGULAR	MASCULINE PLURAL	FEMININE SINGULAR	FEMININE PLURAL
my	il mio	i miei	la mia	le mie
your	il tuo	i tuoi	la tua	le tue
his, her, its	il suo	i suoi	la sua	le sue
your (fml.)	il Suo	i Suoi	la Sua	le Sue
our	il nostro	i nostri	la nostra	le nostre
your	il vostro	i vostri	la vostra	le vostre
their	il loro	i loro	la loro	le loro
your (fml. pl.)	il Loro	i Loro	la Loro	le Loro

11. INDEFINITE ADJECTIVES AND PRONOUNS

some	qualche (*sg.*), alcuni (*pl.*)
any	qualunque, qualsiasi (*no pl.*)
each, every	ogni (*no pl.*), ciascun, ciascuno, ciascuna (*no pl.*)
other, more	altro, altra, altri, altre
no, no one, none of	nessuno, nessun, nessuna (*no pl.*)

12. INDEFINITE PRONOUNS

some	alcuni
someone, somebody	qualcuno
anybody, anyone	chiunque
each one, each person	ognuno
everybody, everyone	tutti (*pl.*)
each, each one	ciascuno
everything	tutto
the other, the others, else (in interrogative or negative sentences), anything else (in interrogative or negative sentences)	l'altro, l'altra, gli altri, le altre, altro
another one	un altro
nothing	niente, nulla
nobody, no one	nessuno (*no pl.*)

13. RELATIVE PRONOUNS

chi	*who*
che	*who, whom, that, which*
cui	*whom, which*

a cui	*to whom, to which*
di cui	*of whom, of which*
in cui	*in which*

a. che: For masculine, feminine, singular, plural; for persons, animals, things. Not used if there is a preposition.

b. cui: Masculine, feminine, singular, plural; for persons, animals, things; used instead of che when there is a preposition.

c. il quale, la quale, i quali, le quali: For persons, animals, things, with the same English meanings as che; can be used with or without prepositions. When used with prepositions, the contracted forms are used, e.g., alla quale, dei quali, etc.

14. PRONOUNS

	SUBJECT	DIRECT OBJECT	INDIRECT OBJECT	WITH PREPOSITION	REFLEXIVE
1st sg.	io	mi	mi	me	mi
2nd sg.	tu	ti	ti	te	ti
3rd m. sg.	lui	lo	gli	lui	si
3rd f. sg.	lei	la	le	lei	si
2nd sg. fml.	Lei	La	Le	Lei	Si
1st pl.	noi	ci	ci	noi	ci
2nd pl.	voi	vi	vi	voi	vi
3rd pl.	loro	li/le	gli/loro	loro	si
2nd pl. fml.	Loro	Li/Le	Gli/Loro	Loro	Si

15. DOUBLE OBJECT PRONOUNS

INDIRECT OBJECT	+ LO	+ LA	+ LI	+ LE	+ NE
mi	me lo	me la	me li	me le	me ne
ti	te lo	te la	te li	te le	te ne
gli/le/ Le	glielo	gliela	glieli	gliele	gliene
ci	ce lo	ce la	ce li	ce le	ce ne
vi	ve lo	ve la	ve li	ve le	ve ne
gli	glielo/ Glielo	gliela/ Gliela	glieli/Glieli	gliele/ Gliele	gliene/ Gliene
loro/ loro	lo … loro/Loro	la … loro/Loro	li … loro/Loro	le … loro/Loro	ne … loro/Loro

16. ADVERBS

a. Many adverbs end in **-mente**.

b. Adjectives ending in **-le** or **-re** drop the final **e** before adding **-mente** if the **l** or **r** is preceded by a vowel.

c. Adverbs may have a comparative and superlative form.

17. PREPOSITIONS

di	*of*
a	*at, to*
da	*from*
in	*in*
con	*with*
su	*above*
per	*through, by means of, on*
tra, fra	*between, among*

Prepositions + Definite Articles

	DI	A	SUL	CON
il	del	al	sul	col
lo	dello	allo	sullo	-
la	della	alla	sulla	-
l'	dell'	all'	sull'	-
i	dei	ai	sui	coi
gli	degli	agli	sugli	-
le	delle	alle	sulle	-

18. NEGATION

a. **Non** (*not*) comes before the verb.

b. Note that **non** can be combined with negative pronouns in the same sentence (double negative).

c. If the negative pronoun begins the sentence, **non** is not used.

19. QUESTION WORDS

Perché?	*Why?*
Come?	*How?*
Quando?	*When?*
Dove?	*Where?*
Quanto/quanta?	*How much?*
Quanti/quante?	*How many?*

20. THE SUBJUNCTIVE

The subjunctive mood expresses doubt, uncertainty, hope, fear, desire, supposition, possibility, probability, or granting. It is mostly found in clauses dependent upon another verb.

The subjunctive is used:

a. after verbs expressing hope, wish, desire, command, doubt.

b. after verbs expressing an opinion (penso, credo).

c. after expressions made with a form of essere and an adjective or an adverb (è necessario, è facile, è possibile), or some impersonal expressions like bisogna, importa, etc.

d. after conjunctions such as sebbene, quantunque, per quanto, benché, affinché, prima che (subjunctive to express a possibility; indicative to express a fact).

21. "IF" CLAUSES

An "*if*" clause can express:

a. REALITY. In this case, the indicative present and future is used.

b. POSSIBILITY. The imperfect subjunctive and the conditional present are used to express possibility in the present. The past perfect subjunctive and the past conditional are used to express a possibility in the past.

c. IMPOSSIBILITY or COUNTERFACTUALITY. Use the same construction as in (b); the only difference is that we know that the condition cannot be fulfilled.

amare
to love, to like

io	noi
tu	voi
lui/lei/Lei	loro/Loro

Present		Imperative	
amo	amiamo		Amiamo!
ami	amate	Ama!	Amate!
ama	amano	Ami!	Amino!

Past		Imperfect	
ho amato	abbiamo amato	amavo	amavamo
hai amato	avete amato	amavi	amavate
ha amato	hanno amato	amava	amavano

Future		Conditional	
amerò	ameremo	amerei	ameremmo
amerai	amerete	ameresti	amereste
amerà	ameranno	amerebbe	amerebbero

Future Perfect		Past Conditional	
avrò amato	avremo amato	avrei amato	avremmo amato
avrai amato	avrete amato	avresti amato	avreste amato
avrà amato	avranno amato	avrebbe amato	avrebbero amato

Past Perfect		Subjunctive	
avevo amato	avevamo amato	ami	amiamo
avevi amato	avevate amato	ami	amiate
aveva amato	avevano amato	ami	amino

temere
to fear

io	noi
tu	voi
lui/lei/Lei	loro/Loro

Present		Imperative	
temo	temiamo		Temiamo!
temi	temete	Temi!	Temete!
teme	temono	Tema!	Temano!

Past		Imperfect	
ho temuto	abbiamo temuto	temevo	temevamo
hai temuto	avete temuto	temevi	temevate
ha temuto	hanno temuto	temeva	temevano

Future		Conditional	
temerò	temeremo	temerei	temeremmo
temerai	temerete	temeresti	temereste
temerà	temeranno	temerebbe	temerebbero

Future Perfect		Past Conditional	
avrò temuto	avremo temuto	avrei temuto	avremmo temuto
avrai temuto	avrete temuto	avresti temuto	avreste temuto
avrà temuto	avranno temuto	avrebbe temuto	avrebbero temuto

Past Perfect		Subjunctive	
avevo temuto	avevamo temuto	tema	temiamo
avevi temuto	avevate temuto	tema	temiate
aveva temuto	avevano temuto	tema	temano

Intermediate Italian

sentire
to hear

io	noi
tu	voi
lui/lei/ Lei	loro/Loro

Present		Imperative	
sento	sentiamo		Sentiamo!
senti	sentite	Senti!	Sentite!
sente	sentono	Senta!	Sentano!

Past		Imperfect	
ho sentito	abbiamo sentito	sentivo	sentivamo
hai sentito	avete sentito	sentivi	sentivate
ha sentito	hanno sentito	sentiva	sentivano

Future		Conditional	
sentirò	sentiremo	sentirei	sentiremmo
sentirai	sentirete	sentiresti	sentireste
sentirà	sentiranno	sentirebbe	sentirebbero

Future Perfect		Past Conditional	
avrò sentito	avremo sentito	avrei sentito	avremmo sentito
avrai sentito	avrete sentito	avresti sentito	avreste sentito
avrà sentito	avranno sentito	avrebbe sentito	avrebbero sentito

Past Perfect		Subjunctive	
avevo sentito	avevamo sentito	senta	sentiamo
avevi sentito	avevate sentito	senta	sentiate
aveva sentito	avevano sentito	senta	sentano

capire
to understand

io	noi
tu	voi
lui/lei/Lei	loro/Loro

Present		Imperative	
capisco	capiamo		Capiamo!
capisci	capite	Capisci!	Capite!
capisce	capiscono	Capisca!	Capiscano!

Past		Imperfect	
ho capito	abbiamo capito	capivo	capivamo
hai capito	avete capito	capivi	capivate
ha capito	hanno capito	capiva	capivano

Future		Conditional	
capirò	capiremo	capirei	capiremmo
capirai	capirete	capiresti	capireste
capirà	capiranno	capirebbe	capirebbero

Future Perfect		Past Conditional	
avrò capito	avremo capito	avrei capito	avremmo capito
avrai capito	avrete capito	avresti capito	avreste capito
avrà capito	avranno capito	avrebbe capito	avrebbero capito

Past Perfect		Subjunctive	
avevo capito	avevamo capito	capisca	capiamo
avevi capito	avevate capito	capisca	capiate
aveva capito	avevano capito	capisca	capiscano

essere
to be

io	noi
tu	voi
lui/lei/ Lei	loro/Loro

Present		Imperative	
sono	siamo		Siamo!
sei	siete	Sii!	Siate!
è	sono	Sia!	Siano!

Past		Imperfect	
sono stato/a	siamo stati/e	ero	eravamo
sei stato/a	siete stati/e	eri	eravate
è stato/a	sono stati/e	era	erano

Future		Conditional	
sarò	saremo	sarei	saremmo
sarai	sarete	saresti	sareste
sarà	saranno	sarebbe	sarebbero

Future Perfect		Past Conditional	
sarò stato/a	saremo stati/e	sarei stato/a	saremmo stati/e
sarai stato/a	sarete stati/e	saresti stato/a	sareste stati/e
sarà stato/a	saranno stati/e	sarebbe stato/a	sarebbero stati/e

Past Perfect		Subjunctive	
ero stato/a	eravamo stati/e	sia	siamo
eri stato/a	eravate stati/e	sia	siate
era stato/a	erano stati/e	sia	siano

avere
to have

io	noi
tu	voi
lui/lei/ Lei	loro/Loro

Present		Imperative	
ho	abbiamo		Abbiamo!
hai	avete	Abbi!	Abbiate!
ha	hanno	Abbia!	Abbiano!

Past		Imperfect	
ho avuto	abbiamo avuto	avevo	avevamo
hai avuto	avete avuto	avevi	avevate
ha avuto	hanno avuto	aveva	avevano

Future		Conditional	
avrò	avremo	avrei	avremmo
avrai	avrete	avresti	avreste
avrà	avranno	avrebbe	avrebbero

Future Perfect		Past Conditional	
avrò avuto	avremo avuto	avrei avuto	avremmo avuto
avrai avuto	avrete avuto	avresti avuto	avreste avuto
avrà avuto	avranno avuto	avrebbe avuto	avrebbero avuto

Past Perfect		Subjunctive	
avevo avuto	avevamo avuto	abbia	abbiamo
avevi avuto	avevate avuto	abbia	abbiate
aveva avuto	avevano avuto	abbia	abbiano

andare
to go

io	noi
tu	voi
lui/lei/ Lei	loro/Loro

Present		Imperative	
vado	andiamo		Andiamo!
vai	andate	Va!/Va'!/Vai!	Andate!
va	vanno	Vada!	Vadano!

Past		Imperfect	
sono andato/a	siamo andati/e	andavo	andavamo
sei andato/a	siete andati/e	andavi	andavate
è andato/a	sono andati/e	andava	andavano

Future		Conditional	
andrò	andremo	andrei	andremmo
andrai	andrete	andresti	andreste
andrà	andranno	andrebbe	andrebbero

Future Perfect		Past Conditional	
sarò andato/a	saremo andati/e	sarei andato/a	saremmo andati/e
sarai andato/a	sarete andati/e	saresti andato/a	sareste andati/e
sarà andato/a	saranno andati/e	sarebbe andato/a	sarebbero andati/e

Past Perfect		Subjunctive	
ero andato/a	eravamo andati/e	vada	andiamo
eri andato/a	eravate andati/e	vada	andiate
era andato/a	erano andati/e	vada	vadano

bere
to drink

io	noi
tu	voi
lui/lei/ Lei	loro/Loro

Present		Imperative	
bevo	beviamo		Beviamo!
bevi	bevete	Bevi!	Bevete!
beve	bevono	Beva!	Bevano!

Past		Imperfect	
ho bevuto	abbiamo bevuto	bevevo	bevevamo
hai bevuto	avete bevuto	bevevi	bevevate
ha bevuto	hanno bevuto	beveva	bevevano

Future		Conditional	
berrò	berremo	berrei	berremmo
berrai	berrete	berresti	berreste
berrà	berranno	berrebbe	berrebbero

Future Perfect		Past Conditional	
avrò bevuto	avremo bevuto	avrei bevuto	avremmo bevuto
avrai bevuto	avrete bevuto	avresti bevuto	avreste bevuto
avrà bevuto	avranno bevuto	avrebbe bevuto	avrebbero bevuto

Past Perfect		Subjunctive	
avevo bevuto	avevamo bevuto	beva	beviamo
avevi bevuto	avevate bevuto	beva	beviate
aveva bevuto	avevano bevuto	beva	bevano

dare
to give

io	noi
tu	voi
lui/lei/ Lei	loro/Loro

Present		Imperative	
do	diamo		Diamo!
dai	date	Dai!/Dà!/Da'!	Date!
dà	danno	Dia!	Diano!

Past		Imperfect	
ho dato	abbiamo dato	davo	davamo
hai dato	avete dato	davi	davate
ha dato	hanno dato	dava	davano

Future		Conditional	
darò	daremo	darei	daremmo
darai	darete	daresti	dareste
darà	daranno	darebbe	darebbero

Future Perfect		Past Conditional	
avrò dato	avremo dato	avrei dato	avremmo dato
avrai dato	avrete dato	avresti dato	avreste dato
avrà dato	avranno dato	avrebbe dato	avrebbero dato

Past Perfect		Subjunctive	
avevo dato	avevamo dato	dia	diamo
avevi dato	avevate dato	dia	diate
aveva dato	avevano dato	dia	diano

dire
to say

io	noi
tu	voi
lui/lei/ Lei	loro/Loro

Present		Imperative	
dico	diciamo		Diciamo!
dici	dite	Di'!/Dì!	Dite!
dice	dicono	Dica!	Dicano!

Past		Imperfect	
ho detto	abbiamo detto	dicevo	dicevamo
hai detto	avete detto	dicevi	dicevate
ha detto	hanno detto	diceva	dicevano

Future		Conditional	
dirò	diremo	direi	diremmo
dirai	direte	diresti	direste
dirà	diranno	direbbe	direbbero

Future Perfect		Past Conditional	
avrò detto	avremo detto	avrei detto	avremmo detto
avrai detto	avrete detto	avresti detto	avreste detto
avrà detto	avranno detto	avrebbe detto	avrebbero detto

Past Perfect		Subjunctive	
avevo detto	avevamo detto	dica	diciamo
avevi detto	avevate detto	dica	diciate
aveva detto	avevano detto	dica	dicano

dovere
to owe, to be obliged, to have to

io	noi
tu	voi
lui/lei/ Lei	loro/Loro

Present		Imperative	
devo (debbo)	dobbiamo		Dobbiamo!
devi	dovete	Devi!	Dovete!
deve	devono (debbono)	Debba!	Debbano!

Past		Imperfect	
ho dovuto	abbiamo dovuto	dovevo	dovevamo
hai dovuto	avete dovuto	dovevi	dovevate
ha dovuto	hanno dovuto	doveva	dovevano

Future		Conditional	
dovrò	dovremo	dovrei	dovremmo
dovrai	dovrete	dovresti	dovreste
dovrà	dovranno	dovrebbe	dovrebbero

Future Perfect		Past Conditional	
avrò dovuto	avremo dovuto	avrei dovuto	avremmo dovuto
avrai dovuto	avrete dovuto	avresti dovuto	avreste dovuto
avrà dovuto	avranno dovuto	avrebbe dovuto	avrebbero dovuto

Past Perfect		Subjunctive	
avevo dovuto	avevamo dovuto	debba	dobbiamo
avevi dovuto	avevate dovuto	debba	dobbiate
aveva dovuto	avevano dovuto	debba	debbano

fare
to do

io	noi
tu	voi
lui/lei/ Lei	loro/Loro

Present		Imperative	
faccio	facciamo		Facciamo!
fai	fate	Fa!/Fai!/Fa'!	Fate!
fa	fanno	Faccia!	Facciano!

Past		Imperfect	
ho fatto	abbiamo fatto	facevo	facevamo
hai fatto	avete fatto	facevi	facevate
ha fatto	hanno fatto	faceva	facevano

Future		Conditional	
farò	faremo	farei	faremmo
farai	farete	faresti	fareste
farà	faranno	farebbe	farebbero

Future Perfect		Past Conditional	
avrò fatto	avremo fatto	avrei fatto	avremmo fatto
avrai fatto	avrete fatto	avresti fatto	avreste fatto
avrà fatto	avranno fatto	avrebbe fatto	avrebbero fatto

Past Perfect		Subjunctive	
avevo fatto	avevamo fatto	faccia	facciamo
avevi fatto	avevate fatto	faccia	facciate
aveva fatto	avevano fatto	faccia	facciano

potere
to be able, can

io	noi
tu	voi
lui/lei/ Lei	loro/Loro

Present		Imperative	
posso	possiamo		Possiamo!
puoi	potete	Puoi!	Possiate!
può	possono	Possa!	Possano!

Past		Imperfect	
ho potuto	abbiamo potuto	potevo	potevamo
hai potuto	avete potuto	potevi	potevate
ha potuto	hanno potuto	poteva	potevano

Future		Conditional	
potrò	potremo	potrei	potremmo
potrai	potrete	potresti	potreste
potrà	potranno	potrebbe	potrebbero

Future Perfect		Past Conditional	
avrò potuto	avremo potuto	avrei potuto	avremmo potuto
avrai potuto	avrete potuto	avresti potuto	avreste potuto
avrà potuto	avranno potuto	avrebbe potuto	avrebbero potuto

Past Perfect		Subjunctive	
avevo potuto	avevamo potuto	possa	possiamo
avevi potuto	avevate potuto	possa	possiate
aveva potuto	avevano potuto	possa	possano

rimanere
to stay

io	noi
tu	voi
lui/lei/ Lei	loro/Loro

Present		Imperative	
rimango	rimaniamo		Rimaniamo!
rimani	rimanete	Rimani!	Rimanete!
rimane	rimangono	Rimanga!	Rimangano!

Past		Imperfect	
sono rimasto/a	siamo rimasti/e	rimanevo	rimanevamo
sei rimasto/a	siete rimasti/e	rimanevi	rimanevate
è rimasto/a	sono rimasti/e	rimaneva	rimanevano

Future		Conditional	
rimarrò	rimarremo	rimarrei	rimarremmo
rimarrai	rimarrete	rimarresti	rimarreste
rimarrà	rimarranno	rimarrebbe	rimarrebbero

Future Perfect		Past Conditional	
sarò rimasto/a	saremo rimasti/e	sarei rimasto/a	saremmo rimasti/e
sarai rimasto/a	sarete rimasti/e	saresti rimasto/a	sareste rimasti/e
sarà rimasto/a	saranno rimasti/e	sarebbe rimasto/a	sarebbero rimasti/e

Past Perfect		Subjunctive	
ero rimasto/a	eravamo rimasti/e	rimanga	rimaniamo
eri rimasto/a	eravate rimasti/e	rimanga	rimaniate
era rimasto/a	erano rimasti/e	rimanga	rimangano

sapere
to know

io	noi
tu	voi
lui/lei/Lei	loro/Loro

Present		Imperative	
so	sappiamo		Sappiamo!
sai	sapete	Sappi!	Sappiate!
sa	sanno	Sappia!	Sappiano!

Past		Imperfect	
ho saputo	abbiamo saputo	sapevo	sapevamo
hai saputo	avete saputo	sapevi	sapevate
ha saputo	hanno saputo	sapeva	sapevano

Future		Conditional	
saprò	sapremo	saprei	sapremmo
saprai	saprete	sapresti	sapreste
saprà	sapranno	saprebbe	saprebbero

Future Perfect		Past Conditional	
avrò saputo	avremo saputo	avrei saputo	avremmo saputo
avrai saputo	avrete saputo	avresti saputo	avreste saputo
avrà saputo	avranno saputo	avrebbe saputo	avrebbero saputo

Past Perfect		Subjunctive	
avevo saputo	avevamo saputo	sappia	sappiamo
avevi saputo	avevate saputo	sappia	sappiate
aveva saputo	avevano saputo	sappia	sappiano

scegliere
to choose

io	noi
tu	voi
lui/lei/ Lei	loro/Loro

Present		Imperative	
scelgo	scegliamo		Scegliamo!
scegli	scegliete	Scegli!	Scegliete!
sceglie	scelgono	Scelga!	Scelgano!

Past		Imperfect	
ho scelto	abbiamo scelto	sceglievo	sceglievamo
hai scelto	avete scelto	sceglievi	sceglievate
ha scelto	hanno scelto	sceglieva	sceglievano

Future		Conditional	
sceglierò	sceglieremo	sceglierei	sceglieremmo
sceglierai	sceglierete	sceglieresti	scegliereste
sceglierà	sceglieranno	sceglierebbe	sceglierebbero

Future Perfect		Past Conditional	
avrò scelto	avremo scelto	avrei scelto	avremmo scelto
avrai scelto	avrete scelto	avresti scelto	avreste scelto
avrà scelto	avranno scelto	avrebbe scelto	avrebbero scelto

Past Perfect		Subjunctive	
avevo scelto	avevamo scelto	scelga	scegliamo
avevi scelto	avevate scelto	scelga	scegliate
aveva scelto	avevano scelto	scelga	scelgano

uscire
to go out

io	noi
tu	voi
lui/lei/ Lei	loro/Loro

Present | ## Imperative

		Imperative	
esco	usciamo		Usciamo!
esci	uscite	Esci!	Uscite!
esce	escono	Esca!	Escano!

Past | ## Imperfect

		Imperfect	
sono uscito/a	siamo usciti/e	uscivo	uscivamo
sei uscito/a	siete usciti/e	uscivi	uscivate
è uscito/a	sono usciti/e	usciva	uscivano

Future | ## Conditional

		Conditional	
uscirò	usciremo	uscirei	usciremmo
uscirai	uscirete	usciresti	uscireste
uscirà	usciranno	uscirebbe	uscirebbero

Future Perfect | ## Past Conditional

		Past Conditional	
sarò uscito/a	saremo usciti/e	sarei uscito/a	saremmo usciti/e
sarai uscito/a	sarete usciti/e	saresti uscito/a	sareste usciti/e
sarà uscito/a	saranno usciti/e	sarebbe uscito/a	sarebbero usciti/e

Past Perfect | ## Subjunctive

		Subjunctive	
ero uscito/a	eravamo usciti/e	esca	usciamo
eri uscito/a	eravate usciti/e	esca	usciate
era uscito/a	erano usciti/e	esca	escano

vedere
to see

io	noi
tu	voi
lui/lei/ Lei	loro/Loro

Present		Imperative	
vedo	vediamo		Vediamo!
vedi	vedete	Vedi!/Ve'!	Vedete!
vede	vedono	Veda!	Vedano!

Past		Imperfect	
ho visto	abbiamo visto	vedevo	vedevamo
hai visto	avete visto	vedevi	vedevate
ha visto	hanno visto	vedeva	vedevano

Future		Conditional	
vedrò	vedremo	vedrei	vedremmo
vedrai	vedrete	vedresti	vedreste
vedrà	vedranno	vedrebbe	vedrebbero

Future Perfect		Past Conditional	
avrò visto	avremo visto	avrei visto	avremmo visto
avrai visto	avrete visto	avresti visto	avreste visto
avrà visto	avranno visto	avrebbe visto	avrebbero visto

Past Perfect		Subjunctive	
avevo visto	avevamo visto	veda	vediamo
avevi visto	avevate visto	veda	vediate
aveva visto	avevano visto	veda	vedano

venire
to come

io	noi
tu	voi
lui/lei/ Lei	loro/Loro

Present		Imperative	
vengo	veniamo		Veniamo!
vieni	venite	Vieni!	Venite!
viene	vengono	Venga!	Vengano!

Past		Imperfect	
sono venuto/a	siamo venuti/e	venivo	venivamo
sei venuto/a	siete venuti/e	venivi	venivate
è venuto/a	sono venuti/e	veniva	venivano

Future		Conditional	
verrò	verremo	verrei	verremmo
verrai	verrete	verresti	verreste
verrà	verranno	verrebbe	verrebbero

Future Perfect		Past Conditional	
sarò venuto/a	saremo venuti/e	sarei venuto/a	saremmo venuti/e
sarai venuto/a	sarete venuti/e	saresti venuto/a	sareste venuti/e
sarà venuto/a	saranno venuti/e	sarebbe venuto/a	sarebbero venuti/e

Past Perfect		Subjunctive	
ero venuto/a	eravamo venuti/e	venga	veniamo
eri venuto/a	eravate venuti/e	venga	veniate
era venuto/a	erano venuti/e	venga	vengano

volere
to want

io	noi
tu	voi
lui/lei/Lei	loro/Loro

Present		Imperative	
voglio	vogliamo		vogliamo!
vuoi	volete	vogli!	vogliate!
vuole	vogliono	voglia!	vogliano!

Past		Imperfect	
ho voluto	abbiamo voluto	volevo	volevamo
hai voluto	avete voluto	volevi	volevate
ha voluto	hanno voluto	voleva	volevano

Future		Conditional	
vorrò	vorremo	vorrei	vorremmo
vorrai	vorrete	vorresti	vorreste
vorrà	vorranno	vorrebbe	vorrebbero

Future Perfect		Past Conditional	
avrò voluto	avremo voluto	avrei voluto	avremmo voluto
avrai voluto	avrete voluto	avresti voluto	avreste voluto
avrà voluto	avranno voluto	avrebbe voluto	avrebbero voluto

Past Perfect		Subjunctive	
avevo voluto	avevamo voluto	voglia	vogliamo
avevi voluto	avevate voluto	voglia	vogliate
aveva voluto	avevano voluto	voglia	vogliano

Glossary

Note that the following abbreviations will be used in this glossary: (m.) = masculine, (f.) = feminine, (inv.) = invariable, (sg.) = singular, (pl.) = plural, (fml.) = formal/polite, (infml.) = informal/familiar. If a word has two grammatical genders, (m./f.) or (f./m.) is used.

Italian-English

A

a *to, at, in, by*
  a + definite article *in the style of*
  A dopo. *See you later.*
  a tempo pieno *full-time*
  A presto. *See you soon.*
  a proposito *by the way*
  a proposito di … *speaking of …*
  a volte *sometimes*
abbastanza *fairly, enough*
abbigliamento (m.) *clothing*
  negozio (m.) di abbigliamento *clothing store*
abbondante *abundant, plentiful*
  cena (f.) abbondante *large dinner*
abbracciarsi *to hug*
abitabile *habitable*
  cucina (f.) abitabile *eat-in kitchen*
abitare *to live*
abito (m.) *suit (men's), dress (women's)*
  abito da uomo *men's suit*
accessorio (m.) *accessory*
accettare *to accept*
accettazione (f.) *reception desk*
accomodante *accommodating*
accompagnare *to accompany*
accordo (m.) *agreement*
  essere d'accordo *to agree*
  d'accordo *agreed, O.K.*
acqua (f.) *water*
  acqua minerale *mineral water*
  acqua minerale naturale *still mineral water*
  acqua minerale frizzante *sparkling mineral water*
adatto *appropriate*
addormentarsi *to fall asleep*

adesso *now*
adolescente (m./f.) *teenager*
adorabile *adorable*
adulto/a (m./f.) *adult*
aereo (m.) *airplane*
  in aereo *by plane*
aerobico *aerobic*
  fare ginnastica aerobica *to do aerobics*
aeroporto (m.) *airport*
affari (m. pl.) *business*
  uomo (m.) d'affari *businessman*
  donna (f.) d'affari *businesswoman*
affatto *completely*
  non … affatto *not … at all*
affermare *to claim*
affettare *to slice*
affettato (m.) *sliced cold meat*
  affettati misti *mixed cold cuts*
affinché *in order that, so that*
affittare *to rent*
affollato *crowded*
affrettato *fast, rushed*
affumicato *smoked*
agenzla (f.) *agency*
aggettivo (m.) *adjective*
aggiungere *to add*
agitarsi *to get nervous*
agosto (m.) *August*
aiutare *to help*
  aiutare a … *to help … ing*
aiutarsi *to help each other*
aiuto (m.) *help*
albergo (m.) *hotel*
albero (m.) *tree*
albicocca (f.) *apricot*
albicocco (m.) *apricot tree*
alcuni/e *a few, some*
alimentari (m. pl.) *groceries*

negozio (m.) **di alimentari** *grocery store*
alla brace *grilled/barbecued*
   carne alla brace *grilled/barbecued meat*
allegare *to attach*
   allegare un file *to attach a file*
   allegare un documento *to attach a document*
allegato (m.) *attachment*
allenatore/trice (m./f.) *coach*
alloggio (m.) *accommodation, apartment*
allora *then, well then, so*
alluce (m.) *big toe*
almeno *at least*
alpino *alpine*
   sci (m.) **alpino** *alpine skiing*
alternare *to alternate*
alto *tall*
altro *other*
   un altro/un'altra *another*
   tutti gli altri *everyone else*
alzarsi *to get up*
amaramente *bitterly*
amare *to love*
   Ti amo. *I love you.*
amaro *sour, bitter*
ambientazione (f.) *settings*
americano *American*
   futbol (m.) **americano** *American football*
amicizia (f.) *friendship*
   fare amicizia *to make friends*
amico (m.)/**amici** (m. pl.) *friend*
ammalato *ill, sick*
amore (m.) *love*
   storie (f. pl.) **d'amore** *love stories*
ampio *spacious, wide*
ananas (m. sg./pl.) *pineapple*
anche *also, too*
ancora *again, still, yet*
andare *to go*
   andare a … *to go … ing*
   andare a trovare *to go visit*
   andare in barca a vela *to sail*
   andare in bicicletta *to ride a bike*
   Andiamoci. *Let's go there.*
   Come va? *How's it going?*
   Va meglio. *It's better.*
   Va' avanti. *Go ahead.*
   Vacci. *Go there.*
anello (m.) *ring*

animale (m.) *animal*
anniversario (m.) *anniversary*
   Buon anniversario. *Happy anniversary.*
anno (m.) *year*
   anno scorso *last year*
   Ho … anni. *I am … years old.*
   Quanti anni hai? *How old are you?* (infml.)
   tutti gli anni *every year*
annoiarsi *to get bored*
anticipo (m.) *advance*
   essere in anticipo *to be early*
antico *ancient*
antipasto (m.) *appetizer*
antipatico *unfriendly*
antistress (m. sg./pl.) *anti-stress*
anzi *on the contrary*
aperitivo (m.) *aperitif*
aperto *open*
   all'aperto *outdoors*
apparecchiare *to set (a table)*
appartamento (m.) *apartment*
appena *just*
appetito (m.) *appetite*
   Buon appetito. *Enjoy your meal.*
apprendere *to learn*
appuntamento (m.) *appointment*
aprile (m.) *April*
aprire *to open*
   aprire un documento *to open a document*
   aprire un file *to open a file*
arabo *Arab*
aragosta (f.) *lobster*
arancia (f.) *orange (fruit)*
arancione (inv.) *orange (color)*
archeologico (m.)/**archeologici** (m. pl.) *archeological*
architetto (m.) *architect*
aria (f.) *air*
   aria condizionata *air conditioning*
armadietto (m.) *medicine cabinet*
armadio (m.) *closet, wardrobe*
aroma (m.) *aroma*
arrivare *to arrive*
Arrivederci. *Good-bye* (infml.)
   ArrivederLa. *Good-bye* (sg. fml.)
arrosto *roast*
arte (f.) *art*
   arte moderna *modern art*

articolo (m.) *article*
artista (m./f.) *artist*
asciugamano (m.) *towel*
ascoltare *to listen to*
aspettare *to wait for*
asse (f.) *board*
  asse da stiro *ironing board*
assistente (m./f.) *assistant*
assolutamente *absolutely*
assorbire *to absorb*
astronauta (m./f.) *astronaut*
atleta (m./f.) *athlete*
attaccare *to attach*
attento *attentive, careful*
  Sta' attento! *Pay attention!/Be careful!/Watch out!*
attenzione (f.) *attention*
  fare attenzione *to pay attention*
attico (m.)/**attici** (m. pl.) *penthouse*
attività (f.)/**attività** (f. pl.) *activity*
attore (m.) *actor*
attorno *around*
  attorno a … *around …*
attrice (f.) *actress*
attuale *current*
autobus (m.) *bus*
automobile (f.) *car*
autore/trice (m./f.) *author*
autunno (m.) *fall*
  in/d'autunno *in the fall*
avanti *forward, before, ahead*
  Va' avanti. *Go ahead.*
avere *to have*
  avere bisogno di … *to need …*
  avere caldo *to be hot*
  avere freddo *to be cold*
  avere in comune *to share*
  avere fretta *to be in a hurry*
  avere la febbre *to have a fever*
  avere male a … *to have a pain in …*
  avere paura (di) *to be afraid (of)*
  avere ragione *to be right*
  avere sete *to be thirsty*
  avere sonno *to be sleepy*
  avere tempo *to have time*
  avere torto *to be wrong*
  avere un dolore a … *to have a pain in …*
  avere voglia di … *to feel like …*

  Ho … anni. *I am … years old.*
  Quanti anni hai? *How old are you?* (infml.)
avocado (m. sg./pl.) *avocado*
avvocato (m.) *lawyer*
azione (f.) *action*
  film (m. pl.) **d'azione** *action movies*

B

baciarsi *to kiss*
bagno (m.) *bathroom*
  costume (m.) **da bagno** *bathing trunks, bathing suit*
  fare il bagno *to take a bath*
  vasca (f.) **(da bagno)** *bath tub*
bagnoschiuma (m.) *bath gel*
ballare *to dance*
ballo (m.) *dance*
bambino/a (m./f.) *baby, child (from 0 to 10 years old)*
banana (f.) *banana*
banca (f.) *bank*
banchiere/a (m./f.) *banker*
bar (m.) *café*
barba (f.) *beard*
  crema (f.) **da barba** *shaving cream*
  farsi la barba *to shave*
barca (f.) *boat*
  andare in barca a vela *to sail*
barocco (m.) *baroque*
barzelletta (f.) *joke*
baseball (m.) *baseball*
basilico (m.) *basil*
basket (m.) *basketball*
basso *short, low*
bastare *to be enough*
  Basta così! *That's enough!*
beato *lucky*
  Beati voi. *Lucky you.* (pl.)
  Beato te! *Lucky you!* (sg. infml.)
Beh … *Well …*
beige (inv.) *beige*
bello *beautiful*
  bellissimo *very beautiful*
  Che bello! *How nice!/How beautiful!*
  Che bel piatto! *What a beautiful dish!*
  Fa bello. *It's beautiful. (weather)*
  fare bella figura *to make a good impression*
benché *although*

benda (f.) *bandage*
bene *well*
  (Sto) bene, grazie. *Fine, thanks.*
  Benissimo! *Wonderful!/Very well!*
  Molto bene, grazie. *Very well, thanks.*
  Va bene. *All right.*
Bentornato. *Welcome back.*
benvenuto *welcome*
bere *to drink*
  qualcosa da bere *something to drink*
bevanda (f.) *drink*
bianco *white*
  vino (m.) bianco *white wine*
bibita (f.) *soft drink, soda*
biblioteca (f.) *library*
bicchiere (m.) *glass*
bichini (m.) *bikini*
bici (f. sg./pl.) *bike*
bicicletta (f.) *bicycle*
  andare in bicicletta *to ride a bike*
biglietto (m.) *ticket*
biliardo (m.) *pool, billiards*
biologia (f.) *biology*
birra (f.) *beer*
bisogno (m.) *need*
  avere bisogno di … *to need …*
  essere nel bisogno *to need*
bistecca (f.) *beefsteak*
blu (inv.) *blue*
blue jeans (m. pl.) *jeans*
bocca (f.) *mouth*
  In bocca al lupo! *Break a leg! (lit. In the mouth of the wolf!)*
bocciare *to reject*
  essere bocciato *to fail (an exam)*
bollire *to boil*
bollitore (m.) *tea kettle*
borotalco (m.) *powder (talcum)*
borsa (f.) *bag, purse*
bosco (m.) *wood*
botte (f.) *cask*
bottiglia (f.) *bottle*
boutique (f.) *boutique*
braccialetto (m.) *bracelet*
braccio (m.) *arm*
  braccia (f. pl.) *arms*
braciola (f.) *chop*
  braciola di maiale *pork chop*

bravo *skillful, talented, nice*
broccolo (m.) *broccoli*
bruschetta (f.) *bruschetta*
brutto *ugly*
  Fa brutto. *It's bad. (weather)*
bucato (m.) *laundry*
  detersivo (m.) per il bucato *laundry detergent*
  fare il bucato *to do the laundry*
bugia (f.) *lie*
buono/buon (before masculine nouns except when they begin with the letter s followed by a consonant, or with the letter z) *good*
  Buon anniversario. *Happy anniversary.*
  Buon appetito. *Enjoy your meal.*
  Buon compleanno. *Happy birthday.*
  Buon giorno. *Good morning.*
  Buon Natale. *Merry Christmas.*
  Buon pomeriggio. *Good afternoon. (from 1 p.m. to 6 p.m.)*
  Buon riposo. *Have a good rest.*
  Buon viaggio. *Have a good trip.*
  Buona cena. *Enjoy your dinner./Have a good dinner.*
  Buona fortuna. *Good luck.*
  Buona giornata. *Have a good day.*
  Buona notte. *Good night.*
  Buona passeggiata. *Enjoy your walk./Have a good walk.*
  Buona sera. *Good evening.*
  Buona serata. *Have a good evening.*
  Buone feste. *Happy holidays.*
burro (m.) *butter*
business (m. sg./pl.) *business*

C

C'è … *There is …*
  C'è il sole. *It's sunny.*
  C'è nebbia. *It's foggy.*
  C'è un temporale. *It's stormy.*
  C'è vento. *It's windy.*
cachemire (m.) *cashmere*
  di cachemire *made out of cashmere*
cadere *to fall*
caffè (m. sg./pl.) *coffee, coffee shop*
caffetteria (f.) *coffee shop*
caffettiera (f.) *coffee maker (stovetop)*
calcio (m.) *soccer*
caldo (m.) *heat*

avere caldo *to be hot*
Fa caldo. *It's hot.*
calpestare *to tread on*
calze (f. pl.) *socks*
cambiare *to change*
　cambiare canale *to flip channels*
camera (f.) *room, bedroom, cabinet*
　camera da letto *bedroom*
　camera doppia *double room*
　　(two twin-size beds)
　camera matrimoniale *double room*
　　(one queen-size bed)
　camera singola *single room (one twin bed)*
cameriera (f.) *waitress*
cameriere (m.) *waiter*
camicetta (f.) *blouse*
camicia (f.) *shirt*
camminare *to walk*
　camminare in montagna *to go hiking*
campagna (f.) *countryside, country*
　in campagna *to the country*
campeggio (m.) *camping*
　fare il campeggio *to go camping*
campione/essa (m./f.) *champion*
campo (m.) *field*
canale (m.) *channel*
　cambiare canale *to flip channels*
cancellare *to delete*
candeggina (f.) *bleach*
canottiera (f.) *undershirt*
cantare *to sing*
canzone (f.) *song*
capacità (f. sg./pl.) *ability*
capelli (m. pl.) *hair*
capire *to understand*
capo/a (m./f.) *boss*
cappello (m.) *hat*
cappotto (m.) *coat (to the knees or longer)*
cappuccino (m.) *cappuccino*
carino *cute, pretty*
carne (f.) *meat*
　carne alla brace *grilled/barbecued meat*
caro *expensive*
carota (f.) *carrot*
carta (f.) *paper, card*
　carta di credito *credit card*
　carta igienica *toilet paper*
　giocare a carte *to play cards*

cartella (f.) *file*
cartina (f.) *map*
casa (f.) *house, home*
　a casa *at home*
　in giro per la casa *around the house*
casalinga (f.) *stay-at-home mom*
casalingo (m.) *stay-at-home dad*
caso (m.) *chance, case*
　in ogni caso *in any event*
　per caso *by any chance*
cassetto (m.) *drawer*
cattivo *naughty*
caviglia (f.) *ankle*
cavo (m.) *cable*
　cavo adsi *cable (dsl)*
cd rom (m.) *CD-ROM*
celebrare *to celebrate*
celibe (m.) *single (man)*
cellulare (m.) *cell phone*
cena (f.) *dinner*
Buona cena. *Enjoy your dinner./Have a good*
　dinner.
centimetro (m.) *centimeter*
cento *hundred*
centro (m.) *center*
　centro acquisti, centro
　　commerciale *shopping mall*
　centro informazioni *information center*
　in centro *downtown, to/in the city*
cercare *to look for*
　cercare di … *to try to …*
cerimonia (f.) *ceremony*
cerotto (m.) *bandage*
certamente *certainly*
certo *some, a few*
certo/a (m./f.) *certain, certain ones*
cervello (m.) *brain*
cetriolo (m.) *cucumber*
chatroom (f.) *chatroom*
che *what* (question); *what, how* (exclamation);
　who, whom, which, that (relative pronoun); *that*
　(conjunction); than (comparative)
Che bello! *How nice!/How beautiful!*
Che cosa? *What?*
Che ora è?/Che ore sono? *What time is it?*
Che tempo fa? *What's the weather like?*
meno … che *less … than*
Non c'è di che. *Don't mention it.*

più … che *more/-er … than*
sia … che *as/so … as, both … and*
chi *who* (question); *he/she who, the one who,*
  whoever (relative pronoun)
  Di chi è … ? *Whose … is it?*
  Di chi sono … ? *Whose … are they?*
chiamare *to call, to telephone*
chiamarsi *to be named*
  Mi chiamo … *My name is …*
  Si chiama … *His/Her name is …*
chiaro (adjective) *clear*
chiaro (adverb), **chiaramente** *clearly*
chiedere *to ask, to ask for*
  chiedere (un) consiglio *to ask for advice*
chiesa (f.) *church*
chilo (m.) *kilo*
chilometro *kilometer*
chimica (f.) *chemistry*
chimico (m. pl *chimici*) *chemical*
chitarra (f.) *guitar*
chiudere *to close*
  chiudere un documento/file *to close a*
    document/file
chiunque *anyone*
ci *us* (direct object pronoun); *to us* (indirect object
  pronoun); *here, there; about/of/on it*
  Andiamoci. *Let's go there.*
  Arrivederci. *Good-bye* (infml.)
  C'è … *There is …*
  Ci penserò. *I'll think about it.*
  Ci sono … *There are …*
  Rieccoci! *Here we are again!*
Ciao. *Hi./Hello./Good-bye.*
  Ciao ciao! *Bye-bye!*
ciascuno *each*
ciascuno/a (m./f.) *each one*
cibo (m.) *food*
ciclismo (m.) *biking*
cielo (m.) *sky*
ciglio (m.) *eyelash*
  ciglia (f. pl.) *eyelashes*
Cina (f.) *China*
cinema (m. sg./pl.) *movie theater*
cinese (m.) *Chinese (language)*
  parlare cinese *to speak Chinese*
cinquanta *fifty*
cinque *five*
  tra cinque minuti *in five minutes*

cintura (f.) *belt*
ciotola (f.) *bowl*
cipolla (f.) *onion*
circa *about*
circo (m.) *circus*
città (f. sg./pl.) *city*
  città natale *hometown*
  fuori città *out of town*
  in giro per la città *around town*
cittadina (f.) *town*
cittadinanza (f.) *citizenship*
civile *civil*
  stato (m.) civile *marital status*
classe (f.) *classroom, class*
classico (m.)/**classici** (m. pl.) *classical*
  musica (f.) classica *classical music*
cliente (m./f.) *customer*
clima (m.) *climate*
club (m. sg./pl.) *club*
colazione (f.) *breakfast*
  fare colazione *to have breakfast*
collana (f.) *necklace*
collega (m./f.) *colleague*
collina (f.) *hill*
collo (m.) *neck*
colloquio (m.) *talk, conversation, interview*
  colloquio di lavoro *job interview*
colonia (f.) *cologne*
coltello (m.) *knife*
coltivare *to grow*
comandare *to command*
come *how, as*
  Com'è? *How is … ?*
  Come mi sta? *How do I look?*
  Come sono? *How are … ?*
  Come sta? *How are you doing* (fml.)?
  Come stai? *How are you doing* (infml.)?
  Come va? *How's it going?*
  così … come *as/so … as*
  Ma come! *How's it possible!/How can this be!*
cominciare *to begin*
cominciare a … *to begin to …*
commedia (f.) *comedy*
commerciante (m./f.) *vendor*
commercio (m.) *business, commerce*
comodo *comfortable*
compagnia (f.) *company*
competenza (f.) *competence*

compiere *to complete*
compleanno (m.) *birthday*
  Buon compleanno. *Happy birthday.*
complimento (m.) *compliment*
  Complimenti! *Congratulations!*
comprare *to buy*
computer (m., pl.) *computer*
comune (m.) *common*
  avere in comune *to share*
comunità (f. sg./pl.) *community*
comunque *in any case*
con *with*
  con talento *talented*
concerto (m.) *concert*
condividere *to share*
condizionato *conditionin*
  aria (f.) condizionata *air conditioned*
condizione (f.) *condition, situation*
  a condizione che … *provided that …*
condominio (m.)/condomini (m. pl.) *apartment building*
confessare *to confess*
congiuntivo (m.) *subjunctive mood (grammar)*
  congiuntivo presente *present subjunctive*
conoscere *to know (a person), to meet (a person for the first time)*
conoscersi *to know each other*
consiglio (m.) *advice*
  chiedere (un) consiglio *to ask for advice*
contadino/a (m./f.) *farmer*
contare *to count*
contemporaneo *contemporary*
  romanzi (m. pl.) contemporanei *contemporary novels*
contento *happy*
  contento di … *happy to …*
continuare *to continue*
  orario (m.) continuato *open all day*
conto (m.) *check, bill*
contorno (m.) *side dish*
  di/per contorno *as a side dish*
controllare *to check*
convincere *to convince*
  convincere a … *to convince to …*
convinto *convinced*
coordinare *to coordinate*
coppia (f.) *couple*
corda (f.) *rope*

  saltare la corda *to jump rope*
correre *to run*
corso (m.) *course*
cortile (m.) *back yard, courtyard*
corto *short*
cosa (f.) *thing*
  Che cosa? *What?*
  cose da fare *things to do*
  mille cose *tons of things, a thousand things*
  Tu cosa prendi? *What are you having?*
così *so*
  Basta così! *That's enough!*
  così … come *as/so … as*
  Così, così. *So so./Not bad.*
costa (f.) *coast, rib*
  di velluto a coste *made out of corduroy*
  velluto a coste *corduroy*
costare *to cost*
  Quanto costa? *How much does it cost?*
costo (m.) *cost*
  a tutti i costi *at all costs*
costoso *expensive*
costume (m.) *costume*
  costume da bagno *bathing trunks, bathing suit*
cotone (m.) *cotton*
cottura (f.) *cooking*
cravatta (f.) *tie*
credenza (f.) *cupboard*
credere *to believe*
  Non credo. *I don't think so.*
credito (m.) *credit*
  carta (f.) di credito *credit card*
crema (f.) *cream*
  crema da barba *shaving cream*
crescere *to grow, to raise*
croce (f.) *tail (of coin)*
  fare testa o croce *to flip a coin*
cucchiaio (m.) *spoon*
cucina (f.) *kitchen*
  cucina a gas *stove*
  cucina abitabile *eat-in kitchen*
  cucina elettrica *stove*
cucinare *to cook*
cugino/a (m./f.) *cousin*
cui *which, whom* (relative pronoun)
  il modo in cui … *the way in which …*
  la ragione/il motivo per cui … *the reason*

why …
cultura (f.) *culture*
cuocere *to cook*
cuore (m.) *heart*
curare *to treat, to cure*
cuscino (m.) *pillow*

D

da *from, to, at, for, since*
  dal lunedì al venerdì *from Monday to Friday*
  dalle … alle … *from … to … (time periods)*
  dalle undici meno un quarto alle tre *from 10:45 a.m. to 3:00 p.m.*
dare *to give*
  dare una festa *to have a party*
data (f.) *date, day*
dati (m. pl.) *data*
  dati anagrafici *personal information*
davanti *in front*
  davanti a … *in front of …*
davvero *really*
debole *weak*
decidere *to decide*
  decidere di … *to decide to …*
decimo *tenth*
decollare *to take off*
delizioso *delicious*
denaro (m.) *money*
dente (m.) *tooth*
dentista (m./f.) *dentist*
deodorante (m.) *deodorant*
depresso *depressed*
descrivere *to describe*
deserto (m.) *desert*
desiderare *to want, to desire*
destra (f.)
  (a) destra *right, on the right, to the right*
determinare *to determine*
detersivo (m.) *detergent*
  detersivo per il bucato *laundry detergent*
  detersivo per i piatti *dishwashing detergent*
di *of, from, than*
  di + definite article *some, any*
  Di chi è … ? *Whose … is it?*
  Di chi sono … ? *Whose … are they?*
  Di dov'è? *Where are you from? (sg. fml.)/Where is he/she from?*
  Di dove sei? *Where are you from? (infml.)*

di legno *wooden*
di lei *her*
di lui *his*
di mattina *in the morning, from 4 to 11 a.m.*
di notte *at night, from midnight to 3 a.m*
di pomeriggio *in the afternoon, from 1 to 5 p.m.*
di sera *in the evening, from 6 to 11 p.m.*
di solito *usually*
È di … *It belongs to …*
È ora di … *It's time to …*
meno … di *less … than*
più … di *more/-er … than*
Sono di … *I'm from …*
dicembre (m.) *December*
diciannove *nineteen*
diciassette *seventeen*
diciotto *eighteen*
dieci *ten*
dietro *behind* (adv.)
differenza (f.) *difference*
difficile *difficult*
dimagrire *to lose weight*
dimenticare
  dimenticare di … *to forget, to forget to … (do something)*
diploma (m.) *diploma*
dire *to say, to tell*
  Non c'è di che. *Don't mention it.*
direttore (m.) *director*
diritto *straight*
  sempre diritto *straight ahead*
discorso (m.) *speech, talk*
discoteca (f.) *disco, club*
disoccupato/a (m./f.) *unemployed*
dispiacere *to displease, to upset*
  Mi dispiace. *I'm sorry.*
disponibile *available*
disponibilità (f.) *availability*
distruggere *to destroy*
dito (m.) *finger*
  dita (f. pl.) *fingers*
divano (m.) *sofa, couch*
diventare *to become*
diverso *different*
divertente *amusing, funny*
divertirsi *to have fun, to enjoy oneself*
divorziarsi *to get a divorce*

divorziarsi da ... *to divorce ... (someone)*
doccia (f.) *shower*
  fare la doccia *to take a shower*
docciaschiuma (m.) *bath gel*
documentario (m.) *documentary*
documento (m.) *document, file*
  allegare un documento *to attach a file*
  aprire un documento *to open a file*
  chiudere un documento *to close a file*
  inviare un documento *to send a file*
  salvare un documento *to save a file*
dodici *twelve*
dolce *sweet*
dolce (m.) *dessert*
dollaro (m.) *dollar*
  un milione di dollari *a million dollars*
dolore (m.) *pain*
  avere un dolore a ... *to have a pain in ...*
domanda (f.) *question*
  fare una domanda *to ask a question*
domani *tomorrow*
domenica (f.) *Sunday*
donna (f.) *woman*
  donna d'affari *businesswoman*
  donna poliziotto *police woman*
dopo *after*
  A dopo. *See you later.*
doppio *double*
  camera (f.) **doppia** *double room (two twin-size beds)*
dormire *to sleep*
  farsi una bella dormita *to take a nice long nap*
dottore/essa (m./f.) *doctor*
dove *where*
  Di dov'è? *Where are you from?* (sg. fml.)/*Where is he/she from?*
  Di dove sei? *Where are you from?* (infml.)
  Dov'è ... ? *Where is ... ?*
  Dove sono ... ? *Where are ... ?*
dovere *must, to have to*
dovuto *due*
  dovuto a ... *due to ...*
dramma (m.) *drama*
dubitare *to doubt*
due *two*
  due ore e mezzo *two and a half hours*
  duemila *two thousand*
  Sono le due. *It's two (o'clock).*

dunque *therefore*
durare *to last*
dvd (m.) *DVD player*

E

e/ed (before a vowel) *and*
  ... e Lei? *... and you?* (sg. fml.)
  ... e tu? *... and you?* (infml.)
eccellente *excellent*
eccetto *except*
eccezionale *exceptional*
ecco *here*
  Ecco ... *Here is ...*
economia (f.) *economics*
edificio (m.) *building*
elegante *elegant*
elegantemente *elegantly*
elementare *elementary*
  la prima elementare *the first grade at elementary school*
elettricista (m.) *electrician*
elettrico *electric*
  cucina (f.) **elettrica** *electric stove*
elettrocardiogramma (m.) *electrocardiogram*
elettronica (f.) *electronics*
  negozio (m.) **di elettronica** *electronics store*
eliminare *to delete*
email (f.)/**mail** (inv.) *e-mail*
  mandare un'email/una mail *to send an e-mail*
enorme *enormous*
entrambi/e *both (of them)*
entrare *to come in*
entusiasticamente *enthusiastically*
erba (f.) *grass*
erboristeria (f.) *herbalist's shop*
ereditare *to inherit*
esagerare *to exaggerate, to go too far*
esagerato *exaggerated*
esame (m.) *exam*
escursione (f.) *hike, excursion*
  fare un'escursione *to go hiking*
esistere *to exist*
esperienza (f.) *experience*
esperto/a (m./f.) *expert*
essere *to be*
  C'è ... *There is ...*
  C'è il sole. *It's sunny.*

C'è nebbia. *It's foggy.*
C'è un temporale. *It's stormy.*
C'è vento. *It's windy.*
Ci sono … *There are …*
Di chi è … ? *Whose … is it ?*
Di chi sono … ? *Whose … are they?*
È di … *It belongs to …*
È l'una di notte. *It's 1:00 a.m.*
È nuvoloso. *It's cloudy.*
È ora di … *It's time to …*
essere bocciato *to fail*
essere d'accordo *to agree*
essere impauriti *to be afraid of*
essere in anticipo *to be early*
essere in cerca di … *to be looking for …*
essere in orario *to be on time*
essere in ritardo *to be late*
essere in sovrappeso *to be overweight*
essere nel bisogno *to need*
essere puntuale *to be on time*
essere promosso *to pass*
Sono di … *I'm from …*
estate (f.) *summer*
  d'estate *in the summer*
estero *foreign*
  all'estero *abroad*
  viaggiare all'estero *to travel abroad*
età (f./f/ pl.) *age*
euro (m. sg./pl.) *euro*
Europa (f.) *Europe*
europeo *European*
extra (inv.) *extra*

F

fa *ago*
  due giorni fa *two days ago*
  un mese fa *a month ago*
fabbrica (f.) *factory*
faccia (f.) *face*
facile *easy*
falegname (m.) *carpenter*
falso *false*
fame (f.) *hunger*
  avere fame *to be hungry*
famiglia (f.) *family*
  famiglia numerosa *large family*
famoso *famous*
fantastico (m.)/fantastici (m. pl.) *fantastic*

fare *to do, to make, to be*
  Che tempo fa? *What's the weather like?*
  Fa bello. *It's beautiful. (weather)*
  Fa brutto *It's bad. (weather)*
  Fa caldo. *It's hot.*
  Fa freddo. *It's cold.*
  Fammi vedere. *Let me see.*
fare amicizia *to make friends*
fare attenzione *to pay attention*
fare bella figura *to make a good impression*
fare colazione *to have breakfast*
fare giardinaggio *to do gardening*
fare ginnastica *to exercise*
fare ginnastica aerobica *to do aerobics*
fare il bagno *to take a bath*
fare il bucato *to do the laundry*
fare il campeggio *to go camping*
fare il footing *to jog*
fare il trasloco *to move (to a new house)*
fare la doccia *to take a shower*
fare il bucato *to do the laundry*
fare la spesa/le spese *to go shopping, to do*
  grocery shopping
fare le valige *to pack (a suitcase)*
fare pari *to draw, to tie*
fare paura *to be scary*
fare rumore *to make noise*
fare spese *to shop*
fare sport *to practice sports*
fare testa o croce *to flip a coin*
fare un'escursione *to go hiking*
fare un giro *to go for a walk/ride*
fare un giro a piedi *to go for a walk*
fare un pisolino *to take a nap*
fare un viaggio *to take a trip*
fare una domanda *to ask a question*
fare una foto/fotografia *to take a picture*
fare una gita *to take a trip*
fare una passeggiata *to take a walk*
fare una pausa *to take a break*
fare una vacanza *to go on a vacation*
fare vedere *to show*
farmacia (f.) *drugstore, pharmacy*
farsi *to get, to become*
  farsi la barba *to shave*
  farsi una bella dormita *to take a nice long nap*
  farsi una bella mangiata *to have a nice big*
    meal

fatto (m.) *fact*
fattore (m.) *factor*
favola (f.) *fairy tale*
favore (m.) *favor*
  Per favore. *Please.*
fax (m. sg./pl.) *fax machine*
febbraio (m.) *February*
febbre (f.) *fever*
  avere la febbre *to have a fever*
fegato (m.) *liver*
felice *happy*
femmina (f.) *female*
ferie (f. pl.) *vacation*
  in ferie *on vacation*
fermarsi *to stop*
ferro (m.) *iron (metal)*
  ferro da stiro *iron (appliance)*
festa (f.) *party, holiday*
  Buone feste. *Happy holidays.*
  dare una festa *to have a party*
fettina (f.) *thin slice*
fettuccine (f. pl.) *fettuccine*
fiaba (f.) *fairy tale*
fianco (m.) *hip*
fidanzato *engaged*
fidanzato/a (m./f.) *fiancé(e)*
fiera (f.) *trade fair*
figlia (f.) *daughter*
  figlia di mia moglie (di mio
    marito) *stepdaughter*
figlio (m.) *son*
  figlio di mia moglie (di mio marito) *stepson*
figura (f.) *figure, illustration*
  fare bella figura *to make a good impression*
file (m.) *file*
  allegare un file *to attach a file*
  aprire un file *to open a file*
  chiudere un file *to close a file*
  inviare un file *to send a file*
film (m. sg./pl.) *movie, film*
  film d'azione *action movies*
finalista (m./f.) *finalist*
finalmente *finally*
finché *until*
fine settimana (m. sg./pl.) *weekend*
finestra (f.) *window*
finire *to finish*
  finire di ... *to finish ... ing*

per finire *to end/finish*
fino (a) *up to, until, till*
  fino a tardi *until late*
  fino in fondo *until the end*
fiore (m.) *flower*
Firenze (f.) *Florence*
fisso *fixed, permanent*
  lavoro (m.) fisso *steady job*
fiume (m.) *river*
follia (f.) *folly*
fondo *bottom*
  di fondo *long distance*
  fino in fondo *until the end*
  in fondo a ... *the bottom/end of ...*
  sci (m.) di fondo *cross-country skiing*
footing (m.) *jogging*
  fare il footing *to jog*
foresta (f.) *forest*
forma (f.) *form, shape*
  in ottima forma *in great shape*
formaggio (m.) *cheese*
formazione (f.) *training, education*
forno (m.) *oven*
  forno a microonde *microwave oven*
  maiale (m.) al forno *roast pork*
forse *maybe, perhaps*
forte (adjective) *strong*
forte (adverb) *loudly*
fortuna (f.) *luck*
  Buona fortuna. *Good luck.*
fortunato *lucky*
foto (f. sg./pl.) *photograph*
  fare una foto *to take a picture*
fotografia (f.) *photograph, photography*
  fare una fotografia *to take a picture*
foulard (m.) *scarf (square)*
fra *between, among, in*
  fra ... e ... *between ... and ...*
  fra mezz'ora *in half an hour*
  fra tre quarti d'ora *in forty-five minutes*
fragola (f.) *strawberry*
francamente *frankly*
francese *French*
fratello (m.) *brother*
frattempo *meantime*
  nel frattempo *in the meantime*
freddo (m.) *cold*
  avere freddo *to be cold*

Fa freddo. *It's cold.*
frequentare *to attend*
fresco *fresh*
fretta (f.) *hurry*
  avere fretta *to be in a hurry*
  in fretta *in a hurry, quickly*
frigorifero (m.) **(frigo)** *refrigerator*
fronte (f.) *forehead*
  di fronte *opposite*
  di fronte a … *facing … , in front of …*
frullatore (m.) *blender*
frutta (f.) *fruit*
  frutta fresca *fresh fruit*
fucsia (inv.) *fuchsia*
fulmine (m.) *lightning*
fungo (m.) *mushroom*
fuori *outside*
  fuori città *out of town*
futbol (m.) *football*
  futbol americano *American football*

G

gabinetto *toilet*
galleria (f.) *gallery*
gamba (f.) *leg*
  in gamba *talented* (colloquial)
gamberetto (m.) *shrimp*
gambero (m.) *shrimp, crawfish*
gara (f.) *event*
garage (m. sg./pl.) *garage*
gas (m. sg./pl.) *gas*
  cucina (f.) **a gas** *gas stove*
gelato (m.) *ice cream*
generale *general*
genetico (m.)/**genetici** (m. pl.) *genetic*
genitore (m.)/**genitrice** (f.)/**genitori** (pl.) *parent*
gennaio (m.) *January*
gente (f.) *people*
gentile *kind*
Germania (f.) *Germany*
ghiaccio (m.) *ice*
hockey (m.) **su ghiaccio** *ice hockey*
già *already*
giacca (f.) *jacket*
giaccone (m.) *coat (above the knees)*
giallo *yellow*
giardinaggio (m.) *gardening*
fare giardinaggio *to do gardening*

giardino (m.) *garden*
ginnastica (f.) *gymnastics*
  fare ginnastica *to exercise*
  fare ginnastica aerobica *to do aerobics*
  scarpe (f. pl.) **da ginnastica** *sneakers*
ginocchio (m.) *knee*
  ginocchia (f. pl.)/**ginocchi** (m. pl.) *knees*
giocare *to play*
  giocare a carte *to play cards*
  giocare a tennis *to play tennis*
giocatore/trice (m./f.) *player*
giornale (m.) *newspaper*
giornale radio (m.) *news (on the radio)*
giornalista (m./f.) *journalist*
giornata (f.) *day*
  Buona giornata. *Have a good day.*
  giornata piena *full/busy day*
giorno (m.) *day*
  Buon giorno. *Good morning.*
  due giorni fa *two days ago*
  fra qualche giorno *in a few days*
  pochi giorni *a few days*
  tutti i giorni *every day*
giovane *young*
giovedì (m. sg./pl.) *Thursday*
girare *to turn*
giro (m.) *circle, tour*
  fare un giro *to go for a walk/ride*
  fare un giro a piedi *to go for a walk*
  in giro per la casa *around the home*
  in giro per la città *around town*
gita (f.) *day trip, short trip*
  fare una gita *to take a trip*
giugno (m.) *June*
giusto (adjective) *right, correct*
giusto (adverb) *exactly, correctly*
gli *the* (m. pl.) *(in front of s + consonant, z, ps, gn, in front of vowels); to him, to it, to them* (indirect object pronoun)
gnomo (m.) *gnome*
gomito (m.) *elbow*
gonna (f.) *skirt*
grado (m.) *degree*
grande *big*
  grande magazzino (m.) *department store*
grandinare *to hail*
  Grandina. *It's hailing.*
grasso (adjective) *fat*

grasso (m.) *fat*
grattugiare *to grate*
grave *serious*
Grazie. *Thank you.*
  Grazie mille. *Thanks a lot.*
  Molto bene, grazie. *Very well, thanks.*
Grecia (f.) *Greece*
greco *Greek*
grigio *gray*
griglia (f.) *grill*
  pesce (m.) alla griglia *grilled fish*
grosso *large, thick*
gruppo (m.) *group, band (music)*
  gruppi (pl.) inglesi *British bands*
guadagnare *to earn*
guancia (f.) *cheek*
guanti (m. pl.) *gloves*
guardare *to watch, to look at*
  guardare la tivù/tele/televisione *to watch*
    television
  guardare lo sport in/alla televisione *to*
    watch sports on TV
guida (f.) *guide*
guidare *to drive*

H

hobby (m./m. pl) *hobby*
hockey (m.) *hockey*
  hockey su ghiaccio *ice hockey*
hotel (m. sg./pl.) *hotel*

I

i *the* (m. pl.) (in front of consonants)
idea (f.) *idea*
  nessuna idea *no idea*
idraulico/a (m./f.) *plumber*
ieri *yesterday*
  ieri sera *last night*
igienico *hygienic*
  carta (f.) igienica *toilet paper*
il *the* (m. sg.) (in front of a consonant)
immaginare *to imagine*
imparare *to learn*
impaurire *to scare*
  essere impauriti da *to be afraid of*
impegnato *busy*
impegno (m.) *obligation, engagement*
imperfetto (m.) *imperfect*

impiegato/a (m./f.) *employee, clerk*
importante *important*
imprenditore (m.) *businessman*
imprenditrice (f.) *businesswoman*
improvvisamente *suddenly*
in *in, at, to, on, by*
  in centro *downtown, to/in the city*
  in gamba *talented* (colloquial)
  in giro per la casa *around the home*
  in giro per la città *around town*
  in vacanza *on vacation*
incontrare *to meet (a person casually)*
incontrarsi *to meet each other*
incrocio (m.) *intersection*
indagine (f.) *study, research*
indeciso *undecided*
indicare *to show, to indicate*
indirizzo (m.) *address*
indossare *to wear*
infarto (m.) *heart attack*
infatti *in fact*
infermiere/a (m./f.) *nurse*
influenza (f.) *influence*
informatica (f.) *computer science*
informatico (adjective) *computer*
ingegnere (m.) *engineer*
inglese *English*
  gruppi (m. pl.) inglesi *British bands (music)*
inglese (m.) *English (language)*
ingrassare *to gain weight*
ingrediente (m.) *ingredient*
ingresso (m.) *hall*
innamorato *in love*
inoltrare *to forward*
inoltre *besides, moreover*
insalata (f.) *salad*
  insalata mista *mixed salad*
insegnante (m./f.) *teacher*
insegnare *to teach*
insieme *together*
  insieme a te *(together) with you*
insistere *to insist*
insonnolito *sleepy*
intellettivo *intellectual*
  quoziente (m.) intellettivo *intelligence*
    quotient (IQ)
intelligente *intelligent*
interessante *interesting*

interessantissimo *very interesting*
interessare *to interest*
interesse (m.) *interest*
internet (m.) *internet*
intero *whole, entire*
interrompere *to interrupt*
intervallo (m.) *intermission*
intervista (f.) *interview*
  interviste (pl.) alla televisione *talk show*
intestino (m.) *intestine*
intorno *around*
  intorno a mezzanotte *around midnight*
  intorno al mondo *around the world*
invecchiare *to grow old*
invece *instead*
invernale (adjective) *winter*
inverno (m.) *winter*
  d'inverno *in winter*
inviare *to send*
  inviare un file/documento *to send a file/ document*
invitare *to invite*
io *I*
iscrivere *to enroll*
isola (f.) *island*
istituto (m.) *institute*
  istituto tecnico *professional school*
istruzione (f.) *education*
Italia (f.) *Italy*
italiano *Italian*

L

l' *the* (m. sg./f. sg.) (in front of a vowel)
la *the* (f. sg.) (in front of a consonant); *her, it* (direct object pronoun)
La *you* (sg. fml.) (direct object pronoun)
lago (m.) *lake*
  al lago *at the lake*
lampada (f.) *lamp*
lampeggiare *to flash*
lampione (m.) *lamp post*
lampo (m.) *lightning*
lana (f.) *wool*
lasagne (f. pl.) *lasagna*
lasciare *to leave, to let*
latinoamericano *Latin American*
latte (m.) *milk*
lattina (f.) *can*

lattuga (f.) *lettuce*
laurea (f.) *degree, university degree*
laurearsi *to graduate*
lavabiancheria (f.) *washing machine*
lavabo (m.) *sink (wash basin)*
lavanderia (f.) *laundry*
lavandino (m.) *sink (kitchen)*
lavapiatti (f.) *dishwasher*
lavare *to wash*
lavare i piatti *to do the dishes*
lavarsi *to wash oneself*
lavastoviglie (f.) *dishwasher*
lavatrice (f.) *washing machine*
lavorare *to work*
lavoro (m.) *job, work*
  Che lavoro fai? *What do you do?*
  colloquio (m.) di lavoro *job interview*
  lavoro fisso *steady job*
  lavoro part-time *part-time job*
  lavoro temporaneo *summer job*
  per lavoro *on business*
le *the* (f. pl.) (in front of consonants and vowels); *them* (f.) (direct object pronoun); *to her, to it* (indirect object pronoun)
Le *to you* (sg. fml.) (indirect object pronoun)
leggere *to read*
leggero *light*
legno (m.) *wood*
di legno *wooden*
lei *she* (subject pronoun); *her, it* (direct object, disjunctive pronoun)
  a lei *to her, to it* (indirect object, disjunctive pronoun)
Lei *you* (sg. fml.) (subject pronoun); *you* (sg. fml.) (direct object, disjunctive pronoun)
  a Lei *to you* (sg. fml.) (indirect object, disjunctive pronoun)
lentamente *slowly*
lenzuolo (m.) *bed sheet*
  lenzuola (f. pl.) *bed sheets*
lettera (f.) *letter*
letteratura (f.) *literature*
letto (m.) *bed*
  camera (f.) da letto *bedroom*
  letto matrimoniale *double bed*
  stanza (f.) da letto *bedroom*
lettore (m.) *reader, player*
  lettore cd *CD-ROM drive*

lettore cd-rom *CD-ROM drive*
lettore di cd *CD player*
lezione (f.) *lesson*
li *them* (m.) (direct object pronoun)
lì *there*
  lì vicino *near there*
libero *free*
  tempo (m.) **libero** *free time*
libreria (f.) *bookstore, bookcase (in a house or office)*
libro (m.) *book*
  libro (di testo) *textbook*
liceo (m.) *high school*
lingua (f.) *language, tongue*
  lingua straniera *foreign language*
lino (m.) *linen*
  di lino *made out of linen*
lista (f.) *list*
  lista dei vini *wine list*
litro (m.) *liter*
livello (m.) *level*
lo *the* (m. sg.) (in front of s + consonant, z, ps, gn); *him, it* (direct object pronoun)
  Lo so. *I know.*
  Non lo so. *I don't know.*
lontano (adjective) *distant*
lontano (adverb) *far*
loro *they* (subject pronoun); *them* (direct object, disjunctive pronoun)
  a loro *to them* (indirect object, disjunctive pronoun)
Loro *you* (pl. fml.) (subject pronoun)
loro (inv.) *their*
lotteria (f.) *lottery*
luglio (m.) *July*
lui *he* (subject pronoun); *him, it* (direct object, disjunctive pronoun)
  a lui *to him, to it* (indirect object, disjunctive pronoun)
luna (f.) *moon*
lunedì (m. sg./pl.) *Monday*
  il lunedì *on Mondays*
lungo (adjective) *long*
lungo (preposition) *along*
luogo (m.) *place*
lupo (m.) *wolf*
  In bocca al lupo! *Break a leg! (lit. In the mouth of the wolf!)*

Crepi il lupo. *Thank you. (In response to In bocca al lupo! Lit. May the wolf die.)*

M

ma *but*
  Ma come! *How's it possible!/How can this be!*
macchina (f.) *car, machine*
  in macchina *by car*
  macchina del caffè *espresso machine*
  macchina fotografica *camera*
macelleria (f.) *butcher shop*
madre (f.) *mother*
  marito (m.) **di mia madre** *stepfather*
maestro/a (m./f.) *teacher (nursery school and elementary school)*
magari *I wish, perhaps*
magazzino (m.) *warehouse*
  grande magazzino *department store*
maggio (m.) *May*
maggiore *older, elder*
maglietta (f.) *T-shirt*
maglioncino (m.) *light sweater*
maglione (m.) *sweater*
Magro *thin*
mai *ever, never (in negative sentences)*
  Mai! *Never!*
  mai più *never again*
maiale (m.) *pork*
  braciola (f.) **di maiale** *pork chop*
  maiale al forno *roast pork*
malato *sick*
malattia (f.) *disease*
male *badly*
  avere male a … *to have a pain in …*
  Fa male. *It hurts.*
mamma (f.) *mom*
manca (f.) *left (hand)*
  Manca un quarto alle quattro. *It's 3:45.*
mancia (f.) *tip*
mancino *left-handed*
mandare *to send*
  mandare un'email *to send an e-mail*
mangiare *to eat*
  farsi una bella mangiata *to have a nice big meal*
mano (f.)/**mani** (f. pl.) *hand*
manzo (m.) *beef*
mappa (f.) *map*

maratona (f.) *marathon*
marciapiede (m.) *sidewalk*
mare (m.) *sea, seaside*
  al mare *at the beach*
marito (m.) *husband*
  figlia (f.) di mia moglie (di mio
    marito) *stepdaughter*
  figlio (m.) di mia moglie (di mio
    marito) *stepson*
  marito di mia madre *stepfather*
marrone *brown*
martedì (m. sg./pl.) *Tuesday*
marzo (m.) *March*
maschio (m.) *male*
matematica (f.) *math*
materia (f.) *subject*
matrimoniale *matrimonial*
  camera (f.) matrimoniale *double room (one*
    queen-size bed)
  letto (m.) matrimoniale *double bed*
matrimonio (m.) *wedding*
mattina (f.) *morning*
  di mattina *in the morning, from 4 to 11 a.m.*
  Sono le undici e un quarto di mattina.
    It's 11:15 a.m.
  tutte le mattine *every morning*
maturità (f.) *high school degree*
me *me* (direct object, disjunctive pronoun)
  a me *to me* (indirect object, disjunctive pronoun)
meccanico (m.)/meccanici (m. pl.) *mechanic*
media (f.) *average*
medicina (f.) *medicine*
medico (m.) *medical doctor*
meglio (adverb) *better, the best*
  Va meglio. *It's better.*
meglio (inv.) *better*
mela (f.) *apple*
melanzana (f.) *eggplant*
melone (m.) *melon*
memoria (f.) *memory*
meno *less*
  a meno che ... non *unless ...*
  meno ... di/che *less ... than*
  Sono le quattro meno un quarto. *It's 3:45.*
mento (m.) *chin*
mentre *while*
menù (m.) *menu*
meraviglioso *wonderful, marvelous*

mercato (m.) *market*
mercoledì (m. sg./pl.) *Wednesday*
mescolare *to mix*
mese (m.) *month*
  mese prossimo *next month*
  un mese fa *a month ago*
messaggio (m.) *message*
  messaggio immediato *instant message*
messinscena (f.) *production (theater)*
mettersi *to put on*
  Si mette ... *He/She wears/puts on ...*
metrò (m. in Milan/f. in Rome) *subway, metro*
metro (m.) *meter*
mettere *to put*
  mettere in ordine *to put things away*
  metterci *to take (time)*
mezzanotte (f.) *midnight*
  È mezzanotte. *It's midnight.*
  intorno a mezzanotte *around midnight*
mezzo *half, half hour*
  alle sette e mezza *at seven thirty (7:30)*
  due ore e mezzo *two and a half hours*
  fra mezz'ora *in half an hour*
  mezze stagioni *half seasons (spring and fall)*
mezzo (m.) *means*
  mezzo di trasporto *means of transportation*
mezzogiorno (m.) *noon*
  È mezzogiorno. *It's noon.*
mi *me* (direct object pronoun); *to me* (indirect
  object pronoun)
  Mi chiamo ... *My name is ...*
  Mi dispiace. *I'm sorry.*
  Mi piace/piacciono ... (sg./pl.) *I like ...*
microonda (f.) *microwave*
  forno (m.) a microonde *microwave oven*
miele (m.) *honey*
migliore (adjective) *better, the best*
Milano (f.) *Milan*
miliardo (m.)/miliardi (m. pl.) *billion*
milione (m.)/milioni (m. pl.) *million*
  un milione di dollari *a million dollars*
mille (m.)/mila (m. pl.) *thousand*
  duemila *two thousand*
  Grazie mille. *Thanks a lot.*
  mille cose (f. pl.) *tons of things,*
    a thousand things
minerale *mineral*
  acqua (f.) minerale *mineral water*

acqua minerale naturale *still mineral water*
acqua minerale frizzante *sparkling*
  mineral water
minestra (f.) *soup*
minore *younger*
minuto (m.) *minute*
  tra cinque minuti *in five minutes*
mio *my*
  figlia (f.) di mia moglie (di mio
    marito) *stepdaughter*
  figlio (m.) di mia moglie (di mio
    marito) *stepson*
  marito (m.) di mia madre *stepfather*
  (la mia) ragazza (f.) *(my) girlfriend*
  (il mio) ragazzo (m.) *(my) boyfriend*
  moglie (f.) di mio padre *stepmother*
  Piacere mio. *Pleased to meet you, too.*
misto *mixed*
  affettati (m. pl.) misti *mixed cold cuts*
  insalata (f.) mista *mixed salad*
misura (f.) *size (shirts)*
misurare *to measure*
mobili (m. pl.) *furniture*
moda (f.) *fashion*
  sfilata (f.) di moda *fashion show*
modello/a (m./f.) *model (fashion)*
modem (m.) *modem*
moderno *modern*
  arte moderna *modern art*
modo (m.) *way, manner*
  il modo in cui … *the way in which …*
moglie (f.) *wife*
molto (adjective) *much, many, a lot of*
  molto tempo *long time*
molto (adverb) *very*
  Molto bene, grazie. *Very well, thanks.*
  Molto piacere! *Very pleased to meet you!*
molto/a (m./f.) (noun) *much, many, a lot*
momento (m.) *moment*
  in questo momento *right now*
  Un momento. *Wait a second.*
mondo (m.) *world*
  del mondo *in the world*
  intorno al mondo *around the world*
monitor (m.) *monitor, screen*
montagna (f.) *mountain*
  camminare in montagna *to go hiking*
  in montagna *to the mountains*

monumento (m.) *monument*
moquette (f.) *carpet (wall-to-wall)*
morire *to die*
moschea (f.) *mosque*
mostra (f.) *exhibition*
mostrare *to show*
motivo (m.) *reason*
  il motivo per cui … *the reason why …*
moto (f. sg./pl.) *motorbike*
motocicletta (f.) *motorbike*
mouse (m.) (computer) *mouse*
municipio (m.) *city hall, municipal building*
muovere *to move*
muratore/trice (m./f.) *construction worker*
muro (m.) *wall*
muscolo (m.) *muscle*
museo (m.) *museum*
musica (f.) *music*
  musica classica *classical music*
  musica pop *pop music*
musicista (m./f.) *musician*
mutande (f. pl.) *boxers*
mutandine (f. pl.) *underpants (women's)*

N

Napoli (f.) *Naples*
nascere *to be born*
nascita (f.) *birth*
naso (m.) *nose*
natale *native*
  città (f.) natale *hometown*
Natale (m.) *Christmas*
  Buon Natale. *Merry Christmas.*
natura (f.) *nature*
naturale *natural*
  acqua (f.) minerale naturale *still mineral water*
ne *about it/them, of it/them*
  Ce ne sono tre. *There are three of them.*
neanche *not even*
nebbia (f.) *fog*
  C'è nebbia. *It's foggy.*
necessario *necessary*
negozio (m.) *store*
  negozio di abbigliamento *clothing store*
  negozio di alimentari *grocery store*
  negozio di elettronica *electronics store*
  negozio di scarpe *shoe store*
nemmeno *not even*

nero *black*
nervoso *nervous*
nessuno *no*
  nessuna idea *no idea*
nessuno/a (m./f.) *none, nobody*
neve (f.) *snow*
nevicare *to snow*
  Nevica. *It's snowing.*
niente *nothing*
  niente di buono da mangiare *nothing good*
    to eat
nipote (m./f.) *nephew, niece, grandson,*
  granddaughter
no *no*
nocivo *harmful*
noi *we* (subject pronoun); *us* (direct object,
  disjunctive pronoun)
  a noi *to us* (indirect object, disjunctive pronoun)
noioso *boring*
nome (m.) *name*
non *not*
  Non c'è di che. *Don't mention it.*
  Non lo so. *I don't know.*
nonna (f.) *grandmother*
nonno (m.) *grandfather*
nono *ninth*
normale *normal*
normalmente *normally*
norvegese (m./f.) *Norwegian*
nostro *our*
notare *to notice*
notizie (f. pl.) *news*
notte (f.) *night*
  Buona notte. *Good night.*
  di notte *at night, from midnight to 3 a.m.*
  È l'una di notte. *It's 1:00 a.m.*
novanta *ninety*
nove *nine*
novembre (m.) *November*
nubile (f.) *single (woman)*
nulla *nothing*
numero (m.) *number, size (shoes)*
numeroso *numerous, large (family)*
  famiglia (f.) numerosa *large family*
nuotare *to swim*
nuoto (m.) *swimming*
nuovo *new*
  di nuovo *again*

nuvola (f.) *cloud*
nuvoloso *cloudy*
  È nuvoloso. *It's cloudy.*

O

O *or*
occhiali (m. pl.) *eyeglasses*
  occhiali da sole *sunglasses*
occhio (m.) *eye*
occupato *busy*
oceano (m.) *ocean*
offrire *to offer*
oggi *today*
ogni *each, every*
  in ogni caso *in any event*
  ogni volta *every time*
ognuno/a (m./f.) *everyone*
olio (m.) *oil*
oliva (f.) *olive*
ombrello (m.) *umbrella*
omeopatia (f.) *homeopathy*
omeopatico (m.)/omeopatici (m.
  pl.) *homeopathic*
opera (f.) *work, opera*
  opere d'arte *works of art*
operaio/a (m./f.) *worker*
opuscolo (m.) *brochure*
ora (f.) *hour*
  Che ora è?/Che ore sono? *What time is it?*
  due ore e mezzo *two and a half hours*
  È ora di … *It's time to …*
  fra mezz'ora *in half an hour*
orario (m.) *time*
  essere in orario *to be on time*
  orario continuato *open all day*
  orario ridotto *shorter working hours*
ordinare *to order*
ordine (m.) *order*
  mettere in ordine *to put things away*
orecchini (m. pl.) *earrings*
orecchio (m.) *ear*
  orecchi (m. pl.)/orecchie (f. pl.) *ears*
organizzare *to organize*
  viaggio (m.) organizzato *guided tour*
ormai *by now, almost*
orologio (m.) *watch*
orto (m.) *vegetable garden, orchard*
ospedale (m.) *hospital*

ospite (m./f.) *guest (male and female)*
osso (m.) *bone*
   ossa (f. pl.) *bones*
ossobuco (m.) *osso buco*
ostello (m.) *youth hostel*
ottanta *eighty*
ottavo *eighth*
ottimo *excellent*
   in ottima forma *in great shape*
otto *eight*
ottobre (m.) *October*
ovvio *obvious*

P

padre (m.) *father*
   moglie (f.) di mio padre *stepmother*
paese (m.) *town (small), village*
paesino (m.) *village (small)*
pagare *to pay*
   pagare il conto (dell'hotel) *to check out*
pagina (f.) *page*
   pagina web *webpage*
paio (m.) *pair*
   paio di scarpe *pair of shoes*
palazzina (f.) *(4-5 story) apartment building*
palazzo (m.) *palace, mansion, apartment building*
palestra (f.) *gym(nasium), health club*
palla (f.) *ball*
   palla a volo *volleyball*
pallacanestro (f.) *basketball*
pallone (m.) *ball*
pancetta (f.) *bacon*
pancia (f.) *stomach (below the waist), belly*
pane (m.) *bread*
panino (m.) *sandwich*
panorama (m.) *panorama*
pantaloni (m. pl.) *pants*
papà (m.) *dad*
parcheggiare *to park*
parco (m.) *park*
   parco giochi *playground*
parecchio (adjective) *a lot of, several*
parecchio/a (m./f.) (noun) *a lot, several*
parente (m./f.) *relative*
parete (f.) *wall*
pari (inv.) *equal, same*
   fare pari *to draw, to tie*

Parigi (f.) *Paris*
parlare *to speak*
   parlare cinese *to speak Chinese*
parmigiano (m.) *Parmesan cheese*
parolaccia (f.) *bad word*
parte (f.) *part*
partecipare *to participate*
partire *to leave*
   a partire da . . . *starting from . . .*
partita (f.) *game*
part-time *part-time*
   lavoro (m.) part-time *part-time job*
passaporto (m.) *passport*
passare *to pass*
passato (m.) *past (tense)*
   passato prossimo *present perfect (grammar)*
passeggiata (f.) *walk*
   Buona passeggiata. *Enjoy your walk./Have a good walk.*
   fare una passeggiata *to take a walk*
passione (f.) *passion*
   passione per . . . *passion for . . .*
pasta (f.) *pasta*
pasticceria (f.) *bakery*
patata (f.) *potato*
patto (m.) *condition*
   a patto che . . . *provided that . . .*
paura (f.) *fear*
   avere paura (di) *to be afraid (of)*
   fare paura *to be scary*
pausa (f.) *break*
   fare una pausa *to take a break*
pavimento (m.) *floor (inside a house or apartment)*
paziente (m./f.) *patient*
pazienza (f.) *patience*
peccato (m.) *sin*
   Peccato! *Too bad!*
pediatra (m./f.) *pediatrician*
pelle (f.) *skin, leather*
   di pelle *made out of leather*
penne (f. pl.) *penne (pasta)*
pensare *to think*
   pensare a . . . *to think about . . . (something/somebody)*
   pensare di . . . *to think about . . . (doing somehing)*
pensionato/a (m./f.) *retired*

Glossary

pentirsi *to repent, to regret*
pentola (f.) *pan, pot*
pepe (m.) *pepper (spice)*
peperone (m.) *pepper (vegetable)*
per *for, through, by*
  detersivo (m.) per i piatti *dishwashing detergent*
  detersivo (m.) per il bucato *laundry detergent*
  in giro per la casa *around the house*
  in giro per la città *around town*
  passione per … *passion for …*
  per caso *by any chance*
  per contorno *as a side dish*
  Per favore. *Please.*
  per lavoro *on business*
  per le sette *by seven (o'clock)*
  pronto per … *ready to …*
pera (f.) *pear*
perché *why, because*
perdere *to lose*
  perdere tempo *to waste time*
perfetto *perfect*
pericoloso *dangerous*
periferia (f.) *suburbs*
periferico *suburban*
periodo (m.) *period*
  in questo periodo *in this period, currently*
permettere *to allow*
permettersi *to allow, to afford*
però *however, but*
persona (f.) *person*
  di persona *in person*
  persona sportiva *athletic person*
  persone (pl.) *people*
pesca (f.) *peach*
pesce (m.) *fish*
  pesce alla griglia *grilled fish*
petto (m.) *chest*
pezzo (m.) *piece*
piacere *to be pleasing (to someone)*
  Mi piace/piacciono … (sg./pl.) *I like …*
  Piacere. *Pleased to meet you.*
  Piacere mio. *Pleased to meet you, too.*
  Molto piacere! *Very pleased to meet you!*
piacevole *pleasant*
pianeta (m.) *planet*
pianista (m./f.) *pianist*
piano (adjective) *smooth, simple*

piano (adverb) *slowly, softly*
piano (m.) *floor*
  piano terra *ground floor*
  primo piano *first floor (second floor in the U.S.)*
pianoforte (m.) *piano*
  suonare il pianoforte *to play the piano*
pianta (f.) *plant*
piantare *to plant*
pianterreno *ground floor*
piantina (f.) *map*
piatto (m.) *plate, dish*
  detersivo (m.) per i piatti *dishwashing detergent*
  lavare i piatti *to do the dishes*
  primo (piatto) *first course*
  secondo (piatto) *main course*
piazza (f.) *square*
piccolo *small*
piede (m.) *foot*
  a piedi *on foot*
  fare un giro a piedi *to go for a walk*
pieno *full*
  a pieno tempo *full-time*
  giornata (f.) piena *full day*
pietra (f.) *stone*
pigiama (m.) *pajamas*
pioggia (f.) *rain*
piovere *to rain*
  Piove. *It's raining.*
pisolino (m.) *nap*
  fare un pisolino *to take a nap*
più *more*
  mai più *never again*
  non … più *no longer, no more*
  più … di/che *more/-er … than*
piuttosto *rather*
plastica (f.) *plastic*
  di plastica *made from plastic*
plurale (m.) *plural*
poco (adjective) *little, few*
  pochi giorni *a few days*
poco/a (m./f.) (noun) *little, few*
  un poco/un po' *a little*
poema (m.) *poem*
poi *then*
  E poi? *And then?*
poker (m. sg./pl.) *poker*

poliziotto (m.) *policeman*
pollice (m.) *thumb*
pollo (m.) *chicken*
polmone (m.) *lung*
polso (m.) *wrist*
pomeriggio (m.) *afternoon*
  Buon pomeriggio. *Good afternoon. (from 1 p.m. to 6 p.m.)*
  di pomeriggio *in the afternoon*
pomodoro (m.) *tomato*
pop (inv.) *pop*
  musica (f.) pop *pop music*
porta (f.) *door*
portare *to carry, to take, to wear*
porto (m.) *harbor*
posate (f. pl.) *silverware*
possessivo *possessive*
possibile *possible*
posta (f.) *mail*
  posta elettronica *e-mail*
postale (adjective) *mail*
  ufficio postale *post office*
posto (m.) *place*
potere *can, to be able to*
  Posso … ? *May I … ?/Can I … ?*
pranzo (m.) *lunch*
  sala (f.) da pranzo *dining room*
praticare *to play*
  praticare uno sport *to play a sport*
prato (m.) *meadow*
preferire *to prefer*
Prego. *You're welcome.*
prendere *to take, to have (food and drink)*
  Tu cosa prendi? *What are you having?*
prenotare *to reserve*
prenotazione (f.) *reservation*
preoccupare *to worry*
  Sono preoccupato. *I'm worried.*
preparare *to prepare*
prepararsi *to get ready*
preposizione (f.) *preposition*
presentare *to present, to introduce*
presentazione (f.) *introduction*
presente (adjective) *present*
  congiuntivo (m.) presente *present subjunctive*
pressione (f.) *pressure*
presso *at, with*
presto *soon, early*

A presto. *See you soon.*
prezzo (m.) *price*
prima *sooner, in advance*
  prima che … , prima di … *before …*
  prima di tutto *first of all*
primavera (f.) *spring*
  in primavera *in the spring*
primo *first*
  per primo *as first course*
  primo (piatto) (m.) *first course*
  primo piano *first floor (second floor in the U.S.)*
primogenito/a (m./f.) *first-born*
privato *private*
probabile *likely*
probabilmente *probably*
problema (m.) *problem*
prodotto (m.) *product*
professionale *professional*
professore/essa (m./f.) *professor*
profondamente *deep*
profumo (m.) *perfume*
progettare *to plan*
programma (m.) *program*
proibire *to prohibit*
promettere *to promise*
  promettere di … *to promise to … (do something)*
promuovere *to promote*
  essere promosso *to pass (an exam)*
pronome (m.) *pronoun*
pronto *ready, fast*
  pronto per … *ready to …*
  pronto soccorso (m.) *emergency room*
proposito (m.) *intention*
  a proposito *by the way*
proprio *exactly, just, really*
prossimo *next, close*
  mese (m.) prossimo *next month*
  passato (m.) prossimo *present perfect (grammar)*
  prossima settimana (f.) *next week*
  trapassato (m.) prossimo *past perfect (grammar)*
provare *to try, to try on*
provincia (f.) *province*
psichiatra (m./f.) *psychiatrist*
psicologo (m./f.) *psychologist*

pubblicare *to publish*
pulire *to clean*
pulirsi *to clean oneself*
pulito *clean*
pullman (m.) *tour bus*
puntuale *punctual*
  essere puntuale *to be on time*
purché *provided that*
purtroppo *unfortunately*

Q

quaderno (m.) *notebook*
quadro (m.) *painting, picture*
qualche *a few, some*
  fra qualche giorno *in a few days*
  qualche volta *sometimes*
qualcosa *something, anything*
  qualcosa da bere *something to drink*
  qualcosa di bello da fare *anything interesting/cool to do*
qualcuno *someone, anyone*
quale *which*
qualsiasi *any*
qualunque *any*
quando *when*
quanto *how many, how much*
  Da quanto tempo … ? *How long has it been since … ?*
  Quanti anni hai? *How old are you?*
  Quanto costa? *How much does it cost?*
  tanto … quanto *as much/many … as*
quaranta *forty*
  Sono le tre e quarantacinque. *It's 3:45.*
quartiere (m.) *neighborhood*
quarto *fourth*
quarto (m.) *quarter*
  fra tre quarti d'ora *in forty-five minutes*
  Manca un quarto alle quattro. *It's 3:45.*
  Sono le quattro meno un quarto. *It's 3:45.*
  Sono le tre e tre quarti. *It's 3:45.*
  Sono le undici e un quarto di mattina. *It's 11:15 a.m.*
quasi *almost*
quattordici *fourteen*
quattro *four*
  Manca un quarto alle quattro. *It's 3:45.*
  Sono le quattro. *It's four (o'clock).*
  Sono le quattro meno un quarto. *It's 3:45.*

quello *that*
questo *this*
  in questo momento *right now*
  in questo periodo *in this period, currently*
  questa sera *this evening*
  questa settimana *this week*
qui *here*
  qui vicino *nearby*
quindi *therefore, so*
quindici *fifteen*
  Sono le tre e quindici. *It's 3:15.*
quinto *fifth*
quotidiano *daily*
  vita (f.) **quotidiana** *everyday life*
quoziente (m.) *quotient*
  quoziente intellettivo *intelligence quotient (IQ)*

R

raccogliere *to pick up*
raccontare *to tell*
radersi *to shave*
ragazza (f.) *girl (from 14 to 35 years old)*
  la mia ragazza (f.) *my girlfriend*
ragazzina (f.) *girl (from 11 to 13 years old)*
ragazzino (m.) *boy (from 11 to 13 years old)*
ragazzo (m.) *boy (from 14 to 35 years old)*
  il mio ragazzo *my boyfriend*
raggiungere *to reach*
ragione (f.) *reason*
  avere ragione *to be right*
  la ragione per cui … *the reason why …*
ragù (m. sg./pl.) *meat sauce*
raramente *rarely*
rasoio (m.) *razor*
ravioli (m. pl.) *ravioli*
reception (f. sg./pl.) *reception desk*
regalo (m.) *gift*
reggiseno (m.) *bra*
regista (m./f.) *movie director*
registrarsi (all'hotel) *to check in*
regolarmente *regularly*
rene (m.) *kidney*
residenza (f.) *residence*
respirare *to breathe*
restare *to stay*
ricco *rich*
ricercatore/trice (m./f.) *researcher, scientist*

ricetta (f.) *recipe*
ricevere *to receive*
ricordare *to remember*
  ricordarsi di … *to remember to … (do something)*
ridotto *reduced*
  orario (m.) ridotto *shorter working hours*
riecco *here again*
  Rieccoci ! *Here we are again !*
riempirsi *to fill*
  riempirsi di … *to fill up with …*
rilassarsi *to relax*
rimanere *to remain*
rinascimentale (adjective) *Renaissance*
Rinascimento (m.) *Renaissance*
riposo (m.) *rest*
  Buon riposo. *Have a good rest.*
riso (m.) *rice*
rispettivamente *respectively*
rispondere *to reply*
rispondere (a) *to answer*
  rispondere al telefono *to answer the phone*
ristorante (m.) *restaurant*
ritardo (m.) *delay*
  essere in ritardo *to be late*
ritornare *to return, to go back*
riunione (f.) *meeting*
  sala (f.) delle riunioni *meeting room*
riuscire *to manage, to be able*
  riuscire a … *to manage to … , to be able to …*
rivista (f.) *magazine, journal*
roba (f.) *stuff*
  un sacco di roba *a bunch/lot of stuff*
roccia (f.) *rock*
Roma (f.) *Rome*
romantico (m.)/ romantici (m. pl.) *romantic*
romanzo (m.) *novel*
  romanzi (m. pl.) contemporanei *contemporary novels*
rompere *to break*
rosa (inv.) *pink*
rosolare *to sauté, to brown*
rosso *red*
  vino (m.) rosso *red wine*
rumore (m.) *noise*
  fare rumore *to make noise*
rumoroso *noisy*
rurale *rural*

S

sabato (m.) *Saturday*
sabbia (f.) *sand*
sacco (m.) *bag*
  un sacco di … *a lot of …*
  un sacco di roba *a bunch/lot of stuff*
sala (f.) *room*
  sala da pranzo *dining room*
  sala delle riunioni *meeting room*
salario (m.) *salary*
salato *expensive*
sale (m.) *salt*
salone (m.) *living room*
saltare *to jump*
  saltare la corda *to jump rope*
salutarsi *to greet each other*
salute (f.) *health*
saluto (m.) *greeting*
salvare *to save*
  salvare un documento *to save a document*
Salve. *Hello.*
sangue (m.) *blood*
sano *healthy*
sapere *to know (a fact), to know how*
  Lo so. *I know.*
  Non lo so. *I don't know.*
saponetta (f.) *soap (bar)*
sapore (m.) *taste, flavor*
Sardegna (f.) *Sardinia*
sbattere *to beat*
sbucciare *to peel*
scaffale (m.) *shelf*
  scaffale (dei libri) *book shelf*
scala (f.) *stairs, staircase*
scarpe (f. pl.) *shoes*
  negozio (m.) di scarpe *shoe store*
  paio (m.) di scarpe *pair of shoes*
  scarpe da ginnastica *sneakers*
  scarpe da tennis *tennis shoes, sneakers*
scatola (f.) *box, carton*
scegliere *to choose*
scelta (f.) *choice*
scheda (f.) *report card*
schedario (m.) *file cabinet*
schermo (m.) *monitor, screen*
schiena (f.) *back*
sci (m.)/sci (m., pl.) *skiing*

sci alpino *alpine skiing*
sci di fondo *cross-country skiing*
sciare *to ski*
sciarpa (f.) *scarf (long)*
scodella (f.) *bowl (small, for one person)*
scolare *to drain*
scolastico (m.)/scolastici (m. pl.) *scholastic*
scopa (f.) *broom*
scorso *last*
  anno (m.) scorso *last year*
  settimana (f.) scorsa *last week*
scrittore/trice (m./f.) *writer*
scrivania (f.) *desk*
scrivere *to write*
scultura (f.) *sculpture*
scuola (f.) *school*
  scuola superiore *high school*
scusare *to excuse*
  Scusa. *Excuse me.* (infml.)
  (Mi) scusi. *Excuse me.* (sg. fml.)
  Scusami. *I'm sorry.*
se *if*
sé *himself, herself, itself, oneself*
secco *dry*
secondo *second*
  di secondo *as main course*
  secondo (piatto) (m.) *main course*
secondo (preposition) *according to*
secondogenito/a (m./f.) *second-born*
sedere (m.) *behind*
sedia (f.) *chair*
sedici *sixteen*
segretario/a (m./f.) *secretary*
seguire *to follow*
sei *six*
selvaggio *wild*
semaforo (m.) *street light, traffic light*
sembrare *to seem*
seminterrato (m.) *basement*
sempre *always*
  sempre diritto *straight ahead*
seno (m.) *breast*
sentire *to hear*
sentirsi *to feel*
Mi sento bene. *I am well.*
  sentirsi di … *to feel like …*
senza *without*
  senza che … *without …*

sera (f.) *evening*
  Buona sera. *Good evening. (from 6 to 11 p.m.)*
  di sera *in the evening*
  ieri sera *last night*
  questa sera *this evening*
  vestito (m.) da sera *evening gown*
serata (f.) *evening*
  Buona serata. *Have a good evening.*
servire *to serve*
servizio (m.) *bathroom*
sessanta *sixty*
sesto *sixth*
seta (f.) *silk*
  di seta *made of silk*
sete (f.) *thirst*
  avere sete *to be thirsty*
settanta *seventy*
sette *seven*
  alle sette e mezza *at seven thirty (7:30)*
  per le sette *by seven (o'clock)*
  Siamo in sette. *There are seven of us.*
settembre (m.) *September*
settimana (f.) *week*
  due volte alla settimana *twice a week*
  fine settimana (m. sg./pl.) *weekend*
  prossima settimana *next week*
  questa settimana *this week*
  settimana scorsa *last week*
settimo *seventh*
sfilata (f.) *parade, march*
  sfilata di moda *fashion show*
shampo (m.) *shampoo*
si *one, they, people (impersonal pronoun)*
sì *yes*
sia … che *as/so … as, both … and*
Sicilia (f.) *Sicily*
sicuro *sure*
signora (f.) *Mrs., lady*
signore (m.) *Mr., gentleman*
silenzioso *silent*
simile *similar*
simpatico *friendly, nice*
sindaco (m.) *mayor*
sinfonia (f.) *symphony*
singolo *single*
  camera (f.) singola *single room (one twin bed)*
sinistra (f.) *left*
  (a) sinistra *on the left, to the left*

sintomo (m.) *symptom*
sistema (m.) *system*
sito (m.) *site*
  sito web *website*
slip (m. pl.) *underpants (men's)*
smettere *to quit, to stop*
  smettere di … *to quit/stop … ing*
smog (m.) *smog*
sneakers (m. pl.) *sneakers*
soccorso (m.) *aid, rescue*
  pronto soccorso *emergency room*
sociale *social*
soddisfatto *satisfied*
sofà (m.) *sofa, couch*
soffitto (m.) *ceiling*
soggiorno (m.) *living room*
soldi (m. pl.) *money*
sole (m.) *sun*
  C'è il sole. *It's sunny.*
solito *usual*
  del solito *than usual*
  di solito *usually*
solo *alone, lonely, only, just*
soltanto *only*
sonno (m.) *sleep*
  avere sonno *to be sleepy*
sopracciglio (m.) *eyebrow*
  sopracciglia (f. pl.) *eyebrows*
  soprattutto *above all*
sorella (f.) *sister*
sorprendere *to surprise*
sorpresa (f.) *surprise*
  Che sorpresa! *What a surprise!*
sostanza (f.) *substance*
sostituto/a (m./f.) *substitute*
sottile *thin*
sotto *under*
sottopiano (m.) *basement*
sovrappeso (m. sg./pl.) *overweight*
  essere in sovrappeso *to be overweight*
spaghetti (m. pl.) *spaghetti*
spalla (f.) *shoulder*
spazioso *spacious*
specchio (m.) *mirror*
spedire *to send*
spendere *to spend*
sperare *to hope*
  sperare di … *to hope to …*

spesa (f.) *shopping*
  fare la spesa/le spese *to go shopping, to do grocery shopping*
  fare spese *to shop*
spesso *often*
spettacolo (m.) *performance, play (theater)*
spezzatino (m.) *stew*
spiaggia (f.) *beach*
splendere *to shine*
sporco *dirty*
sport (m. sg./pl.) *sport*
  guardare lo sport in/alla televisione *to watch sports on TV*
  fare sport *to practice sports*
  praticare uno sport *to play a sport*
sportivo *athletic, casual*
  persona (f.) sportiva *athletic person*
sposarsi *to get married*
  Si sposa. *He/She is getting married.*
  sposarsi con … *to marry … (someone)*
sposato *married*
spumante (m.) *sparkling wine*
spuntino (m.) *snack*
squadra (f.) *team*
squisito *exquisite, delicious*
stadio (m.) *stadium*
staff (m.) *staff*
stage (m. sg./pl.) *internship*
stagione (f.) *season*
  mezze stagioni *half seasons (spring and fall)*
stagno (m.) *pond*
stampante (f.) *printer*
stanco *tired*
stanza (f.) *room, chatroom*
  stanza da letto *bedroom*
stare *to stay, to be feeling, to be*
  Come mi sta? *How do I look?*
  Come sta? *How are you doing (sg. fml.)?/How is he?*
  Come stai? *How are you doing (infml.)?*
  stare per … *to be about to …*
stasera *this evening, tonight*
stato (m.) *state*
  stato civile *marital status*
stazione (f.) *station*
  stazione (dei treni) *train station*
stella (f.) *star*
stereo (m. sg./pl.) *stereo*

stesso *same*
  allo stesso tempo *at the same time*
stimolante *exciting*
stomaco (m.) *stomach (above the waist)*
storia (f.) *story, history*
  storie (pl.) d'amore *love stories*
strada (f.) *street, road*
straniero *foreign*
  lingua (f.) straniera *foreign language*
  turisti (m./f. pl.) stranieri *foreign tourists*
strano *strange*
stressante *stressful*
stressato *stressed, under stress*
studente/essa (m./f.) *student*
  studente universitario *university student*
studiare *to study*
studio (m.) *study, office*
su *on, upon, over, about*
subito *immediately*
succedere *to happen*
succo (m.) *juice*
suo *his, her, its*
Suo *your* (sg. fml.)
suocera (f.) *mother-in-law*
suocero (m.) *father-in-law*
suonare *to play (an instrument), to ring (a bell)*
  suonare il pianoforte *to play the piano*
superiore *superior, higher*
  scuola (f.) superiore *high school*
supermercato (m.) *supermarket*
svegliarsi *to wake up*
svelto *fast*

T

taglia (f.) *size (dresses, pants)*
tagliare *to cut, to slice*
tagliatelle (f. pl.) *tagliatelle (pasta)*
tailleur (m. sg./pl.) *suit (women's)*
  tailleur pantalone *pant suit*
tanto (adjective) *so much, so many, a lot of*
  tanto … quanto *as much/many … as*
tanto (adverb) *so, so much, very*
  Tanto vale … *(One) might as well …*
tanto/a (m./f.) (noun) *so much, so many*
tappetino (m.) *mouse pad*
tappeto (m.) *carpet, rug*
tardi *late*
  fino a tardi *until late*

tassista (m./f.) *taxi driver*
tastiera (f.) *keyboard*
tavolo (m.) *table*
taxi (m.) *taxi*
tazza (f.) *cup*
te *you* (sg. infml.) (direct object, disjunctive pronoun)
  a te *to you* (sg. infml.) (indirect object, disjunctive pronoun)
tè (m.) *tea*
teatro (m.) *theater*
tecnico *technical*
  istituto (m.) tecnico *professional school*
teenager (m./f. sg./pl.) *teenager*
tele (f.) *television*
  guardare la tele *to watch television*
telefonare *to telephone*
telefonarsi *to call each other*
telefonino (m.) *cell phone*
telefono (m.) *telephone*
  rispondere al telefono *to answer the phone*
telegiornale (m.) *news (on TV)*
telegramma (m.) *telegram*
televisione (f.) *television*
  guardare la televisione *to watch television*
  guardare lo sport in/alla televisione *to watch sports on TV*
  interviste (f. pl.) alla televisione *talk show*
televisore (m.) *television*
temperatura (f.) *temperature*
tempio (m.) *temple*
tempo (m.) *time, weather*
  a tempo pieno *full-time*
  avere tempo *to have time*
  Che tempo fa? *What's the weather like?*
  Da quanto tempo … ? *How long has it been since … ?*
  molto tempo *long time*
  perdere tempo *to waste time*
  tempo libero *free time*
temporale (m.) *storm*
  C'è un temporale. *It's stormy.*
temporaneo *temporary*
  lavoro (m.) temporaneo *summer job*
tenda (f.) *curtain*
tendere *to have a tendency*
tendine (m.) *tendon*
tennis (m. sg./pl.) *tennis*
  giocare a tennis *to play tennis*

scarpe (f. pl.) da tennis *tennis shoes, sneakers*
televisivo (adjective) *television*
  trasmissione (f.) televisiva *television program*
terme (f. pl.) *spa*
terra (f.) *land*
terra (inv.) *ground*
piano (m.) terra *ground floor*
terribile *terrible*
terrina (f.) *bowl*
terzo *third*
terzogenito/a *third-born*
tesi (f.)/tesi (f., pl.) *thesis*
test (m.) *test*
testa (f.) *head*
  fare testa o croce *to flip a coin*
TG (m.) *news (on TV)*
ti *you* (sg. infml.) (direct object pronoun); *to you* (sg. infml.) (indirect object pronoun)
tipo (m.) *type, kind*
tirare *to draw*
  Tira vento. *It's windy.*
titolo (m.) *title*
tivù (f.) *television*
  guardare la tivù *to watch television*
tornare *to return, to go back*
torre (f.) *tower*
torta (f.) *cake*
tortellini (m. pl.) *tortellini*
torto (m.) *fault*
  avere torto *to be wrong*
tra *between, among, in*
  tra ... e ... *between ... and ...*
  tra cinque minuti *in five minutes*
tradizionale *traditional*
traffico (m.) *traffic*
tranquillizzare *to calm down*
trapassato (m.) prossimo *past perfect*
trasferirsi *to move, to transfer*
traslocare *to move (to a new house)*
trasloco (m.) *move, removal*
  fare il trasloco *to move (to a new house)*
trasmissione (f.) *program*
  trasmissione televisiva *television program*
trasparente *transparent*
trasporto (m.) *transportation*
  mezzo (m.) di trasporto *means of transportation*
trattoria (f.) *family style restaurant*

tre *three*
  fra tre quarti d'ora *in forty-five minutes*
  Sono le tre. *It's three (o'clock).*
  Sono le tre e quarantacinque. *It's 3:45.*
  Sono le tre e tre quarti. *It's 3:45.*
tredici *thirteen*
treno (m.) *train*
  in treno *train station*
  stazione (f.) (dei treni) *by train*
trenta *thirty*
  Sono le tre e trenta. *It's 3:30.*
triste *sad*
troppo *too (much/many)*
troppo/a (m./f.) *too much, too many*
trovare *to find*
  andare a trovare *to go visit*
  venire a trovare *to come visit*
tu *you* (sg. infml.) (subject pronoun)
tuo *your* (sg. infml.)
tuonare *to thunder*
tuono (m.) *thunder*
tuorlo (m.) *yolk*
turista (m./f.) *tourist*
  turisti (pl.) stranieri *foreign tourists*
tutto *all*
  a tutti i costi *at all costs*
  di tutti *of all*
  prima di tutto *first of all*
  tutte le mattine *every morning*
  tutti gli altri *everyone else*
  tutti gli anni *every year*
  tutti i giorni *every day*

U

ubriaco *drunk*
ufficio (m.) *office*
  in ufficio *in the office*
  ufficio postale *post office*
ultimo *last, final*
un (m.)/uno (m. in front of s + consonant, z, ps, gn)/una (f.)/un' (m./f. in front of a vowel) *a, one*
  È l'una di notte. *It's 1:00 a.m.*
undicesimo *eleventh*
undici *eleven*
  Sono le undici e un quarto di mattina. *It's 11:15 a.m.*
università (f. sg./pl.) *university*
universitario (adjective) *university*

studente (m.) universitario *university student*
uno *one*
uomo (m.)/uomini (m. pl.) *man*
  abito da uomo *men's suit*
  uomo d'affari *businessman*
uovo (m.) *egg*
  uova (f. pl.) *eggs*
uragano (m.) *hurricane*
urbano *urban*
usare *to use*
uscire *to go out*
utile *useful*
  Posso esserLe utile? *How can I help you?/Can I assist you?* (sg. fml.)
uva (f.) *grapes*
  un grappolo d'uva *a bunch of grapes*

V

vacanza (f.) *vacation, holiday*
  fare una vacanza *to go on vacation*
  in vacanza *on vacation*
vagamente *vaguely*
valere *to be worth*
  Tanto vale … *(One) might as well …*
valigia (f.) *suitcase*
  fare le valige/valigie *to pack*
varietà (f.) *variety*
  varietà di scelta *variety of choices*
vasca (f.) *tub*
  vasca (da bagno) *bath tub*
vecchio *old*
vedere *to see, to meet (a person)*
  Fammi vedere. *Let me see.*
  fare vedere *to show*
  visto che … *given that … /since …*
vedersi *to see each other*
vela (f.) *sail*
  andare in barca a vela *to sail*
vela (f.) *sailing*
velluto (m.) *velvet*
  di velluto a coste *made out of corduroy*
  velluto a coste *corduroy*
veloce *fast, quick*
velocemente *quickly*
venditore (m.) *salesman*
venditrice (f.) *saleswoman*
venerdì (m. sg./pl.) *Friday*
Venezia (f.) *Venice*

venire *to come*
  venire a trovare *to come visit*
venti *twenty*
ventidue *twenty-two*
ventilatore (m.) *fan*
ventiquattro *twenty-four*
ventitré *twenty-three*
vento (m.) *wind*
  C'è vento. *It's windy.*
  Tira vento. *It's windy.*
ventre (m.) *stomach (below the waist)*
ventuno *twenty-one*
veramente *actually, really*
verde *green*
verdura (f.) *vegetable*
vergine (f.) *virgin*
verità (f. sg./pl.) *truth*
vero *true, right*
versare *to pour*
versione (f.) *version*
vestirsi *to get dressed*
vestito (m.) *dress*
  vestito da sera *evening gown*
veterinario/a (m./f.) *veterinarian*
vi *you* (pl.) (direct object pronoun); *to you* (pl.) (indirect object pronoun)
via (f.) *street, way, path*
viaggiare *to travel*
  viaggiare all'estero *to travel abroad*
viaggio (m.) *travel, trip*
  Buon viaggio. *Have a good trip.*
  fare un viaggio *to take a trip*
  viaggio organizzato *guided tour*
viale (m.) *avenue, path*
vicino *near*
  lì vicino *near there*
  qui vicino *nearby*
  vicino a … *near …*
video (m.) *monitor, screen*
villetta (f.) *small house*
vincere *to win*
vino (m.) *wine*
  lista (f.) dei vini *wine list*
  vino bianco *white wine*
  vino rosso *red wine*
viola (inv.) *purple*
visitare *to visit, to go sightseeing*
vista (f.) *view*

vita (f.) *life, waist*
  da una vita *for a very long time, since always*
  vita quotidiana *everyday life*
vitello (m.) *veal*
vivere *to live*
  vivere a ... *to live in ...*
voglia (f.) *wish, desire*
  avere voglia di ... *to feel like ...*
voi *you* (pl.) (subject pronoun); *you* (pl.) (direct object, disjunctive pronoun)
  a voi *to you* (pl.) (indirect object, disjunctive pronoun)
volentieri *gladly*
volere *to want*
  Ti voglio bene. *I care about you./I love you.*
  volerci *to take (time)*
  Vorrei ... *I would like ...*
volta (f.) *time*
  a volte *sometimes*
  due volte alla settimana *twice a week*
  ogni volta *every time*
  qualche volta *sometimes*
voltare *to turn*
vostro *your* (pl.)
votazione (f.) *grade*
voto (m.) *grade*
vuoto *empty*

W

water (m.) *toilet*
web log (blog) (m.) *web log (blog)*
web page (f.) *webpage*
weekend (m. sg./pl.) *weekend*

Z

zaino (m.) *backpack*
zero *zero*
zia (f.) *aunt*
zio (m.)/**zii** (m., pl.) *uncle*
zoo (m.)/**zoo** (m., pl.) *zoo*
zucchero (m.) *sugar*
zucchino (m.) *zucchini*

English-Italian

A

a *un/uno* (in front of s + consonant, z, ps, gn)/*una*
  a lot *parecchio/a* (m./f.), *molto/a* (m./f.) (noun)
  a lot of *tanto, parecchio, molto, un sacco di*
  a lot of stuff *un sacco di roba*
a.m. *di mattina, di notte*
  It's 11:15 a.m. *Sono le undici e un quarto di mattina.*
  It's 1:00 a.m. *È l'una di notte.*
ability *capacità (f., pl. capacità)*
able (to be) *riuscire, potere*
  able to ... (to be) *riuscire a ...*
about *circa, su*
  about it *ci, ne*
  about them *ne*
  I'll think about it. *Ci penserò.*
about to ... (to be) *stare per ...*
above all *soprattutto*
abroad *all'estero*
  travel abroad *viaggiare all'estero*
absolutely *assolutamente*
absorb (to) *assorbire*
abundant *abbondante*
accept (to) *accettare*
accessory *accessorio* (m.)
accommodating *accomodante*
accommodation *alloggio* (m.)
accompany (to) *accompagnare*
according to ... *secondo ...*
action *azione* (f.)
  action movies *film* (m. pl.) *d'azione*
activity *attività (f., pl. attività)*
actor *attore* (m.)
actress *attrice* (f.)
actually *veramente*
add (to) *aggiungere*
address *indirizzo* (m.)
adjective *aggettivo* (m.)
adorable *adorabile*
adult *adulto/a* (m./f.)
advance *anticipo* (m.)
  in advance *prima*
advice *consiglio* (m.)
  ask for advice (to) *chiedere (un) consiglio*
aerobic *aerobico*

afford (to) *permettersi*
afraid (to be) *avere paura*
  afraid of (to be) *avere paura di/essere impauriti da*
after *dopo*
afternoon *pomeriggio* (m.)
  Good afternoon. (from 1 p.m. to 6 p.m.) *Buon pomeriggio.*
  in the afternoon *di pomeriggio*
again *ancora, di nuovo*
  never again *mai più*
age *età (f., pl. età)*
agency *agenzia* (f.)
ago *fa*
  a month ago *un mese fa*
  two days ago *due giorni fa*
agree (to) *essere d'accordo*
agreed *d'accordo*
agreement *accordo* (m.)
ahead *avanti*
  Go ahead. *Va' avanti.*
aid *soccorso* (m.)
air *aria* (f.)
  air conditioning *aria condizionata*
airplane *aereo* (m.)
  by plane *in aereo*
airport *aeroporto* (m.)
all *tutto*
  above all *soprattutto*
  All right. *Va bene.*
  at all costs *a tutti i costi*
  first of all *prima di tutto*
  not … at all *non … affatto*
  of all *di tutti*
  open all day *orario* (m.) *continuato*
allow (to) *permettere, permettersi*
almost *quasi, ormai*
alone *solo*
along *lungo*
alpine *alpino*
  alpine skiing *sci* (m.) *alpino*
already *già*
also *anche*
alternate (to) *alternare*
although *benché*
always *sempre*
American *americano*
  American football *futbol americano* (m.)

among *fra, tra*
amusing *divertente*
ancient *antico*
and *e* (ed before a vowel)
  … and you? (fml.) *… e Lei?*
  … and you? (infml.) *… e tu?*
animal *animale* (m.)
ankle *caviglia* (f.)
anniversary *anniversario* (m.)
  Happy anniversary. *Buon anniversario.*
another *un altro/un'altra*
answer (to) *rispondere (a)*
  answer the phone (to) *rispondere al telefono*
anti-stress *antistress* (m., pl. *antistress*)
any *qualsiasi, qualunque, di + definite article*
anyone *chiunque, qualcuno*
anything *qualcosa*
  anything interesting/cool to do *qualcosa di bello da fare*
apartment *appartamento* (m.), *alloggio* (m.)
  apartment building *condominio* (m., pl.: *condomini*)
  apartment building (4-5 story building) *palazzo* (m.), *palazzina* (f.)
aperitif *aperitivo* (m.)
appetite *appetito* (m.)
appetizer *antipasto* (m.)
apple *mela* (f.)
appointment *appuntamento* (m.)
appropriate *adatto*
apricot *albicocca* (f.)
  apricot tree *albicocco* (m.)
April *aprile* (m.)
Arab *arabo*
archeological *archeologico (m. pl archeologici)*
architect *architetto* (m.)
arm *braccio* (m.)
arms *braccia* (f. pl.)
aroma *aroma* (m.)
around *attorno, intorno*
  around … *attorno a …*
  around midnight *intorno a mezzanotte*
  around the home/house *in giro per la casa*
  around the world *intorno al mondo*
  around town *in giro per la città*
  arrive (to) *arrivare*
art *arte* (f.)
  modern art *arte moderna*

article *articolo* (m.)

artist *artista* (m./f.)

as *come*

  as a side dish *di/per contorno*

  as first course *per primo*

  as main course *di secondo*

  as many/much … as *tanto … quanto*

  as/so … as *così … come, sia … che*

  (One) might as well … *Tanto vale …*

ask (to), ask for (to) *chiedere*

  ask a question (to) *fare una domanda*

  ask for advice (to) *chiedere (un) consiglio*

assistant *assistente* (m./f.)

astronaut *astronauta* (m./f.)

at *a, da, in, presso*

  at all costs *a tutti i costi*

  at home *a casa*

  at least *almeno*

  at night, from midnight to 3 a.m *di notte*

  at seven thirty (7:30) *alle sette e mezza*

  at the beach *al mare*

  at the lake *al lago*

  at the same time *allo stesso tempo*

  not … at all *non … affatto*

athlete *atleta* (m./f.)

athletic *sportivo*

  athletic person *persona* (f.) *sportiva*

attach (to) *attaccare*

  attach (a file) (to) *allegare un file/documento*

attachment *allegato* (m.)

attend (to) *frequentare*

attention *attenzione* (f.)

  pay attention (to) *fare attenzione*

  Pay attention! *Sta' attento!*

attentive *attento*

August *agosto* (m.)

aunt *zia* (f.)

author *autore/trice* (m./f.)

availability *disponibilità* (f.)

available *disponibile*

avenue *viale* (m.)

average *media* (f.)

avocado *avocado (m., pl. avocado)*

B

baby *bambino/a* (m./f.)

back *schiena* (f.)

  go back (to) *ritornare, tornare*

back yard *cortile* (m.)

backpack *zaino* (m.)

bacon *pancetta* (f.)

bad *cattivo*

  It's bad. (weather) *Fa brutto.*

  Not bad. *Così, così.*

  Too bad! *Peccato!*

bad word *parolaccia* (f.)

badly *male*

bag *sacco* (m.), *borsa* (f.)

baked pork *maiale* (m.) *al forno*

bakery *pasticceria* (f.)

ball *palla* (f.), *pallone* (m.)

banana *banana* (f.)

band (music) *gruppo* (m.)

  British bands *gruppi* (pl.) *inglesi*

bandage *benda* (f.), *cerotto* (m.)

bank *banca* (f.)

banker *banchiere/a* (m./f.)

barbeque *alla brace*

baroque *barocco* (m.)

baseball *baseball* (m.)

basement *seminterrato* (m.), *sottopiano* (m.)

basil *basilico* (m.)

basketball *basket* (m.), *pallacanestro* (f.)

bath gel *bagnoschiuma* (m.), *docciaschiuma* (m.)

bath tub *vasca* (f.) *(da bagno)*

  take a bath (to) *fare il bagno*

bathing trunks/suit *costume* (m.) *da bagno*

bathroom *bagno* (m.), *servizio* (m.)

be (to) *essere, fare, stare*

beach *spiaggia* (f.)

beard *barba* (f.)

beat (to) *sbattere*

beautiful *bello*

  How beautiful! *Che bello!*

  It's beautiful. (weather) *Fa bello.*

  very beautiful *bellissimo*

  What a beautiful dish! *Che bel piatto!*

because *perché*

become (to) *diventare, farsi*

bed *letto* (m.)

  bed sheet *lenzuolo* (m.)

  bed sheets *lenzuola* (f. pl.)

  double bed *letto matrimoniale*

bedroom *camera* (f.), *camera da letto, stanza* (f.) *da letto*

beef *manzo* (m.)

beefsteak *bistecca* (f.)
beer *birra* (f.)
before *avanti*
  before … *prima che … , prima di …*
begin (to) *cominciare*
  begin to … (to) *cominciare a …*
behind (n.) *sedere* (m.)
  behind (adv.) *dietro*
beige *beige* (inv.)
believe (to) *credere*
belly *pancia* (f.)
belong (It belongs to …) *È di …*
belt *cintura* (f.)
besides *inoltre*
best (the) *migliore, meglio*
better *meglio* (inv.), *migliore, meglio*
  It's better. *Va meglio.*
between *fra, tra*
  between … and … *fra … e … /tra … e …*
bicycle *bicicletta* (f.)
  ride a bike (to) *andare in bicicletta*
big *grande*
  have a nice big meal (to) *farsi una bella mangiata*
bike *bici* (f., pl. bici)
biking *ciclismo* (m.)
bikini *bichini* (m.)
bill *conto* (m.)
billiards *biliardo* (m.)
billion *miliardo (pl. miliardi)*
biology *biologia* (f.)
birth *nascita* (f.)
birthday *compleanno* (m.)
  Happy birthday. *Buon compleanno.*
bitter *amaro*
bitterly *amaramente*
black *nero*
bleach *candeggina* (f.)
blender *frullatore* (m.)
blog *blog* (m.)
blood *sangue* (m.)
blouse *camicetta* (f.)
blue *blu* (inv.)
board *asse* (f.)
  ironing board *asse da stiro*
boat *barca* (f.)
boil (to) *bollire*
bone *osso* (m.)

bones *ossa* (f. pl.)
book *libro* (m.)
bookcase (in a house or office) *libreria* (f.)
bookstore *libreria* (f.)
bored (to get bored) *annoiarsi*
boring *noioso*
born (to be) *nascere*
  first-born *primogenito/a* (m./f.)
  second-born *secondogenito/a* (m./f.)
  third-born *terzogenito/a*
boss *capo/a* (m./f.)
both (of them) *entrambi/e*
  both … and *sia … che*
bottle *bottiglia* (f.)
bottom *fondo*
  the bottom of … *in fondo a …*
boutique *boutique* (f.)
bowl *ciotola* (f.), *terrina* (f.)
  bowl (small, for one person) *scodella* (f.)
box *scatola* (f.)
boxers *mutande* (f. pl.)
boy (from 11 to 13 years old) *ragazzino* (m.)
  boy (from 14 to 35 years old) *ragazzo* (m.)
boyfriend *ragazzo* (m.)
  my boyfriend *il mio ragazzo*
bra *reggiseno* (m.)
bracelet *braccialetto* (m.)
brain *cervello* (m.)
bread *pane* (m.)
break *pausa* (f.)
  take a break (to) *fare una pausa*
break (to) *rompere*
  Break a leg! (lit. In the mouth of the wolf!) *In bocca al lupo!*
  Thank you. (lit. May the wolf die.) *Crepi il lupo. (in response to In bocca al lupo!)*
breakfast *colazione* (f.)
  have breakfast (to) *fare colazione*
breast *seno* (m.)
breathe (to) *respirare*
broccoli *broccolo* (m.)
brochure *opuscolo* (m.)
broom *scopa* (f.)
brother *fratello* (m.)
brown *marrone*
brown (to) *rosolare*
bruschetta *bruschetta* (f.)
building *edificio* (m.)

bus *autobus* (m.)
  tour bus *pullman* (m.)
business *affari* (m. pl.), *business* (m., pl.),
  commercio (m.)
  on business *per lavoro*
businessman *imprenditore* (m.), *uomo* (m.)
  d'affari
businesswoman *imprenditrice* (f.), *donna* (f.)
  d'affari
busy *impegnato, occupato*
  busy day *giornata* (f.) *piena*
but *ma, però*
butcher shop *macelleria* (f.)
butter *burro* (m.)
buy (to) *comprare*
by *per, in, a*
  by any chance *per caso*
  by car *in macchina*
  by now *ormai*
  by plane *in aereo*
  by seven (o'clock) *per le sette*
  by the way *a proposito*
  by train *in treno*
Bye-bye! *Ciao ciao!*

C

cabinet *camera* (f.)
  medicine cabinet *armadietto* (m.)
cable *cavo* (m.)
  cable (dsl) *cavo adsi*
café *bar* (m.)
cake *torta* (f.)
call (to) *chiamare, telefonare*
  call each other (on the phone) (to) *telefonarsi*
calm down (to) *tranquillizzare*
camera *macchina fotografica*
camping *campeggio* (m.)
  go camping (to) *fare il campeggio*
can *potere*
  Can I ... ? *Posso ... ?*
  How can this be! *Ma come!*
can (noun) *lattina* (f.)
cappuccino *cappuccino* (m.)
car *automobile* (f.), *macchina* (f.)
  by car *in macchina*
card *carta* (f.)
  credit card *carta di credito*
  play cards (to) *giocare a carte*

careful *attento*
  Be careful! *Sta' attento!*
carpenter *falegname* (m.)
carpet *tappeto* (m.)
  carpet (wall-to-wall) *moquette* (f.)
carrot *carota* (f.)
carry (to) *portare*
carton *scatola* (f.)
case *caso* (m.)
  in any case *comunque*
cashmere *cachemire* (m.)
  made out of cashmere *di cachemire*
cask *botte* (f.)
casual *sportivo*
CD-ROM *cd rom* (m.)
CD-ROM drive *lettore cd, lettore cd-rom*
ceiling *soffitto* (m.)
celebrate (to) *celebrare*
cell phone *cellulare* (m.), *telefonino* (m.)
center *centro* (m.)
  information center *centro informazioni*
centimeter *centimetro* (m.)
ceremony *cerimonia* (f.)
certain (ones) *certo/a* (m./f.)
certainly *certamente*
chair *sedia* (f.)
champion *campione/essa* (m./f.)
chance *caso* (m.)
  by any chance *per caso*
change (to) *cambiare*
channel *canale* (m.)
  flip channels (to) *cambiare canale*
chatroom *chatroom* (f.)
check *conto* (m.)
check (to) *controllare*
check in (to) *registrarsi (all'hotel)*
check out (to) *pagare il conto (dell'hotel)*
cheek *guancia* (f.)
cheese *formaggio* (m.)
chemical *chimico* (m. pl *chimici*)
chemistry *chimica* (f.)
chest *petto* (m.)
chicken *pollo* (m.)
child (from 0 to 10 years old) *bambino/a* (m./f.)
chin *mento* (m.)
China *Cina* (f.)
Chinese (language) *cinese* (m.)
  speak Chinese (to) *parlare cinese*

choice *scelta* (f.)
  variety of choices *varietà* (f.) *di scelta*
choose (to) *scegliere*
chop *braciola* (f.)
  pork chop *braciola di maiale*
Christmas *Natale* (m.)
  Merry Christmas. *Buon Natale.*
church *chiesa* (f.)
circle *giro* (m.)
circus *circo* (m.)
citizenship *cittadinanza* (f.)
city *città (f., pl. città)*
  in/to the city *in centro*
city hall *municipio* (m.)
civil *civile*
claim (to) *affermare*
classical *classico (m. pl. classici)*
  classical music *musica* (f.) *classica*
classroom, class *classe* (f.)
clean *pulito*
clean (to) *pulire*
  clean oneself (to) *pulirsi*
clear *chiaro*
clearly *chiaro, chiaramente*
clerk *impiegato/a* (m./f.)
climate *clima* (m.)
close *prossimo*
close (to) *chiudere*
  close a file (to) *chiudere un documento/file*
closet *armadio* (m.)
clothing *abbigliamento* (m.)
  clothing store *negozio* (m.) *di abbigliamento*
cloud *nuvola* (f.)
cloudy *nuvoloso*
  It's cloudy. *È nuvoloso.*
club *club (m., pl. club), discoteca* (f.)
coach *allenatore/trice* (m./f.)
coast *costa* (f.)
coat (above the knees) *giaccone* (m.)
  coat (to the knees or longer) *cappotto* (m.)
coffee *caffè (m., pl. caffè)*
coffee maker (stovetop) *caffettiera* (f.)
coffee shop *caffetteria* (f.), *caffè (m., pl. caffè)*
cold (noun) *freddo* (m.)
cold (to be) *avere freddo*
  It's cold. *Fa freddo.*
colleague *collega* (m./f.)
cologne *colonia* (f.)

come (to) *venire*
  come in (to) *entrare*
  come visit (to) *venire a trovare*
comedy *commedia* (f.)
comfortable *comodo*
command (to) *comandare*
commerce *commercio* (m.)
common *comune* (m.)
community *comunità (f., pl. comunità)*
company *compagnia* (f.)
competence *competenza* (f.)
complete (to) *compiere*
completely *affatto*
compliment *complimento* (m.)
computer *computer (m., pl computer);*
  informatico (adjective)
  computer science *informatica* (f.)
concert *concerto* (m.)
condition *patto* (m.), *condizione* (f.)
conditioning *condizionato*
confess (to) *confessare*
Congratulations! *Complimenti!*
construction worker *muratore/trice* (m./f.)
contemporary *contemporaneo*
  contemporary novels *romanzi* (m. pl.)
    contemporanei
continue (to) *continuare*
conversation *colloquio* (m.)
convince (to) *convincere*
  convince to … (to) *convincere a …*
convinced *convinto*
cook (to) *cucinare, cuocere*
cooking *cottura* (f.)
coordinate (to) *coordinare*
corduroy *velluto a coste*
  made out of corduroy *di velluto a coste*
correct *giusto*
correctly *giusto*
cost *costo* (m.)
  at all costs *a tutti i costi*
cost (to) *costare*
  How much does it cost? *Quanto costa?*
costume *costume* (m.)
cotton *cotone* (m.)
couch *divano* (m.), *sofà* (m.)
count (to) *contare*
country *campagna* (f.)
  to the country *in campagna*

countryside *campagna* (f.)
couple *coppia* (f.)
course *corso* (m.)
  as first course *per primo*
  as main course *di secondo*
  first course *primo (piatto)* (m.)
  main course *secondo (piatto)* (m.)
courtyard *cortile* (m.)
cousin *cugino/a* (m./f.)
cream *crema* (f.)
  shaving cream *crema da barba*
credit *credito* (m.)
  credit card *carta* (f.) *di credito*
cross-country skiing *sci* (m.) *di fondo*
crowded *affollato*
cucumber *cetriolo* (m.)
culture *cultura* (f.)
cup *tazza* (f.)
cupboard *credenza* (f.)
cure (to) *curare*
current *attuale*
currently *in questo periodo*
curtain *tenda* (f.)
customer *cliente* (m./f.)
cut (to) *tagliare*
cute *carino*

D

dad *papà* (m.)
  stay-at-home dad *casalingo* (m.)
daily *quotidiano*
dance *ballo* (m.)
dance (to) *ballare*
dangerous *pericoloso*
data *dati* (m. pl.)
date *data* (f.)
daughter *figlia* (f.)
day *giorno* (m.), *giornata* (f.), *data* (f.)
  a few day *pochi giorni* (m. pl.)
  a full day, a busy day *giornata* (f.) *piena*
  day trip *gita* (f.)
every day *tutti i giorni*
  Have a good day. *Buona giornata.*
  in a few days *fra qualche giorno*
  open all day *orario* (m.) *continuato*
  two days ago *due giorni fa*
December *dicembre* (m.)
decide (to) *decidere*

decide to … (to) *decidere di …*
deep *profondamente*
degree *grado* (m.), *laurea* (f.)
  high school degree *maturità* (f.)
  university degree *laurea* (f.)
delay *ritardo* (m.)
delete (to) *cancellare, eliminare*
delicious *delizioso, squisito*
dentist *dentista* (m./f.)
deodorant *deodorante* (m.)
department store *grande magazzino* (m.)
depressed *depresso*
describe (to) *descrivere*
desert *deserto* (m.)
desire *voglia* (f.)
desire (to) *desiderare*
desk *scrivania* (f.)
dessert *dolce* (m.)
destroy (to) *distruggere*
detergent *detersivo* (m.)
  dishwashing detergent *detersivo per i piatti*
  laundry detergent *detersivo per il bucato*
determine (to) *determinare*
die (to) *morire*
difference *differenza* (f.)
different *diverso*
difficult *difficile*
dining room *sala* (f.) *da pranzo*
dinner *cena* (f.)
  Enjoy your dinner./Have a good
    dinner. *Buona cena.*
diploma *diploma* (m.)
director *direttore* (m.)
  movie director *regista* (m./f.)
dirty *sporco*
disco *discoteca* (f.)
disease *malattia* (f.)
dish *piatto* (m.)
do the dishes (to) *lavare i piatti*
  What a beautiful dish! *Che bel piatto!*
dishwasher *lavapiatti* (f.), *lavastoviglie* (f.)
dishwashing detergent *detersivo* (m.) *per i
piatti*
displease (to) *dispiacere*
distant *lontano*
divorce … (someone) (to) *divorziarsi da …*
  get a divorce (to) *divorziarsi*
do (to) *fare*

do aerobics (to) *fare ginnastica aerobica*
do gardening (to) *fare giardinaggio*
do grocery shopping (to) *fare la spesa/le spese*
do the dishes (to) *lavare i piatti*
do the laundry (to) *fare il bucato*
How are you doing (fml.)? *Come sta?*
How are you doing (infml.)? *Come stai?*
things to do *cose* (f. pl.) *da fare*
What do you do? *Che lavoro fai?*
doctor *dottore/essa* (m./f.)
document *documento* (m.)
save a document (to) *salvare un documento*
documentary *documentario* (m.)
dollar *dollaro* (m.)
a million dollars *un milione di dollari*
door *porta* (f.)
double *doppio*
double bed *letto* (m.) *matrimoniale*
double room (one queen-size bed) *camera* (f.) *matrimoniale*
double room (two twin-size beds) *camera* (f.) *doppia*
doubt (to) *dubitare*
downtown *in centro*
drain (to) *scolare*
drama *dramma* (m.)
draw (to) *tirare, fare pari*
drawer *cassetto* (m.)
dress *vestito* (m.), *abito* (m.)
dressed (to get dressed) *vestirsi*
drink *bevanda* (f.)
drink (to) *bere*
something to drink *qualcosa da bere*
drive (to) *guidare*
drugstore *farmacia* (f.)
drunk *ubriaco*
dry *secco*
due *dovuto*
due to ... *dovuto a ...*
DVD player *dvd* (m.)

E

each *ciascuno, ogni*
each one *ciascuno/a* (m./f.)
ear *orecchio* (m.)
ears *orecchi/orecchie* (m. pl./f. pl.)
early *presto*

early (to be) *essere in anticipo*
earn (to) *guadagnare*
earrings *orecchini* (m. pl.)
easy *facile*
eat (to) *mangiare*
eat-in kitchen *cucina* (f.) *abitabile*
nothing good to eat *niente di buono da mangiare*
economics *economia* (f.)
education *istruzione* (f.)
egg *uovo* (m.)
eggs *uova* (f. pl.)
eggplant *melanzana* (f.)
eight *otto*
eighteen *diciotto*
eighth *ottavo*
eighty *ottanta*
elbow *gomito* (m.)
elder *maggiore*
electric *elettrico*
electrician *elettricista* (m.)
electrocardiogram *elettrocardiogramma* (m.)
electronics *elettronica* (f.)
electronics store *negozio* (m.) *di elettronica*
elegant *elegante*
elegantly *elegantemente*
elementary *elementare*
the first grade at elementary school *la prima elementare*
eleven *undici*
It's 11:15 a.m. *Sono le undici e un quarto di mattina.*
eleventh *undicesimo*
e-mail *email, mail (f., pl. email, mail), posta* (f.) *elettronica*
send an e-mail (to) *mandare un'email/una mail*
emergency room *pronto soccorso* (m.)
employee *impiegato/a* (m./f.)
empty *vuoto*
end (to) *per finire*
engaged *fidanzato*
engagement *impegno* (m.)
engineer *ingegnere* (m.)
English *inglese*
British bands (music) *gruppi* (m. pl.) *inglesi*
English (language) *inglese* (m.)
enjoy oneself (to) *divertirsi*

Enjoy your dinner. *Buona cena.*
Enjoy your meal. *Buon appetito.*
Enjoy your walk. *Buona passeggiata.*
enormous *enorme*
enough *abbastanza*
  enough (to be) *bastare*
  That's enough! *Basta così!*
enroll (to) *iscrivere*
enthusiastically *entusiasticamente*
entire *intero*
equal *pari* (inv.)
espresso machine *macchina* (f.) *del caffè*
euro *euro* (m., pl. *euro*)
Europe *Europa* (f.)
European *europeo*
evening *sera* (f.), *serata* (f.)
  evening gown *vestito* (m.) *da sera*
  Good evening (from 6 to 11 p.m.). *Buona sera.*
  Have a good evening. *Buona serata.*
  in the evening *di sera*
  this evening *questa sera*
event *gara* (f.)
  in any event *in ogni caso*
ever *mai*
every *ogni*
  every day *tutti i giorni*
  every morning *tutte le mattine*
  every time *ogni volta*
  every year *tutti gli anni*
everyday life *vita* (f.) *quotidiana*
everyone *ognuno/a* (m./f.)
  everyone else *tutti gli altri*
exactly *giusto, proprio*
exaggerate (to) *esagerare*
exaggerated *esagerato*
exam *esame* (m.)
  fail (an exam) (to) *essere bocciato*
excellent *eccellente, ottimo*
exceptional *eccezionale*
exciting *stimolante*
excursion *escursione* (f.)
excuse (to) *scusare*
  Excuse me. (fml.) *(Mi) scusi.*
  Excuse me. (infml.) *Scusa.*
exercise (to) *fare ginnastica*
exhibition *mostra* (f.)
exist (to) *esistere*

expensive *caro, costoso, salato*
experience *esperienza* (f.)
expert *esperto/a* (m./f.)
exquisite *squisito*
extra *extra* (inv.)
eye *occhio* (m.)
eyebrow *sopracciglio* (m.)
  eyebrows *sopracciglia* (f. pl.)
eyeglasses *occhiali* (m. pl.)
eyelash *ciglio* (m.)
  eyelashes *ciglia* (f. pl.)

F

face *faccia* (f.)
facing … *di fronte a …*
fact *fatto* (m.)
  in fact *infatti*
factor *fattore* (m.)
factory *fabbrica* (f.)
fail (an exam) (to) *essere bocciato*
fairly *abbastanza*
fairy tale *favola* (f.), *fiaba* (f.)
fall *autunno* (m.)
  in the fall *in/d'autunno*
fall (to) *cadere*
  fall asleep (to) *addormentarsi*
false *falso*
family *famiglia* (f.)
  family style restaurant *trattoria* (f.)
  large family *famiglia numerosa*
famous *famoso*
fan *ventilatore* (m.)
fantastic *fantastico* (m. pl. *fantastici*)
far *lontano* (adverb)
  go too far (to) *esagerare*
farmer *contadino/a* (m./f.)
fashion *moda* (f.)
  fashion show *sfilata* (f.) *di moda*
fast *svelto, veloce, affrettato, pronto* (adjective); *veloce* (adverb)
fat *grasso* (m.) (noun); *grasso* (adjective)
father *padre* (m.)
father-in-law *suocero* (m.)
fault *torto* (m.)
favor *favore* (m.)
fax machine *fax* (m., pl. *fax*)
fear *paura* (f.)
February *febbraio* (m.)

feel (to) *sentirsi*
  feel like ... (to) *sentirsi di ... /avere voglia di ...*
  feeling (to be) *stare*
female *femmina* (f.)
fettuccine *fettuccine* (f. pl.)
fever *febbre* (f.)
  have a fever (to) *avere la febbre*
few *poco/a* (m./f.) (noun); *poco* (adjective)
  a few *alcuni/e* (noun); *qualche, certo* (adjective)
  a few days *pochi giorni* (m. pl.)
  in a few days *fra qualche giorno*
fiancé(e) *fidanzato/a* (m./f.)
field *campo* (m.)
fifteen *quindici*
  It's 11:15 a.m. *Sono le undici e un quarto di mattina.*
  It's 3:15. *Sono le tre e quindici.*
fifth *quinto*
fifty *cinquanta*
figure *figura* (f.)
file *documento* (m.), *file* (m.), *cartella* (f.)
  attach a file (to) *allegare un documento/file*
  close a file (to) *chiudere un documento/file*
  open a file (to) *aprire un documento/file*
  send a file (to) *inviare un documento/file*
file cabinet *schedario* (m.)
fill (to) *riempire*
  fill up with ... (to) *riempirsi di ...*
film *film* (m., pl. film)
final *ultimo*
finalist *finalista* (m./f.)
finally *finalmente*
find (to) *trovare*
Fine, thanks. *(Sto) bene, grazie.*
finger *dito* (m.)
fingers *dita* (f. pl.)
finish (to) *finire*
  finish ... ing (to) *finire di ...*
  to finish *per finire*
first *primo*
  as first course *per primo*
  first course *primo (piatto)* (m.)
  first floor (second floor in the U.S.) *primo piano* (m.)
  first of all *prima di tutto*
  first-born *primogenito/a* (m./f.)
  the first grade at elementary school *la prima elementare*
fish *pesce* (m.)
  grilled fish *pesce alla griglia*
five *cinque*
  in five minutes *tra cinque minuti*
fixed *fisso*
flash (to) *lampeggiare*
flavor *sapore* (m.)
flip a coin (to) *fare testa o croce*
flip channels (to) *cambiare canale*
floor *piano* (m.)
  floor (inside a house or apartment) *pavimento* (m.)
  first floor (second floor in the U.S.) *primo piano*
  ground floor *pianterreno* (m.), *piano terra*
Florence *Firenze* (f.)
flower *fiore* (m.)
fog *nebbia* (f.)
  It's foggy. *C'è nebbia.*
follow (to) *seguire*
folly *follia* (f.)
food *cibo* (m.)
foot *piede* (m.)
  on foot *a piedi*
football *futbol* (m.)
  American football *futbol americano*
for *per, da*
  ask for (to) *chiedere*
  be looking for ... (to) *essere in cerca di ...*
  for a very long time *da una vita*
  go for a ride (to) *fare un giro*
  go for a walk (to) *fare un giro/fare un giro a piedi*
  look for (to) *cercare*
  passion for ... *passione per ...*
  wait for (to) *aspettare*
forehead *fronte* (f.)
foreign *straniero, estero*
foreign language *lingua* (f.) *straniera*
  foreign tourists *turisti* (m./f. pl.) *stranieri*
forest *foresta* (f.)
forget (to) *dimenticare*
  forget to ... (do something) (to) *dimenticare di ...*
form *forma* (f.)
forty *quaranta*
  from 10:45 a.m. to 3:00 p.m. *dalle undici meno*

un quarto alle tre
in forty-five minutes *fra tre quarti d'ora*
It's 3:45. *Sono le tre e quarantacinque./Sono le tre e tre quarti./Sono le quattro meno un quarto./Manca un quarto alle quattro.*
forward *avanti*
forward (to) *inoltrare*
four *quattro*
It's four (o'clock). *Sono le quattro.*
fourteen *quattordici*
fourth *quarto*
frankly *francamente*
free *libero*
free time *tempo* (m.) *libero*
French *francese*
fresh *fresco*
fresh fruit *frutta* (f.) *fresca*
Friday *venerdì* (m., pl.)
from Monday to Friday *dal lunedì al venerdì*
friend *amico* (m.)/*amici* (m., pl.)
friendly *simpatico*
friendship *amicizia* (f.)
From *da, di*
from … to … (time periods) *dalle … alle …*
from Monday to Friday *dal lunedì al venerdì*
from 10:45 a.m. to 3:00 p.m. *dalle undici meno un quarto alle tre*
I'm from … *Sono di …*
starting from … *a partire da …*
Where are you from? (fml.)/**Where is he/she from?** *Di dov'è?*
Where are you from? (infml.) *Di dove sei?*
fruit *frutta* (f.)
fresh fruit *frutta fresca*
fuchsia *fucsia* (inv.)
full *pieno*
a full day *giornata* (f.) *piena*
full-time *a tempo pieno*
fun (to have fun) *divertirsi*
funny *divertente*
furniture *mobili* (m. pl.)

G

gain weight (to) *ingrassare*
gallery *galleria* (f.)
game *partita* (f.)
garage *garage* (m., pl.)
garden *giardino* (m.)

gardening *giardinaggio* (m.)
do gardening (to) *fare giardinaggio*
gas *gas* (m., pl. *gas*)
general *generale*
genetic *genetico* (m. pl. *genetici*)
gentleman *signore* (m.)
Germany *Germania* (f.)
get (to) *farsi*
get a divorce (to) *divorziarsi*
get bored (to) *annoiarsi*
get dressed (to) *vestirsi*
get married (to) *sposarsi*
get nervous (to) *agitarsi*
get ready (to) *prepararsi*
get up (to) *alzarsi*
gift *regalo* (m.)
girl (from 11 to 13 years old) *ragazzina* (f.)
girl (from 14 to 35 years old) *ragazza* (f.)
girlfriend *ragazza* (f.)
my girlfriend *la mia ragazza*
give (to) *dare*
given that … *visto che …*
gladly *volentieri*
glass *bicchiere* (m.)
gloves *guanti* (m. pl.)
gnome *gnomo* (m.)
go (to) *andare*
go … ing (to) *andare a …*
Go ahead. *Va' avanti.*
go back (to) *ritornare, tornare*
go camping (to) *fare il campeggio*
go for a ride (to) *fare un giro*
go for a walk (to) *fare un giro/fare un giro a piedi*
go hiking (to) *fare un'escursione/camminare in montagna*
go on a vacation (to) *fare una vacanza*
go out (to) *uscire*
go shopping (to) *fare la spesa/le spese*
go sightseeing (to) *visitare*
Go there. *Vacci.*
go too far (to) *esagerare*
go visit (to) *andare a trovare*
How's it going? *Come va?*
Let's go there. *Andiamoci.*
good *buono* (buon before masculine nouns except when they begin with s followed by another consonant, or with z)

Good afternoon. (from 1 p.m. to 6 p.m.) *Buon pomeriggio.*
Good evening. *Buona sera.*
Good luck. *Buona fortuna.*
Good morning. *Buon giorno.*
Good night. *Buona notte.*
Good-bye (infml.) *Arrivederci./Ciao.*
Good-bye (fml.) *ArrivederLa.*
Have a good day. *Buona giornata.*
Have a good dinner. *Buona cena.*
Have a good evening. *Buona serata.*
Have a good rest. *Buon riposo.*
Have a good trip. *Buon viaggio.*
Have a good walk. *Buona passeggiata.*
make a good impression (to) *fare bella figura*
nothing good to eat *niente di buono da mangiare*
grade *votazione* (f.), *voto* (m.)
   the first grade at elementary school *la prima elementare*
graduate (to) *laurearsi*
granddaughter *nipote* (m./f.)
grandfather *nonno* (m.)
grandmother *nonna* (f.)
grandson *nipote* (m./f.)
grapes *uva* (f.)
   a bunch of grapes *un grappolo* (m.) *d'uva*
grass *erba* (f.)
grate (to) *grattugiare*
Greece *Grecia* (f.)
Greek *greco*
green *verde*
greet each other (to) *salutarsi*
greeting *saluto* (m.)
gray *grigio*
grill *griglia* (f.)
   grilled/barbequed *alla brace*
   grilled fish *pesce* (m.) *alla griglia*
   grilled/barbequed meat *carne alla brace*
groceries *alimentari* (m. pl.)
   do grocery shopping (to) *fare la spesa/le spese*
   grocery store *negozio* (m.) *di alimentari*
ground (adjective) *terra* (inv.)
   ground floor *piano* (m.) *terra, pianterreno*
group *gruppo* (m.)
grow (to) *coltivare, crescere*
   grow old (to) *invecchiare*

guest *ospite* (m./f.)
guide *guida* (f.)
   guided tour *viaggio* (m.) *organizzato*
guitar *chitarra* (f.)
gym(nasium) *palestra* (f.)
gymnastics *ginnastica* (f.)

H

habitable *abitabile*
hail (to) *grandinare*
   It's hailing. *Grandina.*
hair *capelli* (m. pl.)
half, half hour *mezzo, mezz'ora*
   half seasons (spring and fall) *mezze stagioni* (f. pl.)
   in half an hour *fra mezz'ora*
   two and a half hours *due ore e mezzo*
hall *ingresso* (m.)
hand *mano* (f., pl. *mani*)
happen (to) *succedere*
happy *contento, felice*
   Happy anniversary. *Buon anniversario.*
   Happy birthday. *Buon compleanno.*
   Happy holidays. *Buone feste.*
   happy to … *contento di …*
harbor *porto* (m.)
harmful *nocivo*
hat *cappello* (m.)
have (to) *avere*
   have (food and drink) (to) *prendere*
   Have a good day. *Buona giornata.*
   Have a good dinner. *Buona cena.*
   Have a good evening. *Buona serata.*
   Have a good rest. *Buon riposo.*
   Have a good trip. *Buon viaggio.*
   Have a good walk. *Buona passeggiata.*
   have a nice big meal (to) *farsi una bella mangiata*
   have a tendency (to) *tendere*
   have breakfast (to) *fare colazione*
   have fun (to) *divertirsi*
   have to (to) *dovere*
he (subject pronoun) *lui*
   he/she who (relative pronoun) *chi*
head *testa* (f.)
health *salute* (f.)
health club *palestra* (f.)
healthy *sano*

hear (to) *sentire*
heart *cuore* (m.)
heart attack *infarto* (m.)
heat *caldo* (m.)
Hello. *Salve./Ciao.*
help *aiuto* (m.)
help (to) *aiutare*
 help … ing (to) *aiutare a …*
 help each other (to) *aiutarsi*
 How can I help you? (fml.) *Posso esserLe utile?*
her (direct object pronoun) *la*
 her (direct object, disjunctive pronoun) *lei*
 to her (indirect object pronoun) *le*
 to her (indirect object, disjunctive pronoun) *A lei*
 her (possessive) *suo/sua/suoi/sue, di lei*
 His/Her name is … *Si chiama …*
herbalist's shop *erboristeria* (f.)
here *ecco, qui, ci*
 here again *riecco*
 Here is … *Ecco …*
 Here we are again! *Rieccoci!*
herself *sé*
Hi. *Ciao.*
high school *liceo* (m.), *scuola* (f.) *superiore*
high school degree *maturità* (f.)
higher *superiore*
hike *escursione* (f.)
 go hiking (to) *fare un'escursione/camminare in montagna*
hill *collina* (f.)
him (direct object pronoun) *lo*
 him (direct object, disjunctive pronoun) *lui*
 to him (indirect object pronoun) *gli*
 to him (indirect object, disjunctive pronoun) *a lui*
himself *sé*
hip *fianco* (m.)
his *suo/sua/suoi/sue, di lui*
 His/Her name is … *Si chiama …*
history *storia* (f.)
hobby *hobby* (m., pl)
hockey *hockey* (m.)
 ice hockey *hockey su ghiaccio*
holiday *festa* (f.), *vacanza* (f.)
 Happy holidays. *Buone feste.*
home *casa* (f.)
 around the home *in giro per la casa*
 at home *a casa*

stay-at-home dad *casalingo* (m.)
stay-at-home mom *casalinga* (f.)
homeopathic *omeopatico* (m. pl. *omeopatici*)
homeopathy *omeopatia* (f.)
hometown *città* (f.) *natale*
honey *miele* (m.)
hope (to) *sperare*
 hope to … (to) *sperare di …*
hospital *ospedale* (m.)
hot (to be) *avere caldo*
 It's hot. *Fa caldo.*
hotel *albergo* (m.), *hotel* (m., pl. *hotel*)
hour *ora* (f.)
 half hour *mezzo*
 in half an hour *fra mezz'ora*
 shorter working hours *orario* (m.) *ridotto*
 two and a half hours *due ore e mezzo*
house *casa* (f.)
 around the house *in giro per la casa*
 small house *villetta* (f.)
how *come*
 how (exclamation) *che*
 How are you doing? (fml.) *Come sta?*
 How are you doing? (infml.) *Come stai?*
 How can I help you? (fml.) *Posso esserLe utile?*
 How do I look? *Come mi sta?*
 How is … ?/How are … ? *Com'è?/Come sono?*
 How long has it been since … ? *Da quanto tempo … ?*
 how many/much *quanto*
 How much does it cost? *Quanto costa?*
 How nice!/How beautiful! *Che bello!*
 How old are you? (infml.) *Quanti anni hai?*
 How's it going? *Come va?*
 How's it possible!/How can this be! *Ma come!*
 know how (to) *sapere*
however *però*
hug (to) *abbracciarsi*
hundred *cento*
hunger *fame* (f.)
hungry (to be) *avere fame*
hurricane *uragano* (m.)
hurry *fretta* (f.)
 in a hurry *in fretta*
 in a hurry (to be) *avere fretta*

husband *marito* (m.)
hygienic *igienico*

I

I *io*
ice *ghiaccio* (m.)
ice cream *gelato* (m.)
ice hockey *hockey* (m.) *su ghiaccio*
idea *idea* (f.)
  no idea *nessuna idea*
if *se*
ill *ammalato*
illustration *figura* (f.)
imagine (to) *immaginare*
immediately *subito*
imperfect *imperfetto* (m.)
important *importante*
impression (to make a good impression) *fare bella figura*
in *fra, tra, in, a*
  check in (to) *registrarsi (all'hotel)*
  come in (to) *entrare*
  in a few days *fra qualche giorno*
  in a hurry *in fretta*
  in advance *prima*
  in any case *comunque*
  in any event *in ogni caso*
  in fact *infatti*
  in five minutes *tra cinque minuti*
  in forty-five minutes *fra tre quarti d'ora*
  in front *davanti*
  in front of … *davanti a … /di fronte a …*
  in great shape *in ottima forma*
  in half an hour *fra mezz'ora*
  in love *innamorato/a*
  in order that *affinché*
  in person *di persona*
  in the afternoon, from 1 to 5 p.m. *di pomeriggio*
  in the city *in centro*
  in the evening, from 6 to 11 p.m. *di sera*
  in the fall *in/d'autunno*
  in the meantime *nel frattempo*
  in the morning, from 4 to 11 a.m. *di mattina*
  in the office *in ufficio*
  in the spring *in primavera*
  in the style of *a + definite article*
  in the summer *d'estate*
  in the world *del mondo*
  in this period *in questo periodo*
  in winter *d'inverno*
  live in … (to) *vivere a …*
  the way in which … *il modo in cui …*
indicate (to) *indicare*
influence *influenza* (f.)
ingredient *ingrediente* (m.)
inherit (to) *ereditare*
insist (to) *insistere*
instead *invece*
institute *istituto* (m.)
intellectual *intellettivo*
intelligence quotient (IQ) *quoziente* (m.) *intellettivo*
intelligent *intelligente*
intention *proposito* (m.)
interest *interesse* (m.)
interest (to) *interessare*
interesting *interessante*
  anything interesting/cool to do *qualcosa di bello da fare*
  very interesting *interessantissimo*
intermission *intervallo* (m.)
internet *internet* (m.)
internship *stage* (m., pl stage)
interrupt (to) *interrompere*
intersection *incrocio* (m.)
interview *colloquio* (m.), *intervista* (f.)
  job interview *colloquio di lavoro*
intestine *intestino* (m.)
introduce (to) *presentare*
introduction *presentazione* (f.)
invite (to) *invitare*
iron *ferro* (m.) *(metal), ferro da stiro (appliance)*
ironing board *asse* (f.) *da stiro*
island *isola* (f.)
it (direct object pronoun) *lo* (m.), *la* (f.)
  it (direct object, disjunctive pronoun) *lui* (m.), *lei* (f.)
  to it (indirect object pronoun) *gli* (m.), *le* (f.)
  to it (indirect object, disjunctive pronoun) *a lui* (m.), *a lei* (f.)
  about it *ci, ne*
  How long has it been since … ? *Da quanto tempo … ?*
  It hurts. *Fa male.*
  It's bad. (weather) *Fa brutto.*

It's beautiful. (weather) *Fa bello.*
It's better. *Va meglio.*
It's cloudy. *È nuvoloso.*
It's cold. *Fa freddo.*
It's 11:15 a.m. *Sono le undici e un quarto di mattina.*
It's foggy. *C'è nebbia.*
It's four (o'clock). *Sono le quattro.*
It's hailing. *Grandina.*
It's hot. *Fa caldo.*
It's midnight. *È mezzanotte.*
It's noon. *È mezzogiorno.*
It's 1:00 a.m. *È l'una di notte.*
It's raining. *Piove.*
It's snowing. *Nevica.*
It's stormy. *C'è un temporale.*
It's sunny. *C'è il sole.*
It's three (o'clock). *Sono le tre.*
It's 3:15. *Sono le tre e quindici.*
It's 3:45. *Sono le tre e quarantacinque./Sono le tre e tre quarti./Sono le quattro meno un quarto./Manca un quarto alle quattro.*
It's 3:30. *Sono le tre e trenta.*
It's time to … *È ora di …*
It's two (o'clock). *Sono le due.*
It's windy. *C'è vento./Tira vento.*
of it, on it *ci, ne*
What time is it? *Che ora è?/Che ore sono?*
Italian *italiano*
Italy *Italia* (f.)
its *suo/sua/suoi/sue*
itself *sé*

J

jacket *giacca* (f.)
January *gennaio* (m.)
jeans *blue jeans* (m. pl.)
job *lavoro* (m.)
  job interview *colloquio* (m.) *di lavoro*
  part-time job *lavoro part-time*
  steady job *lavoro fisso*
  summer job *lavoro temporaneo*
jog (to) *fare il footing*
jogging *footing* (m.)
joke *barzelletta* (f.)
journal *rivista* (f.)
journalist *giornalista* (m./f.)
juice *succo* (m.)

July *luglio* (m.)
jump (to) *saltare*
  jump rope (to) *saltare la corda*
June *giugno* (m.)
just *appena, proprio, solo*

K

keyboard *tastiera* (f.)
kidney *rene* (m.)
kilo *chilo* (m.)
kilometer *chilometro*
kind (adjective) *gentile*
kind (noun) *tipo* (m.)
kiss (to) *baciarsi*
kitchen *cucina* (f.)
  eat-in kitchen *cucina abitabile*
knee *ginocchio* (m.)
  knees *ginocchia/ginocchi* (f./m. pl.)
knife *coltello* (m.)
know (to) *sapere* (a fact, how), *conoscere* (a person)
  I know. *Lo so.*
  I don't know. *Non lo so.*
  know each other (to) *conoscersi*

L

lady *signora*
lake *lago* (m.)
  at the lake *al lago*
lamp *lampada* (f.)
lamp post *lampione* (m.)
land *terra* (f.)
language *lingua* (f.)
  foreign language *lingua straniera*
large *grosso; numeroso* (family)
  large dinner *cena* (f.) *abbondante*
  large family *famiglia* (f.) *numerosa*
lasagna *lasagne* (f. pl.)
last *scorso, ultimo*
  last night *ieri sera*
  last week *settimana* (f.) *scorsa*
  last year *anno* (m.) *scorso*
last (to) *durare*
late *tardi*
  late (to be) *essere in ritardo*
until late *fino a tardi*
Latin American *latinoamericano*
laundry *bucato* (m.), *lavanderia* (f.)

do the laundry (to) *fare il bucato*
laundry detergent *detersivo* (m.) *per il bucato*
lawyer *avvocato* (m.)
learn (to) *apprendere, imparare*
leather *pelle* (f.)
made out of leather *di pelle*
leave (to) *partire, lasciare*
left *sinistra* (f.)
left (hand) *manca* (f.)
on/to the left *(a) sinistra*
left-handed *mancino*
leg *gamba* (f.)
Break a leg! (lit. In the mouth of the wolf!) *In bocca al lupo!*
Thank you. (lit. May the wolf die.) *Crepi il lupo. (in response to In bocca al lupo!)*
less *meno*
less … than *meno … di/che*
lesson *lezione* (f.)
let (to) *lasciare*
Let me see. *Fammi vedere.*
Let's go there. *Andiamoci.*
letter *lettera* (f.)
lettuce *lattuga* (f.)
level *livello* (m.)
library *biblioteca* (f.)
lie *bugia* (f.)
life *vita* (f.)
everyday life *vita quotidiana*
light *leggero*
light sweater *maglioncino* (m.)
lightning *lampo* (m.), *fulmine* (m.)
like (to) *piacere, amare*
I like … *Mi piace/piacciono …* (sg./pl.)
I would like … *Vorrei …*
likely *probabile*
linen *lino* (m.)
made out of linen *di lino*
list *lista* (f.)
wine list *lista dei vini*
listen to (to) *ascoltare*
liter *litro* (m.)
literature *letteratura* (f.)
little *poco/a* (m./f.) (noun); *poco* (adjective)
a little *un poco/un po'*
live (to) *vivere, abitare*
live in … (to) *vivere a …*
liver *fegato* (m.)

living room *salone* (m.), *soggiorno* (m.)
lobster *aragosta* (f.)
lonely *solo*
long *lungo*
for a very long time *da una vita*
How long has it been since … ? *Da quanto tempo … ?*
long distance *di fondo*
long time *molto tempo*
take a nice long nap (to) *farsi una bella dormita*
look at (to) *guardare*
How do I look? *Come mi sta?*
look for (to) *cercare*
looking for … (to be) *essere in cerca di …*
lose (to) *perdere*
lose weight (to) *dimagrire*
lottery *lotteria* (f.)
loudly *forte* (adverb)
Love *amore* (m.)
in love *innamorato/a*
love stories *storie* (f. pl.) *d'amore*
love (to) *amare*
I love you. *Ti voglio bene. Ti amo.*
low *basso*
luck *fortuna* (f.)
Good luck. *Buona fortuna.*
lucky *beato, fortunato*
Lucky you. *Beati voi.* (pl.)
Lucky you! *Beato te!*
lunch *pranzo* (m.)
lung *polmone* (m.)

M

machine *macchina* (f.)
magazine *rivista* (f.)
mail *posta* (f.) (noun); *postale* (adjective)
e-mail *posta elettronica*
send an e-mail (to) *mandare un'email/una mail*
main course *secondo (piatto)* (m.)
as main course *di secondo*
make (to) *fare*
made from plastic *di plastica*
made out of cashmere *di cachemire*
made out of corduroy *di velluto a coste*
made out of leather *di pelle*
made out of linen *di lino*

made out of silk *di seta*
make a good impression (to) *fare bella figura*
make friends (to) *fare amicizia*
make noise (to) *fare rumore*
male *maschio* (m.)
man *uomo* (m.)/*uomini* (pl.)
  men's suit *abito da uomo*
manage (to) *riuscire*
  manage to . . . (to) *riuscire a . . .*
manner *modo* (m.)
many *molto* (adjective); *molto/a* (m./f.) (noun)
  as many . . . as *tanto . . . quanto*
  how many *quanto*
  so many *tanto* (adjective); *tanto/a* (m./f.) (noun)
  too many *troppo* (adjective); *troppo/a* (m./f.)
    (noun)
map *cartina* (f.), *mappa* (f.), *piantina* (f.)
marathon *maratona* (f.)
March *marzo* (m.)
march *sfilata* (f.)
marital status *stato civile*
market *mercato* (m.)
married *sposato/a*
marry . . . (someone) (to) *sposarsi con . . .*
  get married (to) *sposarsi*
  He/She is getting married. *Si sposa.*
marvelous *meraviglioso*
math *matematica* (f.)
matrimonial *matrimoniale*
May *maggio* (m.)
May I . . . ? *Posso . . . ?*
maybe *forse*
mayor *sindaco* (m.)
me (direct object pronoun) *mi*
  me (direct object, disjunctive pronoun) *me*
  to me (indirect object pronoun) *mi*
  to me (indirect object, disjunctive pronoun) *a me*
meadow *prato* (m.)
means *mezzo* (m.)
  means of transportation *mezzo di trasporto*
meantime *frattempo*
  in the meantime *nel frattempo*
measure (to) *misurare*
Meat *carne* (f.)
  grilled/barbecued meat *carne alla brace*
  meat sauce *ragù* (m., pl.)
  sliced cold meat *affettato* (m.)
mechanic *meccanico* (m.)/*meccanici* (pl.)

medical doctor *medico* (m.)
medicine *medicina* (f.)
  medicine cabinet *armadietto* (m.)
meet (to) *vedere* (a person), *incontrare* (a person
  casually), *conoscere* (a person for the first time)
  meet each other (to) *incontrarsi*
  Pleased to meet you. *Piacere.*
  Pleased to meet you, too. *Piacere mio.*
  Very pleased to meet you! *Molto piacere!*
meeting *riunione* (f.)
  meeting room *sala* (f.) *delle riunioni*
melon *melone* (m.)
memory *memoria* (f.)
menu *menù* (m.)
Merry Christmas. *Buon Natale.*
message *messaggio* (m.)
  instant message *messaggio immediato*
meter *metro* (m.)
metro, subway *metrò* (m. in Milan/f. in Rome)
microwave *microonda* (f.)
  microwave oven *forno* (m.) *a microonde*
midnight *mezzanotte* (f.)
  around midnight *intorno a mezzanotte*
  It's midnight. *È mezzanotte.*
Might as well . . . *Tanto vale . . .*
Milan *Milano* (f.)
milk *latte* (m.)
million *milione* (m.)/*milioni* (pl.)
  a million dollars *milione di dollari*
mineral *minerale*
  mineral water *acqua* (f.) *minerale*
  still mineral water *acqua minerale naturale*
  sparkling mineral water *acqua minerale
    frizzante*
minute *minuto* (m.)
  in five minutes *tra cinque minuti*
  in forty-five minutes *fra tre quarti d'ora*
mirror *specchio* (m.)
mix (to) *mescolare*
mixed *misto*
  mixed cold cuts *affettati* (m. pl.) *misti*
  mixed salad *insalata* (f.) *mista*
model (fashion) *modello/a* (m./f.)
modem *modem* (m.)
modern *moderno*
  modern art *arte* (f.) *moderna*
mom *mamma* (f.)
  stay-at-home mom *casalinga* (f.)

moment *momento* (m.)

Monday *lunedì* (m., pl.)
   from Monday to Friday *dal lunedì al venerdì*
   on Mondays *il lunedì*

money *denaro* (m.), *soldi* (m. pl.)

monitor *monitor* (m.), *schermo* (m.), *video* (m.)

month *mese* (m.)
   a month ago *un mese fa*
   next month *mese prossimo*

monument *monumento* (m.)

moon *luna* (f.)

more *più*
   more/-er ... than *più ... di/che*
   no more *non ... più*

moreover *inoltre*

morning *mattina* (f.)
   every morning *tutte le mattine*
   Good morning. *Buon giorno.*
   in the morning, from 4 to 11 a.m. *di mattina*

mosque *moschea* (f.)

mother *madre* (f.)

mother-in-law *suocera* (f.)

motorbike *motocicletta* (f.), *moto* (f., pl.)

mountain *montagna* (f.)
   to the mountains *in montagna*

mouse *mouse* (m.) (computer)

mouse pad *tappetino* (m.)

mouth *bocca* (f.)

move (to) *muovere, trasferirsi*
   move (to a new house) (to) *traslocare, fare il
      trasloco*

movie *film* (m., pl.)
   action movies *film d'azione*
   movie director *regista* (m./f.)
   movie theater *cinema* (m., pl.: cinema)

Mr. *signore* (m.)

Mrs. *signora* (f.)

much *molto* (adjective); *molto/a* (m./f.) (noun)
   as much ... as *tanto ... quanto*
   how much *quanto*
   How much does it cost? *Quanto costa?*
   so much *tanto* (adjective); *tanto/a* (m./f.) (noun),
      tanto (adverb)
   too much *troppo* (adjective); *troppo/a* (m./f.)
      (noun)

municipal building *municipio* (m.)

muscle *muscolo* (m.)

museum *museo* (m.)

mushroom *fungo* (m.)

music *musica* (f.)
   classical music *musica classica*
   pop music *musica pop*

musician *musicista* (m./f.)

must *dovere*

my *mio/mia/miei/mie*
   My name is ... *Mi chiamo ...*

N

name *nome* (m.)
   His/Her name is ... *Si chiama ...*
   My name is ... *Mi chiamo ...*

named (to be) *chiamarsi*

nap *pisolino* (m.)
   take a nap (to) *fare un pisolino*
   take a nice long nap (to) *farsi una bella
      dormita*

Naples *Napoli* (f.)

native *natale*

natural *naturale*

nature *natura* (f.)

naughty *cattivo*

near *vicino*
   near ... *vicino a ...*
   near there *lì vicino*

nearby *qui vicino*

necessary *necessario*

neck *collo* (m.)

necklace *collana* (f.)

need *bisogno* (m.)
   need (to) *essere nel bisogno*
   need ... (to) *avere bisogno di ...*

neighborhood *quartiere* (m.)

nephew *nipote* (m./f.)

nervous *nervoso*
   get nervous (to) *agitarsi*

never *mai* (in negative sentences)
   Never! *Mai!*
   never again *mai più*

new *nuovo*

news *notizie* (f. pl.), *giornale radio* (m.) (on the
   radio), *telegiornale* (m.) (on TV), *TG* (m.) (on TV)

newspaper *giornale* (m.)

next *prossimo*
   next month *mese* (m.) *prossimo*
   next week *prossima settimana* (f.)

nice *simpatico, bravo*

have a nice big meal (to) *farsi una bella mangiata*

How nice! *Che bello!*

take a nice long nap (to) *farsi una bella dormita*

niece *nipote* (m./f.)

night *notte* (f.)

at night, from midnight to 3 a.m. *di notte*

Good night. *Buona notte.*

last night *ieri sera*

nine *nove*

nineteen *diciannove*

ninth *nono*

ninety *novanta*

no *no* (adverb); *nessuno* (adjective)

no idea *nessuna idea*

no longer *non ... più*

no more *non ... più*

nobody *nessuno/a* (m./f.)

noise *rumore* (m.)

make noise (to) *fare rumore*

noisy *rumoroso*

none *nessuno/a* (m./f.)

noon *mezzogiorno* (m.)

It's noon. *È mezzogiorno.*

normal *normale*

normally *normalmente*

Norwegian *norvegese* (m./f.)

nose *naso* (m.)

not *non*

not ... at all *non ... affatto*

Not bad. *Così, così.*

not even *neanche, nemmeno*

notebook *quaderno* (m.)

nothing *niente, nulla*

nothing good to eat *niente di buono da mangiare*

notice (to) *notare*

novel *romanzo* (m.)

contemporary novels *romanzi* (pl.) *contemporanei*

November *novembre* (m.)

now *adesso*

by now *ormai*

right now *in questo momento*

number *numero* (m.)

numerous *numeroso*

nurse *infermiere/a* (m./f.)

O

O.K. *d'accordo*

obligation *impegno* (m.)

obvious *ovvio*

ocean *oceano* (m.)

October *ottobre* (m.)

of *di*

first of all *prima di tutto*

means of transportation *mezzo* (m.) *di trasporto*

of all *di tutti*

of it *ci, ne*

of them *ne*

out of town *fuori città*

pair of shoes *paio* (m.) *di scarpe*

speaking of ... *a proposito di ...*

There are seven of us. *Siamo in sette.*

There are three of them. *Ce ne sono tre.*

variety of choices *varietà* (f.) *di scelta*

works of art *opere* (f. pl.) *d'arte*

offer (to) *offrire*

office *ufficio* (m.), *studio* (m.)

in the office *in ufficio*

often *spesso*

oil *olio* (m.)

old *vecchio*

grow old (to) *invecchiare*

How old are you? *Quanti anni hai?*

I am ... years old. *Ho ... anni.*

older *maggiore*

olive *oliva* (f.)

on *in, su*

on business *per lavoro*

on foot *a piedi*

on it *ci*

on Mondays *il lunedì*

on the contrary *anzi*

on the left *a sinistra*

on the right *a destra*

on time (to be) *essere in orario, essere puntuale*

on vacation *in ferie, in vacanza*

one *un/uno* (in front of s + consonant, z, ps, gn)/*una*

one (impersonal pronoun) *si*

one (number) *uno*

It's 1:00 a.m. *È l'una di notte.*

the one who, whoever (relative pronoun) *chi*

oneself *sé*
onion *cipolla* (f.)
only *soltanto, solo*
open *aperto*
  open all day *orario* (m.) *continuato*
open (to) *aprire*
  open a file (to) *aprire un documento/file*
opera *opera* (f.)
opposite *di fronte*
or *o*
orange *arancione* (inv.) *(color); arancia* (f.) *(fruit)*
orchard *orto* (m.)
order *ordine* (m.)
  in order that *affinché*
order (to) *ordinare*
organize (to) *organizzare*
osso buco *ossobuco* (m.)
other *altro*
our *nostro/nostra/nostri/nostre*
out of town *fuori città*
outdoors *all'aperto*
outside *fuori*
oven *forno* (m.)
  microwave oven *forno a microonde*
over *su*
overweight *sovrappeso* (m., pl.)
overweight (to be) *essere in sovrappeso*

P

p.m. *di pomeriggio, di sera*
pack (a suitcase) (to) *fare le valige/valigie*
page *pagina* (f.)
pain *dolore* (m.)
  have a pain in … (to) *avere un dolore a … /*
    avere male a …
painting *quadro* (m.)
pair *paio* (m.)
  pair of shoes *paio di scarpe*
pajamas *pigiama* (m.)
pan *pentola* (f.)
panorama *panorama* (m.)
pants *pantaloni* (m. pl.)
  pant suit *tailleur* (m.) *pantalone*
paper *carta* (f.)
  toilet paper *carta igienica*
parade *sfilata* (f.)
parent *genitore/trice* (m./f.)
Paris *Parigi* (f.)

park *parco* (m.)
park (to) *parcheggiare*
Parmesan cheese *parmigiano* (m.)
part *parte* (f.)
participate (to) *partecipare*
part-time *part-time*
  part-time job *lavoro* (m.) *part-time*
party *festa* (f.)
  have a party (to) *dare una festa*
pass (an exam) (to) *passare, essere promosso*
passion *passione* (f.)
  passion for … *passione per …*
passport *passaporto* (m.)
past (tense)
  past perfect *passato* (m.)
trapassato (m.) prossimo
pasta *pasta* (f.)
path *viale* (m.), *via* (f.)
patience *pazienza* (f.)
patient *paziente* (m./f.)
pay (to) *pagare*
  pay attention (to) *fare attenzione*
  Pay attention! *Sta' attento!*
peach *pesca* (f.)
pear *pera* (f.)
pediatrician *pediatra* (m./f.)
peel (to) *sbucciare*
penne (pasta) *penne* (f. pl.)
penthouse *attico* (m., pl. attici)
people *gente* (f.), *persone* (pl.)
people (impersonal pronoun) *si*
pepper (spice) *pepe* (m.) *(spice); peperone* (m.)
  (vegetable)
perfect *perfetto*
performance *spettacolo* (m.)
perfume *profumo* (m.)
perhaps *magari, forse*
period *periodo* (m.)
  in this period *in questo periodo*
permanent *fisso*
person *persona* (f.)
  athletic person *persona sportiva*
  in person *di persona*
personal information *dati* (m. pl.) *anagrafici*
pharmacy *farmacia* (f.)
photograph *foto* (f., pl.), *fotografia* (f.)
  take a picture (to) *fare una foto/fotografia*
photography *fotografia* (f.)

pianist *pianista* (m./f.)
piano *pianoforte* (m.)
 play the piano (to) *suonare il pianoforte*
pick up (to) *raccogliere*
picture *quadro* (m.) *(painting); foto* (f., pl.),
 fotografia (f.) *(photograph)*
 take a picture (to) *fare una foto/fotografia*
piece *pezzo* (m.)
pillow *cuscino* (m.)
pineapple *ananas* (m., plural *ananas)*
pink *rosa* (inv.)
place *luogo* (m.), *posto* (m.)
plan (to) *progettare*
planet *pianeta* (m.)
plant *pianta* (f.)
plant (to) *piantare*
plastic *plastica* (f.)
 made from plastic *di plastica*
plate *piatto* (m.)
play (theater) *spettacolo* (m.)
play (to) *giocare (sport, game); praticare (sport);*
 suonare (instrument)
 play a sport (to) *praticare uno sport*
 play cards (to) *giocare a carte*
 play tennis (to) *giocare a tennis*
 play the piano (to) *suonare il pianoforte*
player *giocatore/trice* (m./f.) *(person); lettore*
 (m.) *(machine)*
 CD player *lettore di cd (ci-di)*
 DVD player *dvd* (m.)
playground *parco giochi*
pleasant *piacevole*
Please. *Per favore.*
pleasing (to someone) (to be) *piacere*
 Pleased to meet you. *Piacere.*
 Pleased to meet you, too. *Piacere mio.*
 Very pleased to meet you! *Molto piacere!*
plentiful *abbondante*
plumber *idraulico/a* (m./f.)
plural *plurale* (m.)
poem *poema* (m.)
poker *poker* (m., pl.)
policeman *poliziotto* (m.)
 policewoman *donna* (f.) *poliziotto*
pond *stagno* (m.)
pool *biliardo* (m.)
pop *pop* (inv.)
 pop music *musica* (f.) *pop*

pork *maiale* (m.)
 baked pork *maiale al forno*
 pork chop *braciola* (f.) *di maiale*
possessive *possessivo*
possible *possibile*
 How's it possible! *Ma come!*
post office *ufficio* (m.) *postale*
pot *pentola* (f.)
potato *patata* (f.)
pour (to) *versare*
powder (talcum) *borotalco* (m.)
practice sports (to) *fare sport*
prefer (to) *preferire*
prepare (to) *preparare*
preposition *preposizione* (f.)
present (adjective) *presente*
 present perfect *passato* (m.) *prossimo*
 present subjunctive *congiuntivo* (m.) *presente*
present (to) *presentare*
pressure *pressione* (f.)
pretty *carino*
price *prezzo* (m.)
printer *stampante* (f.)
private *privato*
probably *probabilmente*
problem *problema* (m.)
product *prodotto* (m.)
production (theater) *messinscena* (f.)
professional
professional school *professionale*
istituto (m.) *tecnico*
professor *professore/essa* (m./f.)
program *trasmissione* (f.), *programma* (m.)
 television program *trasmissione televisiva*
prohibit (to) *proibire*
promise (to) *promettere*
 promise to ... (do something)
  (to) *promettere di ...*
promote (to) *promuovere*
pronoun *pronome* (m.)
provided that ... *a patto che ... / a condizione*
 che ... / purché
province *provincia* (f.)
psychiatrist *psichiatra* (m./f.)
psychologist *psicologo* (m./f.)
publish (to) *pubblicare*
punctual *puntuale*
purple *viola* (inv.)

purse *borsa* (f.)
put (to) *mettere*
put things away (to) *mettere in ordine*
put on (to) *mettersi*
He/She puts on … (to) *Si mette …*

Q

quarter *quarto* (m.)
question *domanda* (f.)
  ask a question (to) *fare una domanda*
quick *veloce*
quickly *velocemente, in fretta*
quit (to) *smettere*
quit … ing (to) *smettere di …*
quotient *quoziente* (m.)
  intelligence quotient (IQ) *quoziente
  intellettivo*

R

rain *pioggia* (f.)
rain (to) *piovere*
  It's raining. *Piove.*
raise (to) *crescere*
rarely *raramente*
rather *piuttosto*
ravioli *ravioli* (m. pl.)
razor *rasoio* (m.)
reach (to) *raggiungere*
read (to) *leggere*
reader *lettore* (m.)
ready *pronto*
  get ready (to) *prepararsi*
  ready to … *pronto per …*
really *veramente, davvero, proprio*
reason *motivo* (m.), *ragione* (f.)
  the reason why … *il motivo per cui … / la
  ragione per cui …*
receive (to) *ricevere*
reception desk *accettazione* (f.), *reception* (f., pl.)
recipe *ricetta* (f.)
red *rosso*
  red wine *vino* (m.) *rosso*
reduced *ridotto*
refrigerator *frigorifero* (m.) *(frigo)*
regret (to) *pentirsi*
regularly *regolarmente*
reject (to) *bocciare*
relative *parente* (m./f.)

relax (to) *rilassarsi*
remain *rimanere*
remember (to) *ricordare*
  remember to … (do something)
    (to) *ricordarsi di …*
removal *trasloco* (m.)
Renaissance *Rinascimento* (m.) (noun);
  rinascimentale (adjective)
rent (to) *affittare*
repent (to) *pentirsi*
reply (to) *rispondere*
report card *scheda* (f.)
rescue *soccorso* (m.)
research *indagine* (f.)
researcher *ricercatore/trice* (m./f.)
reservation *prenotazione* (f.)
reserve (to) *prenotare*
residence *residenza* (f.)
respectively *rispettivamente*
rest *riposo* (m.)
  Have a good rest. *Buon riposo.*
restaurant *ristorante* (m.)
  family style restaurant *trattoria* (f.)
retired *pensionato/a* (m./f.)
return (to) *ritornare, tornare*
rib *costa* (f.)
rice *riso* (m.)
rich *ricco*
ride a bike (to) *andare in bicicletta*
right *destra* (f.) (noun); *vero, giusto* (adjective)
  on/to the right *(a) destra*
  right (to be) *avere ragione*
  right now *in questo momento*
ring *anello* (m.)
ring (a bell) (to) *suonare*
river *fiume* (m.)
road *strada* (f.)
roast *arrosto*
roast pork *maiale* (m.) *al forno*
rock *roccia* (f.)
romantic *romantico* (m., pl. *romantici*)
Rome *Roma* (f.)
room *sala* (f.), *camera* (f.), *stanza* (f.)
  bedroom *camera* (f.), *camera da letto, stanza*
    (f.) *da letto*
  dining room *sala da pranzo*
  double room (one queen-size bed) *camera
    matrimoniale*

double room (two twin-size beds) *camera doppia*
emergency room *pronto soccorso* (m.)
living room *salone* (m.), *soggiorno* (m.)
meeting room *sala delle riunioni*
single room (one twin bed) *camera singola*
study (room) *studio* (m.)
rope *corda* (f.)
  jump rope (to) *saltare la corda*
rug *tappeto* (m.)
run (to) *correre*
rural *rurale*
rushed *affrettato*

S

sad *triste*
sail *vela* (f.)
sail (to) *andare in barca a vela*
sailing *vela* (f.)
salad *insalata* (f.)
  mixed salad *insalata mista*
salary *salario* (m.)
salesman *venditore* (m.)
saleswoman *venditrice* (f.)
salt *sale* (m.)
same *stesso, pari* (inv.)
  at the same time *allo stesso tempo*
sand *sabbia* (f.)
sandwich *panino* (m.)
Sardinia *Sardegna* (f.)
satisfied *soddisfatto*
Saturday *sabato* (m.)
sauté (to) *rosolare*
save (to) *salvare*
  save a document (to) *salvare un documento*
say (to) *dire*
scare (to) *impaurire*
scarf *sciarpa* (f.) (long), *foulard* (m.) (square)
scary (to be) *fare paura*
scholastic *scolastico* (m. pl. *scolastici*)
school *scuola* (f.)
  high school *liceo* (m.), *scuola* (f.) *superiore*
  professional school *istituto* (m.) *tecnico*
  the first grade at elementary school *la prima elementare*
scientist *ricercatore/trice* (m./f.)
screen *monitor* (m.), *schermo* (m.), *video* (m.)
sculpture *scultura* (f.)

sea *mare* (m.)
seaside *mare* (m.)
season *stagione* (f.)
  half seasons (spring and fall) *mezze stagioni*
second *secondo*
  second-born *secondogenito/a* (m./f.)
secretary *segretario/a* (m./f.)
see (to) *vedere*
  Let me see. *Fammi vedere.*
  see each other (to) *vedersi*
  See you later. *A dopo.*
  See you soon. *A presto.*
seem (to) *sembrare*
send (to) *inviare, mandare, spedire*
  send a file (to) *inviare un documento/file*
  send an e-mail (to) *mandare un'email/una mail*
September *settembre* (m.)
serious *grave*
serve (to) *servire*
set (a table) (to) *apparecchiare*
settings *ambientazione* (f.)
seven *sette*
  at seven thirty (7:30) *alle sette e mezza*
  by seven (o'clock) *per le sette*
  There are seven of us. *Siamo in sette.*
seventeen *diciassette*
seventh *settimo*
seventy *settanta*
several *parecchio* (adjective); *parecchio/a* (m./f.) (noun)
shampoo *shampo* (m.)
shape *forma* (f.)
  in great shape *in ottima forma*
share (to) *condividere, avere in comune*
shave (to) *farsi la barba, radersi*
shaving cream *crema* (f.) *da barba*
she (subject pronoun) *lei*
  he/she who (relative pronoun) *chi*
shelf *scaffale* (m.)
  book shelf *scaffale (dei libri)*
shine (to) *splendere*
shirt *camicia* (f.)
shoes *scarpe* (f. pl.)
  pair of shoes *paio* (m.) *di scarpe*
  shoe store *negozio* (m.) *di scarpe*
  tennis shoes *scarpe da tennis*
shop (to) *fare spese*

shopping *spesa* (f.)
  go shopping (to), do grocery shopping
    (to) *fare la spesa/le spese*
shopping mall *centro acquisti, centro*
commerciale
short *corto, basso*
  short trip *gita* (f.)
  shorter working hours *orario* (m.) *ridotto*
shoulder *spalla* (f.)
show (to) *mostrare, indicare, fare vedere*
shower *doccia* (f.)
  take a shower (to) *fare la doccia*
shrimp *gambero* (m.), *gamberetto* (m.)
Sicily *Sicilia* (f.)
sick *malato, ammalato*
side dish *contorno* (m.)
  as a side dish *di/per contorno*
sidewalk *marciapiede* (m.)
sightseeing (to go sightseeing) *visitare*
silent *silenzioso*
silk *seta* (f.)
  made out of silk *di seta*
silverware *posate* (f. pl.)
similar *simile*
simple *piano*
sin *peccato* (m.)
since *da*
  How long has it been since … ? *Da quanto*
    tempo … ?
  since … *visto che …*
  since always *da una vita*
sing (to) *cantare*
single *singolo*
  single (man) *celibe* (m.)
  single (woman) *nubile* (f.)
  single room (one twin bed) *camera* (f.)
    singola
sink (kitchen) *lavandino* (m.) (kitchen); *lavabo*
(m.) (wash basin)
sister *sorella* (f.)
site *sito* (m.)
situation *condizione* (f.)
six *sei*
sixteen *sedici*
sixth *sesto*
sixty *sessanta*
size *taglia* (f.) (dresses, pants), *misura* (f.) (shirts),
numero (m.) (shoes)

ski (to) *sciare*
skiing *sci* (m., pl.)
  alpine skiing *sci alpino*
  cross-country skiing *sci di fondo*
skillful *bravo*
skin *pelle* (f.)
skirt *gonna* (f.)
sky *cielo* (m.)
sleep *sonno* (m.)
sleep (to) *dormire*
sleepy *insonnolito*
  sleepy (to be) *avere sonno*
slice (to) *affettare, tagliare*
  sliced cold meat *affettato* (m.)
slowly *lentamente, piano*
small *piccolo*
smog *smog* (m.)
smoked *affumicato*
smooth *piano*
snack *spuntino* (m.)
sneakers *scarpe* (f. pl.) *da ginnastica, scarpe da*
  tennis, sneakers (m. pl.)
snow *neve* (f.)
snow (to) *nevicare*
  It's snowing. *Nevica.*
so *così, tanto, allora, quindi*
  I don't think so. *Non credo.*
  so … as *così … come/sia … che*
  so many *tanto/a* (m./f.) (noun); *tanto* (adjective)
  so much *tanto/a* (m./f.) (noun); *tanto* (adjective);
    tanto (adverb)
  So so. *Così, così.*
  so that *affinché*
soap (bar) *saponetta* (f.)
soccer *calcio* (m.)
social *sociale*
socks *calze* (f. pl.)
soda *bibita* (f.)
sofa *sofà* (m.), *divano* (m.)
soft drink *bibita* (f.)
softly *piano*
some *alcuni/e, qualche, certo, di + definite article*
someone *qualcuno*
something *qualcosa*
  something to drink *qualcosa da bere*
sometimes *qualche volta, a volte*
son *figlio* (m.)
song *canzone* (f.)

soon *presto*
  See you soon. *A presto.*
sooner *prima*
Sorry (I'm sorry.) *Mi dispiace./Scusami.*
soup *minestra* (f.)
sour *amaro*
spacious *spazioso, ampio*
spaghetti *spaghetti* (m. pl.)
sparkling wine *spumante* (m.)
spa *terme* (f. pl.)
speak (to) *parlare*
  speak Chinese (to) *parlare cinese*
  speaking of ... *a proposito di ...*
speech *discorso* (m.)
spend (to) *spendere*
spoon *cucchiaio* (m.)
sport *sport* (m., pl.)
  play a sport (to) *praticare uno sport*
  practice sports (to) *fare sport*
  watch sports on TV (to) *guardare lo sport in/
   alla televisione*
spring *primavera* (f.)
  in the spring *in primavera*
square *piazza* (f.)
stadium *stadio* (m.)
staff *staff* (m.)
staircase *scala* (f.)
stairs *scale* (f.)
star *stella* (f.)
starting from ... *a partire da ...*
state *stato* (m.)
station *stazione* (f.)
  train station *stazione (dei treni)*
stay (to) *restare, stare*
  stay-at-home dad *casalingo* (m.)
  stay-at-home mom *casalinga* (f.)
steady job *lavoro* (m.) *fisso*
stepdaughter *figlia* (f.) *di mia moglie (di mio
  marito)*
stepfather *marito* (m.) *di mia madre*
stepmother *moglie* (f.) *di mio padre*
stepson *figlio* (m.) *di mia moglie (di mio marito)*
stereo *stereo* (m., pl.)
stew *spezzatino* (m.)
still *ancora*
stomach *stomaco* (m.) *(above the waist); ventre*
  (m.), *pancia* (f.) *(below the waist)*
stone *pietra* (f.)

stop (to) *fermarsi, smettere*
stop ... ing (to) *smettere di ...*
store *negozio* (m.)
  clothing store *negozio di abbigliamento*
  department store *grande magazzino* (m.)
  electronics store *negozio di elettronica*
  grocery store *negozio di alimentari*
  shoe store *negozio di scarpe*
storm *temporale* (m.)
  It's stormy. *C'è un temporale.*
story *storia* (f.)
  love stories *storie* (pl.) *d'amore*
stove (electric, gas) *cucina* (f.) *elettrica, cucina
  *(f.) *a gas*
straight *diritto*
  straight ahead *sempre diritto*
strange *strano*
strawberry *fragola* (f.)
street *strada* (f.), *via* (f.)
street light *semaforo* (m.)
stressed *stressato*
stressful *stressante*
strong *forte*
student *studente/essa* (m./f.)
  university student *studente universitario*
study *indagine* (f.), *studio* (m.) *(room)*
study (to) *studiare*
stuff *roba* (f.)
  a bunch/lot of stuff *un sacco di roba*
subject *materia* (f.)
subjunctive mood (grammar) *congiuntivo* (m.)
  present subjunctive *congiuntivo presente*
substance *sostanza* (f.)
substitute *sostituto/a* (m./f.)
suburban *periferico*
suburbs *periferia* (f.)
subway *metrò* (m. in Milan/f. in Rome)
suddenly *improvvisamente*
sugar *zucchero* (m.)
suit *abito* (m.) *(men's), tailleur* (m., pl.) *(women's)*
  men's suit *abito da uomo*
  pant suit *tailleur pantalone*
suitcase *valigia* (f.)
summer *estate* (f.)
  in the summer *d'estate*
  summer job *lavoro* (m.) *temporaneo*
sun *sole* (m.)
  It's sunny. *C'è il sole.*

Sunday *domenica* (f.)
sunglasses *occhiali da sole*
superior *superiore*
supermarket *supermercato* (m.)
sure *sicuro*
surprise *sorpresa* (f.)
  What a surprise! *Che sorpresa!*
surprise (to) *sorprendere*
sweater *maglione* (m.)
sweet *dolce*
swim (to) *nuotare*
swimming *nuoto* (m.)
symphony *sinfonia* (f.)
symptom *sintomo* (m.)
system *sistema* (m.)

T

table *tavolo* (m.)
tagliatelle (pasta) *tagliatelle* (f. pl.)
tail (of coin) *croce* (f.)
take (to) *portare, prendere*
  take (time) (to) *metterci, volerci*
  take a bath (to) *fare il bagno*
  take a break (to) *fare una pausa*
  take a nap (to) *fare un pisolino*
  take a nice long nap (to) *farsi una bella
    dormita*
  take a picture (to) *fare una foto/fotografia*
  take a shower (to) *fare la doccia*
  take a trip (to) *fare una gita, fare un viaggio*
  take a walk (to) *fare una passeggiata*
take off (to) *decollare*
talented *bravo, con talento; in gamba* (colloquial)
talk *discorso* (m.), *colloquio* (m.)
  talk show *interviste* (f. pl.) *alla televisione*
tall *alto*
taste *sapore* (m.)
taxi *taxi* (m.)
taxi driver *tassista* (m./f.)
tea *tè* (m.)
tea kettle *bollitore* (m.)
teach (to) *insegnare*
teacher *insegnante* (m./f.); *maestro/a* (m./f.)
  (nursery school and elementary school)
team *squadra* (f.)
technical *tecnico*
teenager *adolescente* (m./f.), *teenager* (m./f., pl.
  teenager)

telegram *telegramma* (m.)
telephone *telefono* (m.)
  answer the phone (to) *rispondere al telefono*
  cell phone *cellulare* (m.), *telefonino* (m.)
telephone (to) *telefonare, chiamare*
television *televisione* (f.), *tele* (f.), *tivù* (f.),
  televisore (m.) (noun); *televisivo* (adjective)
  television program *trasmissione* (f.) *televisiva*
  watch television (to)) *guardare la
    televisione/tele/ tivù*
  watch sports on TV (to) *guardare lo sport in/
    alla televisione*
tell (to) *raccontare, dire*
temperature *temperatura* (f.)
temple *tempio* (m.)
temporary *temporaneo*
ten *dieci*
  from 10:45 a.m. to 3:00 p.m. *dalle undici meno
    un quarto alle tre*
tendon *tendine* (m.)
tennis *tennis* (m., pl. *tennis*)
  play tennis (to) *giocare a tennis*
  tennis shoes *scarpe* (f. pl.) *da tennis*
tenth *decimo*
terrible *terribile*
test *test* (m.)
textbook *libro (di testo)*
than *di, che*
  less... than *meno... di/che*
  more/-er... than *più... di/che*
  than usual *del solito*
Thank you. *Grazie.*
Fine, thanks. *(Sto) bene, grazie.*
Thanks a lot. *Grazie mille.*
Very well, thanks. *Molto bene, grazie.*
that (conjunction) *che*
that (demonstrative) *quello*
that (relative pronoun) *che*
the *il* (m. sg.) (in front of a consonant); *lo* (m. sg.)
  (in front of s + consonant, z, ps, gn); *l'* (m. sg./f. sg.)
  (in front of a vowel); *la* (f. sg.) (in front of a
  consonant); *i* (m. pl.) (in front of consonants); *gli* (m.
  pl.) (in front of s + consonant, z, ps, gn, in front of
  vowels); *le* (f. pl.) (in front of consonants or vowels)
theater *teatro* (m.)
  movie theater *cinema* (m., pl.)
their *loro* (inv.)
them (direct object pronoun) *li/le* (m./f.)

them (direct object, disjunctive pronoun) *loro*
to them (indirect object pronoun) *gli*
to them (indirect object, disjunctive pronoun) *a loro*
then *poi, allora*
  And then? *E poi?*
there *lì, ci*
  Go there. *Vacci.*
  Let's go there. *Andiamoci.*
  near there *lì vicino*
  There is... *C'è...*
  There are... *Ci sono...*
  There are seven of us. *Siamo in sette.*
  There are three of them. *Ce ne sono tre.*
therefore *dunque, quindi*
thesis *tesi (f., pl. tesi)*
they (subject pronoun) *loro*
  they (impersonal pronoun) *si*
thick *grosso*
thin *magro, sottile*
thin slice *fettina (f.)*
thing *cosa (f.)*
  things to do *cose da fare*
  tons of things, a thousand things *mille cose*
think (to) *pensare*
  I don't think so. *Non credo.*
  I'll think about it. *Ci penserò.*
  think about... (doing somehing)
    (to) *pensare di...*
  think about... (something/somebody)
    (to) *pensare a...*
third *terzo*
  third-born *terzogenito/a*
thirst *sete (f.)*
thirsty (to be) *avere sete*
thirteen *tredici*
thirty *trenta*
  at seven thirty (7:30) *alle sette e mezza*
  It's 3:30. *Sono le tre e trenta.*
this *questo*
  in this period *in questo periodo*
  this evening *questa sera, stasera*
  this week *questa settimana*
thousand *mille (m.), mila (pl.)*
  two thousand *duemila*
three *tre*
  from 10:45 a.m. to 3:00 p.m. *dalle undici meno un quarto alle tre*

It's three (o'clock). *Sono le tre.*
It's 3:15. *Sono le tre e quindici.*
It's 3:45. *Sono le tre e quarantacinque./Sono le tre e tre quarti./Sono le quattro meno un quarto./Manca un quarto alle quattro.*
It's 3:30. *Sono le tre e trenta.*
There are three of them. *Ce ne sono tre.*
through *per*
thumb *pollice (m.)*
thunder *tuono (m.)*
thunder (to) *tuonare*
Thursday *giovedì (m., pl.)*
ticket *biglietto (m.)*
tie *cravatta (f.)*
tie (to) *fare pari*
till *fino (a)*
time *tempo (m.), orario (m.), volta (f.)*
  at the same time *allo stesso tempo*
  every time *ogni volta*
  for a very long time *da una vita*
  free time *tempo libero*
  full-time *a pieno tempo*
  have time (to) *avere tempo*
  It's time to... *È ora di...*
  long time *molto tempo*
  on time (to be) *essere in orario, essere puntuale*
  part-time *part-time*
  part-time job *lavoro part-time*
  waste time (to) *perdere tempo*
  What time is it? *Che ora è?/Che ore sono?*
tip *mancia (f.)*
tired *stanco*
title *titolo (m.)*
to *in, a, da*
  from... to... (time periods) *dalle... alle...*
  from Monday to Friday *dal lunedì al venerdì*
  from 10:45 a.m. to 3:00 p.m. *dalle undici meno un quarto alle tre*
  nothing good to eat *niente di buono da mangiare*
  something to drink *qualcosa da bere*
  things to do *cose (f. pl.) da fare*
  to the city *in centro*
  to the country *in campagna*
  to the left *(a) sinistra*
  to the mountains *in montagna*
  to the right *(a) destra*

today *oggi*
toe (big) *alluce* (m.)
together *insieme*
   (together) with you *insieme a te*
toilet *water* (m.), *gabinetto* (m.)
toilet paper *carta* (f.) *igienica*
tomato *pomodoro* (m.)
tomorrow *domani*
tongue *lingua* (f.)
tonight *stasera*
tons of things *mille cose* (f. pl.)
too *anche*
   Pleased to meet you, too. *Piacere mio.*
too (much/many) *troppo/a* (m./f.) (noun); *troppo*
   (adjective)
   go too far (to) *esagerare*
   Too bad! *Peccato!*
tooth *dente* (m.)
tortellini *tortellini* (m. pl.)
tour *giro* (m.)
   guided tour *viaggio* (m.) *organizzato*
   tour bus *pullman* (m.)
tourist *turista* (m./f.)
   foreign tourists *turisti* (pl.) *stranieri*
towel *asciugamano* (m.)
tower *torre* (f.)
town *cittadina* (f.); *paese* (m.) *(small)*
   around town *in giro per la città*
   hometown *città* (f.) *natale*
   out of town *fuori città*
trade fair *fiera* (f.)
traditional *tradizionale*
traffic *traffico* (m.)
traffic light *semaforo* (m.)
train *treno* (m.)
   by train *in treno*
   train station *stazione* (f.) *(dei treni)*
training *formazione* (f.)
transfer (to) *trasferirsi*
transparent *trasparente*
transportation *trasporto* (m.)
   means of transportation *mezzo* (m.) *di
   trasporto*
travel *viaggio* (m.)
travel (to) *viaggiare*
   travel abroad (to) *viaggiare all'estero*
tread on (to) *calpestare*
treat (to) *curare*

tree *albero* (m.)
trip *viaggio* (m.)
   day trip *gita* (f.)
   Have a good trip. *Buon viaggio.*
   short trip *gita* (f.)
   take a trip (to) *fare un viaggio*
true *vero*
truth *verità* (f., pl.)
try (to) *provare*
   try on (to) *provare*
   try to … (to) *cercare di …*
t-shirt *maglietta* (f.)
tub *vasca* (f.)
   bath tub *vasca (da bagno)*
Tuesday *martedì* (m., pl. *martedì*)
turn (to) *girare, voltare*
twelve *dodici*
twenty *venti*
twenty-four *ventiquattro*
twenty-one *ventuno*
twenty-three *ventitré*
twenty-two *ventidue*
twice a week *due volte alla settimana*
two *due*
   It's two (o'clock). *Sono le due.*
   two and a half hours *due ore e mezzo*
   two days ago *due giorni fa*
   two thousand *duemila*
type *tipo* (m.)

U

ugly *brutto*
umbrella *ombrello* (m.)
uncle *zio (m., pl. zii)*
undecided *indeciso*
under *sotto*
   under stress *stressato*
underpants *slip* (m. pl.) *(men's)*; *mutandine* (f. pl.)
   (women's)
undershirt *canottiera* (f.)
understand (to) *capire*
unemployed *disoccupato/a* (m./f.)
unfortunately *purtroppo*
unfriendly *antipatico*
university *università (f., pl. università)* (noun);
   universitario (adjective)
   university degree *laurea* (f.)
   university student *studente* (m.) *universitario*

unless ... *a meno che ... non*
until *finché, fino (a)*
  until late *fino a tardi*
  until the end *fino in fondo*
up to *fino (a)*
upon *su*
upset (to) *dispiacere*
urban *urbano*
us (direct object pronoun) *ci*
  us (direct object, disjunctive pronoun) *noi*
  to us (indirect object pronoun) *ci*
  to us (indirect object, disjunctive pronoun) *a noi*
use (to) *usare*
useful *utile*
usual *solito*
  than usual *del solito*
usually *di solito*

V

vacation *ferie* (f. pl.), *vacanza* (f.)
  on vacation *in ferie, in vacanza*
vaguely *vagamente*
variety *varietà* (f.)
  variety of choices *varietà di scelta*
veal *vitello* (m.)
vegetable *verdura* (f.)
vegetable garden *orto* (m.)
velvet *velluto* (m.)
vendor *commerciante* (m./f.)
Venice *Venezia* (f.)
version *versione* (f.)
very *molto, tanto*
  for a very long time *da una vita*
  very beautiful *bellissimo*
  very interesting *interessantissimo*
  Very pleased to meet you! *Molto piacere!*
  Very well! *Benissimo!*
  Very well, thanks. *Molto bene, grazie.*
veterinarian *veterinario/a* (m./f.)
view *vista* (f.)
village *paese* (m.); *paesino* (m.) (small)
virgin *vergine* (f.)
visit (to) *visitare*
  come visit (to) *venire a trovare*
  go visit (to) *andare a trovare*
volleyball *palla* (f.) *a volo*

W

waist *vita* (f.)
wait for (to) *aspettare*
  Wait a second. *Un momento.*
waiter *cameriere* (m.)
waitress *cameriera* (f.)
wake up (to) *svegliarsi*
walk *passeggiata* (f.)
  Enjoy your walk./Have a good walk. *Buona passeggiata.*
  go for a walk (to) *fare un giro/fare un giro a piedi*
  take a walk (to) *fare una passeggiata*
walk (to) *camminare*
wall *parete* (f.), *muro* (m.)
want (to) *volere, desiderare*
wardrobe *armadio* (m.)
warehouse *magazzino* (m.)
wash (to) *lavare*
  wash oneself (to) *lavarsi*
washing machine *lavatrice* (f.), *lavabiancheria* (f.)
waste time (to) *perdere tempo*
watch *orologio* (m.)
watch (to) *guardare*
  Watch out! *Sta' attento!*
  watch sports on TV (to) *guardare lo sport in/alla televisione*
  watch television (to) *guardare la tivù/tele/televisione*
water *acqua* (f.)
  mineral water *acqua minerale*
  still mineral water *acqua minerale naturale*
  sparkling mineral water *acqua minerale frizzante*
way *via* (f.), *modo* (m.)
  by the way *a proposito*
  the way in which ... *il modo in cui ...*
we (subject pronoun) *noi*
weak *debole*
wear (to) *portare, indossare*
  He/She wears. *Si mette ...*
weather *tempo* (m.)
  What's the weather like? *Che tempo fa?*
web log *web log* (m.)
webpage *web page* (f.), *pagina* (f.) *web*
website *sito* (m.) *web*

wedding *matrimonio* (m.)
Wednesday *mercoledì* (m., pl.)
week *settimana* (f.)
  last week *settimana scorsa*
  next week *prossima settimana*
  this week *questa settimana*
  twice a week *due volte alla settimana*
weekend *fine settimana* (m., pl.), *weekend* (m., pl.)
welcome *benvenuto*
  You're welcome. *Prego.*
  Welcome back. *Bentornato.*
well *bene*
  I am well. *Mi sento bene.*
  (One) might as well ... *Tanto vale ...*
  Very well! *Benissimo!*
  Very well, thanks. *Molto bene, grazie.*
Well ... *Beh ...*
what *che*
  What? *Che cosa?*
  What a beautiful dish! *Che bel piatto!*
  What a surprise! *Che sorpresa!*
  What are you having? *Tu cosa prendi?*
  What do you do? *Che lavoro fai?*
  What time is it? *Che ora è?/Che ore sono?*
  What's the weather like? *Che tempo fa?*
when *quando*
where *dove*
  Where are you from? (fml.)/**Where is he/she from?** *Di dov'è?*
  Where are you from? (infml.) *Di dove sei?*
  Where is ... ?/Where are ... ? *Dov'è ... ?/ Dove sono ... ?*
which *quale* (question); *cui, che* (relative pronoun)
  the way in which ... *il modo in cui ...*
while *mentre*
white *bianco*
  white wine *vino* (m.) *bianco*
who *chi* (question); *che* (relative pronoun)
whoever *chi*
whole *intero*
whom *che, cui*
Whose ... is it ?/Whose ... are they? *Di chi è ... ?/Di chi sono ... ?*
why *perché*
  the reason why ... *il motivo per cui ... / la ragione per cui ...*
wide *ampio*
wife *moglie* (f.)

wild *selvaggio*
win (to) *vincere*
wind *vento* (m.)
  It's windy. *C'è vento./Tira vento.*
window *finestra* (f.)
wine *vino* (m.)
  red wine *vino rosso*
  wine list *lista* (f.) *dei vini*
  white wine *vino bianco*
winter *inverno* (m.) (noun); *invernale* (adjective)
  in winter *d'inverno*
wish *voglia* (f.)
  I wish *magari*
with *con, presso*
  (together) with you *insieme a te*
without *senza*
  without ... *senza che ...*
wolf *lupo* (m.)
woman *donna* (f.)
  businesswoman *donna d'affari*
  policewoman *donna poliziotto*
  saleswoman *venditrice* (f.)
wonderful *meraviglioso*
  Wonderful! *Benissimo!*
wood *legno* (m.), *bosco* (m.)
wooden *di legno*
wool *lana* (f.)
work *lavoro* (m.), *opera* (f.)
  works of art *opere* (pl.) *d'arte*
work (to) *lavorare*
worker *operaio/a* (m./f.)
  construction worker *muratore/trice* (m./f.)
world *mondo* (m.)
  around the world *intorno al mondo*
  in the world *del mondo*
worry (to) *preoccupare*
  I'm worried. *Sono preoccupato.*
worth (to be) *valere*
wrist *polso* (m.)
write (to) *scrivere*
writer *scrittore/trice* (m./f.)
wrong (to be) *avere torto*

Y

year *anno* (m.)
  every year *tutti gli anni*
  I am ... years old. *Ho ... anni.*
  last year *anno scorso*

yellow *giallo*

yes *sì*

yesterday *ieri*

yet *ancora*

yolk *tuorlo* (m.)

you (subject pronoun) *Lei* (sg. fml.), *tu* (sg. infml.), *Loro* (pl. fml.), *voi* (pl.)

   you (direct object pronoun) *La* (sg. fml.), *ti* (sg. infml.), *vi* (pl.)

   you (direct object, disjunctive pronoun) *Lei* (sg. fml.), *te* (sg. infml.), *voi* (pl.)

   to you (indirect object pronoun) *Le* (sg. fml.), *ti* (sg. infml.), *vi* (pl.)

   to you (indirect object, disjunctive pronoun) *a Lei* (sg. fml.), *a te* (sg. infml.), *a voi* (pl.)

young *giovane*

younger *minore*

your *Suo/Sua/Suoi/Sue* (sg. fml.); *tuo/tua/tuoi/tue* (sg. infml.); *Loro/Loro* (pl. fml.); *vostro/vostra/vostri/vostre* (pl. infml.)

youth hostel *ostello* (m.)

Z

zero *zero*

zoo *zoo* (m., pl.)

zucchini *zucchino* (m.)